THE SOUL MATE EXPEDITONS

The

SOUL MATE EXPEDITONS

Lyle Greenfield

are you sitting LLC

The Soul Mate Expeditions is a work of fiction, non-fiction and opinion.
Names, characters, places and events are either a figment of the author's imagination
or they are not. Any resemblance to actual persons or spirits, living or dead, events or
countries, provinces, cities or hamlets is entirely coincidental, or intentional. It depends.

Any grammatical inconsistencies or typographical corrigenda
discovered in this volume were made at the deliberate and sole
discretion the author, unless by oversight or plain nescience.

Published in the United States of America by Are You Sitting LLC, New York
PO Box 440 Amagansett, NY 11930

Cover and book design: Joan Greenfield / Gooddesign Resource
www.gooddesign.net

Guidance and coordination: Karen Schober-Maneely at BookBaby

Please address all inquiries to: author@bangworld.com

For Mary

CONTENTS

FOREWORD

The original stories comprising *The Soul Mate Expeditions* (first section of this collection) were actually written 20 years ago. If you are reading this in the year 2024 it was 25 years ago. If you are reading this in the year 2099 it was100 years ago and I am dead. You're welcome to visit my gravesite in East Hampton, NY and to make a generous contribution to the East Hampton Food Pantry in my name. Thank you!

Regarding the novella, *What Vienna Saw*, the idea was a spore in my brain going back to 1985 and periodically I would deliver a feverish synopsis to a captive audience over dinner and drinks. Several close friends suggested that if I didn't finally commit the story to paper they would send me to my room without supper. Or drinks. Therefore...

As for the Letters to the Editor of *The East Hampton Star*, I discovered in 1998 that it was the policy of this weekly newspaper to publish every signed letter submitted "with the exception those judged to be proselytizing, an invasion of privacy, libelous, or obscene." This idiosyncratic editorial position, in effect since the 1950s, quickly became a psychogenic discharge valve to me and I took unfair advantage, I fear, writing letters of 1,000 to 2,000 words in length, on any viewpoint, fantasy or personal humiliation I cared to share. One devoted reader, Bunny Dell, strongly suggested I put them in a book. As did Jeff Rosner, who frequently gave animated letter readings to unsuspecting houseguests.

So, to those who have graciously encouraged this compilation, I hope you're satisfied. And to those seeing all or any of it for the first time, I hope you're satisfied, too, because its sidewalk resale value will be mere pennies on the dollar.

—L.G.

Signs

Do you remember seeing this sign taped to light poles, phone stands and store windows along West 72nd Street many years ago?

LAUREN
LOST YOUR NUMBER
AFTER CPW TAXI RIDE!
PLEASE CALL MICHAEL:
210-7301

I'm not sure how you could have missed it—I put up over a hundred of them. The taxi ride thing happened in late February, early in the final quarter of the last century. Friday night, and I was attempting to hail a cab at the corner of 72nd and Central Park West, on my way to the East Side to join a friend for dinner. Standing not far away in the blustery cold was a young woman carrying two large shopping bags. A cab pulled up beside me and I glanced over at her.

"I'm sorry, were you waiting for a taxi?" I asked, concerned that I'd inadvertently taken advantage of her unarmed state.

"No, I'm waiting for the bus," she said.

"Well I'm just going over to the East Side to meet a friend, and I could drop you off if you'd like," I offered unselfconsciously.

"Thank you, that'd be great," she said. I helped her into the cab with her bags and off we went.

"I'm apartment-sitting on 72nd Street for a friend who has cats, but I needed to do some things at my own place on East 81st—I don't think the buses are running too frequently." I hadn't noticed before, standing in the near-darkness in a denim jacket, clutching unwieldy bags, but she was beautiful. Her features soft, unguarded, her eyes dark and animated.

"I always take a taxi at night," I said. "In fact, I don't think I've even been on a bus in New York."

Question: What can you do in a five-minute cab ride from West 72nd Street to East 79th and Lexington with a total stranger? Answer: Stare out the window and watch the trees and street lamps go by. Or, you could learn someone's name. Lauren. You could learn that Lauren is a dancer; that she has recently broken up with someone with whom she's been living for six years; that she is happy to be living alone again and feels suddenly like she has friends again; that she doesn't see how anybody could live outside of New York City. And there'd still be time for Lauren to find out that her fellow passenger was married until fairly recently, to a woman he'd met in college; that he had a daughter; that he hadn't really been dating because it's hasn't felt right; that, no, he hadn't seen a movie in probably three months; that he'd left his hometown right after high school.

So, it's possible to fit many years into a five-minute cab ride across the park, with no additional charge on the meter. As we neared my destination I gave Lauren money for the fare, and, looking at her I said, "Well it's been really nice meeting you, and talking with you…kind of unexpected…" Yes, she agreed, she had enjoyed meeting me as well. "Well it might be nice to get together again sometime, maybe for a cab ride and dinner…would you like to do that?" I asked, emboldened by the knowledge that in moments I would be out of the cab, probably never in my life to see this woman again.

"Yes, I think that would be nice," she said to me. I began to get an erection. I'm certain of it. She said it "would be nice" to have dinner with me. Is there any way to overstate the level of our insecurity under certain circumstances? No, there is not.

The car stopped at the corner of 79th and Lexington and I said, "That's great! Tell me your number and I'll give you a call early next week."

"I don't have a pen…do you have anything to write with?" I did not have a pen. The driver had no paper. This moment was beginning to drift, and that could not be permitted. Could we remind ourselves that this is taking place decades ago, before the dawn of the little devices that help us meet people and remember things? Thank you.

"You know what, tell me your number…I'll remember and I'll write it down soon as I get to the restaurant." So Lauren told me her number, and

I repeated it several times and opened the car door. "Great meeting you, Lauren, enjoy your weekend and we'll talk in a few days."

"You too…I'm looking forward to it." I was on the sidewalk, and she was looking back at me from the rear window as the cab pulled away. Do you know what that's like when she's looking back at you as the car is pulling away? Yes, that is exactly right—unless the person looking back at you has just left, with all of her possessions, for good. That's different.

Now I had to find the restaurant where my friend was probably already waiting for me. Wait a minute, what's her number? What was the number? Right! Seven…eight…four…six…eight…seven…two…seven-eight-four-six-eight-seven-two…seveneightfoursixeightseventwo. "Hey man, what's up?" Max said from his stool at the bar.

"Hang on a second, gimme a pen quick, I gotta write something down." Safe. I put the napkin with Lauren's number on it in my back pocket. Safe. Then Max and I did what we often do on a Friday night. We drank, we had a burger at the bar, we searched the room, we talked about our 'love lives'—oh yes, as if there actually were love lives to talk about. I told Max all about meeting Lauren and he said "Great, a dancer, are you on drugs? She's got no fucking job!" Max gave me the update on Florence, his girlfriend. "She's really putting it to me. She wants to see a ring. Ultimatum time. 'It's five years now, Max—I need to know!' I don't know what to do…I'm fucking freaking."

I shook my head slowly in mock empathy and told Max that he was a cultural victim of the ancient tradition of Jewish guilt. "You know you're gonna marry her—why not just get it over with?"

"I can't…I told myself I wasn't going to marry a Jewish girl."

"But you're practically living together! You have the same tastes, like to do the same things…it's the best sex you ever had, isn't that what you said?"

"But she makes me nuts, she's always whining, she doesn't have enough class, her parents are pure garmento…"

I don't understand it, this compulsion to break away from our cultural herd, in search of something 'truer' to our *true* self. Sociologists have written that the availability of higher education to many more Americans since the end of World War II has prepared a new generation for professional, social and geographical choices never before possible for so many. Yes, and made it possible for more people to imagine that the answers are somewhere over the rainbow—the fortune, the inner peace, the trimmer, more confident you. Your soul mate. Never imagining that one end of the rainbow might actually start at your feet.

Max never married Florence. She broke it off, which had been his hope since a preemptive act on her part would reduce his guilt-risk position. Since then he has dated a succession of blond women, who eventually show signs of weariness in the company of his family around the Christmas holidays. Three years after their breakup, Florence was diagnosed with a brain tumor, and seven months later she expired. Max now had enough guilt to power the turbines of a small town on Long Island—probably near Great Neck. He should have married her.

The next day I rose slowly, with no plans and one thought. Sitting on the side of my bed I saw the napkin: 784-6872. I thought about Lauren. How amazing to meet her. You could go to a party every week, rescue a drowning pug puppy at Jones Beach, be selected to judge a National Collegiate Women's Synchronized Swimming competition—and chances are you still wouldn't meet someone. You know, some *One*. And then, on a dark, frigid New York street corner... I had to dial the number. I had to dial the number just to make sure that the voice I'd heard in the taxi was the voice I would hear on my phone. And I would say, "Hi, it's Michael... from the taxi last night. Yeah! Hey, I just wanted to make sure I got your number right...and I did! So, ah, I'll talk to you soon, okay?"

I dialed the number. Seven-eight-four...six-eight-seven-two. It rang a few times. And then she picked up. "Hello."

"Hi, Lauren?"

"This isn't Lauren."

"I'm sorry, is Lauren there?"

"I don't know, mister, does she work here?"

4

"Work where?"

"You've reached the visitor's desk at Roosevelt Hospital." Holy shit.

"I don't think so. Sorry." Holy shit. Oh my God. I dialed the number again. "Hello."

"Sorry." Jesus Christ. I had the wrong number. Saturday morning, I haven't even brushed my teeth yet, and I'm sweating. Calm down. I started dialing other combinations: eight-six-seven-two… "Yeah who is it?"

"Sorry, wrong number."

Six-seven-eight-two… "Lucky Deli can I help you?"

"Sorry." Six-eight-seven-three…

"Hello."

"Hi, is this Lauren?"

"Just a minute…Lori! Somebody on the phone for you! Hang on a sec."

"Hi, this is Lori."

"Lauren? This is Michael."

"No, this is Lori. There's no Lauren here."

"I'm sorry. I guess I've got the wrong number." I tried another fifteen or twenty numbers. Nothing. Could she have intentionally given me the wrong number? No chance. I couldn't have mistaken the way we'd connected. And we said we looked forward to seeing each other again, and now I'm the one who's going to be the liar because I didn't remember her number! What a fucking asshole! I don't know Lauren's last name, she doesn't know mine. I don't know where she lives, or even the building where she's apartment sitting. I don't even know the name of her dance company. This can't be—it's not possible that I have met someone who may be a very special person, who may be meant to have a special place in my life, and I would jar this unique moment from its precious orbit through an act of stupid self-distraction. I am without worth.

Saturday was a bad day. I obsessed on this situation, and I was very unhappy. I took a listless walk in the Park, hoping, ridiculously, to run into Lauren. I didn't call Max to tell him what had happened—or not happened. I couldn't deal with his 'Well now you know what was really meant to be—she had no job anyway, you idiot!' I picked at some food, watched a little football on television. I begged the day to pass. Sunday, repeat.

Monday morning was a cold winter morning, waking me up smartly as soon as I hit the sidewalk. My partner at J. Walter Thompson, John, was already in his office when I arrived. John and I would never begin a day's work, much less a new week, without first recapping the highlights of the night or the weekend before. John's marriage of many years had drifted off the road. There wasn't a lot of talk about the problem, or of getting assistance, either. Just sitting there in the front seat, staring out the windshield. Did you ever do that? Did you ever just stop talking, stop trying to find a way back into the being of the person whom you had once penetrated so deeply, perhaps even exchanged vows with? Do you know what it's like to lie beside that person, inside the bedding you had registered for your wedding, with no emotion, no energy, no life passing between you?

John and his wife separated after a couple of years and subsequently divorced. A few years later, both remarried. All I know—or believe—is that John found his soul mate. Maybe he was just older and weary and experienced enough to be ready when she first entered his hemisphere. But if you saw them together, you'd smile, and you'd be grateful for what you were seeing. Anyway, John said that his weekend had been great—they'd seen a couple of movies and had dinner with her daughters. Lovely.

He quickly changed the subject and asked me how my weekend had been and I told him about meeting Lauren, and losing her number, and freaking out because I had no way to reach her and I had told her that I would call and it was killing me not only because I'd said that I would but because I really believed there was a connection between us and a strange serendipity in the way in which we had met that made it vital for us to reconnect and discover whatever it was we were meant to know about each other. John laughed mercilessly. Nearly everything about our lives was so very different. He commuted from Westchester, Michael commuted from Mars. Or so it must have seemed to him. But we loved each other and our little creative universe at the agency. And he always loved these stories because they seemed to him not so much the dramatic narrative of someone's life, but like colorful balloons being blown up and twisted into different animal shapes before his very eyes—playful distractions from the sameness of his own story. Still, I wasn't going to let him off with a laugh. "Seriously, John, what am I gonna do? I have to contact her and I have to see her, it's not like there's some other choice!"

"Maybe you could run an ad," he joked, "Does she speak English?" John did not know that he was having a near-death experience—I could have killed him.

Run an ad. Good thought. I could run an ad. Maybe I could even put up a few posters on West 72nd Street! At least I would be doing something, stirring the atmosphere, relieving the agony of my own helplessness. Later that morning I called the classifieds department at *New York Magazine,* and over the phone placed the following notice in the "Personals": Lauren: Lost Your Number After CPW Taxi Ride. Please Call Michael. 210-7301 (My number at the office—I didn't want any stalkers or freaks calling me at home.). I felt better already. In a matter of days she could see the ad! Maybe some friend whom she'd told of our meeting would spot it. The quest was on. During lunch, I enlisted John to help me create a poster. He had superior printing skills and so, using a thick black marking device on an 8 1/2 x 11 sheet of paper, he applied the message carefully:

LAUREN
LOST YOUR NUMBER
AFTER CPW TAXI RIDE!
PLEASE CALL MICHAEL:
210-7301

I asked Terri, who ruled the giant copy machine, to make one hundred fifty copies of the page, and she stared at me in disbelief. "You've lost it completely, Michael. You had it once. But now you've lost it. Gone." Truthfully, I think she was enjoying this, seeing me in the possession of something I couldn't control, and to save the one crumb of dignity I might still have on the table I pretended to ignore her rolling eyes. Business as usual. A hundred fifty posters begging someone I didn't know to call me.

John and I worked late in preparation for a presentation we had to make in Detroit the next morning. It would be the 7:30 a.m. American out of LaGuardia. A 5:30 wake-up to catch the 'zombie' flight. I left the office after 10 p.m. and in my bag I carried the posters, a roll of masking tape and a staple gun. The cabby dropped me at the corner of 72nd and Central Park West, exactly where I had first met Lauren. There were snowflakes in the air, and a brisk wind made it bitter. I blew on my hands and looked around—few pedestrians at this hour. Still, I felt embarrassed. Maybe I *had* lost it. But I couldn't turn back now. Just over forty-eight hours ago we had met in this very place. We had to meet again, we had to find out. I took out the masking tape and began taping the posters to light poles and fireboxes at the intersection. I used the staple gun to attach them to trees. I moved west on 72nd, zigzagging back and forth across the street. Every inanimate object was a potential billboard for my sign. Store windows were useful, too, I discovered. After twenty minutes I was lost in the routine, moving involuntarily, no longer thinking about how it 'looked.' Some guy came up behind me at one point and grabbed my ass saying, "Nice," then ran down the block. Thank you so much.

After an hour I was at 72nd and Broadway. It was almost midnight; I still had over thirty posters left, but, looking back at the blocks I'd covered I decided the job was done. Over a hundred signs dotted my field of vision. They wouldn't all be removed by shopkeepers, sanitation workers and agnostics at once. If Lauren was still in the neighborhood in the next several days, she would have to see one of the signs. I felt a burden lifted from me. There was nothing else to do, and there was comfort in that knowledge. I walked home and went to bed. I don't know how I heard the alarm go off at 5:30, how I could end up in an airplane heading for Detroit at 7:30. Automatic pilot.

Our morning meetings were over before noon—time to call the office before rejoining clients for lunch. "Terri it's Michael. Do I have any messages? Carl called? Fuck Carl! Did Lauren call? Yes, Lauren as seen on posters everywhere…did she call? Shit. All right, I'll call you later before we head for the airport." When I got off the phone John was chuckling. "Do

you think she'll see the signs?" I begged him, "I put them everywhere...
everyfuckingwhere!"

"Oh she's seen them," he assured me with a twinkle in his eyes. "She's
already contacted the police by now." Haha. By late afternoon no one had
tried to contact me, Terri reported, but "Have a great flight back and see
ya tomorrow." We landed at LaGuardia just after 9:30. As the taxi made its
way back along 72nd Street, I could see out the windows that they were
still everywhere. She couldn't have missed them! I slept like a baby. Or a
dog. Or an idiot.

On Wednesday my phone rang at 11:45 a.m. "Hello?"

"Hello, Michael?"

"Yes, who's this?"

"It's Lauren." But it didn't sound like Lauren, not that I would know
Lauren's voice on the phone—but this voice sounded strange... under
some sort of influence.

"Right, Lauren, uh, where did we meet?"

"We met at Mr. Goodbar's."

"I don't think we met there and I'm sure I would remember, but thanks
for calling." I hung up, thinking how fucked up this was, thankful I hadn't
advertised my home number. Lauren did not call on Thursday, either.
Terri stopped by my office on her way to the copier to ask if I needed any
more signs printed up. "No, Terri, thank you."

"Hey, I heard a country western song once called "If The Phone Don't
Ring It's Me"...pretty cool title, right?!" Haha. Right. Truth be told—which
we are trying to do here—I was getting over this drama. I had done what
could possibly have been done—in a few more days I would help the New
York City Department of Sanitation with the cleanup of West 72nd Street.
Maybe invite the men to join me at O'Neal's for a cold one.

Sometime after lunch on Friday my phone rang, and the following
conversation transpired: "Hello, this is Michael."

"Hi, this is Lauren."

"Lauren? Lauren who?"

"Lauren who?! Lauren whose name is plastered all over the West Side, I believe."

"Oh Jesus…I'm sorry…I got a call the other day from someone pretty strange, and I kind of gave up thinking I would actually ever hear from you. So…you…saw one of the signs?"

"I was walking on 72nd Street with a friend of mine and actually she saw it first. And then, of course, we saw quite a few of them. How many did you put up?"

"Uh, well, I guess a little over a hundred. God, I feel so dumb. As soon as I left the cab last Friday night I got distracted trying to find this restaurant, and then when I found it and joined my friend inside, I wrote the number down immediately—and of course I discovered the next day that it wasn't your number. And the twenty other numbers I dialed weren't your number, either. And I just felt so shitty about it, after meeting you and enjoying our conversation and telling you that I'd call…You must think I'm crazy."

"Well, truthfully, it is kind of flattering. My friend thought it was pretty amazing. She said, 'So there's at least one romantic left on the planet.'"

"Well, if you enjoyed the posters you'll probably love the ad in *New York Magazine*. I think you'll find it in the current issue."

"Oh my God, you *are* crazy."

"Well maybe you'd have second thoughts about dinner with a 'crazy,' but I'd still like to get together, if you're up for it."

"I guess I'm up for it—I answered the ad, didn't I?"

In the realm of human socialization known as the First Date, there is historical evidence that supports a continuing tradition of maintaining one's 'cool' during the gestation period leading up to said date. This usually means not displaying an unseemly degree of eagerness—often interpreted as desperation—that could possibly cause the other party—the date— to conclude that you have a) low self-esteem b) no critical standards whatsoever c) do not get out of the house very often. Clearly, by virtue of my signage campaign alone, I was in violation of the historical precedents. I was bereft of cool at this moment. Still, I crawled onward.

"How about Saturday night?"

"What?"

"How about dinner Saturday night? Is that too soon, I mean, we could wait…maybe next week would be better?"

"No, no, dinner Saturday should be all right. I have plans in the afternoon, but I'm free for dinner."

Thank you, God. Thank you for sending me on this Sacred Journey, for though i am incapable, as Your mortal primate, of understanding the meaning and mystery of Your circuitous Path, yea nonetheless i am humbled to crawl behind You in the Valley of Eternal Hope. Lauren said that she'd still be in the apartment on West 72nd through the weekend, and suggested I meet her there. I carefully wrote down, then repeated back, all relevant phone and residential information. 8 7 4 - 6 8 7 2. Eight-seven-four! Not seven-eight-four! Jesus. "I'll make a reservation for nine…how 'bout if I come to your place around eight-thirty?"

"That sounds great," she said, "see you then."

"Great, see you then!" Click. 'Eight-seven-four.' I rolled up the "Weekend" section of *The Times* and slapped myself in the face over and over again. Catharsis. But the ordeal was done. A done ordeal. I rejoiced to myself, literally trembling at the thought of seeing Lauren, and reflecting on the amazing events of the past week. And now, behind my desk, what a Friday afternoon I was sitting in! My office filled up with tapioca pudding— just like my Mother used to make—and I flailed my arms gleefully. Terri ran down the hall and peered into my doorway, her eyes popping with astonishment at the tapioca, rising rapidly above desk height.

"Michael! What the hell is happening?"

"Lauren called! We're going out tomorrow night! I don't think that she suspects I'm an idiot! And I feel like I'm getting ready for prom night and I don't know what to wear but I might soil myself or a treasured piece of furniture."

"God, you *are* an idiot. Did you tell John yet?"

"No, could you summon him—I can't move from my chair!"

I have, on a number of occasions in this narrative, referred to God. To be truthful, I cannot tell you with certainty that there is a God, although I now plead for His or Her mercy, should He or She be out there, for ever doubting His or Her existence. On Saturday so powerful was my feeling of elation that I considered it strong evidence of the existence of God. And God made the Heavens, and God made Earth. And Earth is a board game, except that it is round. I spent three hours selecting, from my closet, a combination of jeans, shirt and jacket that I thought would speak most clearly of my personal 'style'—specifically, man-with-limited-wardrobe. I reminded myself that I would also need shoes. By seven-forty, I was dressed and ready. Unfortunately, I wasn't supposed to meet Lauren for another fifty minutes, and she was just a five-minute walk down 72nd Street.

You hate that, too, don't you? You are dressed, you are ready, but it's too early to leave. What are you going to do, walk around the block a few times? Have the fluids checked in your car? Pretend to start reading a magazine? You're screwed, because you're just going display all the signs of twitching inertia—question your shirt, review your shave, examine the spaces between your teeth for trace elements, watch the eighth frame of a regional women's bowling championship. That's what I did. And I kept trying to recreate the image of Lauren—I tried to *see* her. What would she be wearing? Was I starting to perspire? Shit! I haven't even left the apartment! I shouldn't have had a beer this afternoon. I checked my watch. Eight-twelve. I checked my breath, which is difficult to do by yourself. You have to cup both of your hands over your mouth, expel air from the mouth into your cupped hands, and then inhale that air through your nose. I required a dab of toothpaste. Okay, I'm leaving now. Okay, bye-bye. Shoes! Must put shoes on.

Out on 72nd Street, I walked slowly, methodically westward using the traditional technique of placing one foot in front of the other, pushing off on the front foot then lifting the following foot forward until it becomes the leading foot, pushing off, etc. Using this method, I arrived at Lauren's building in nine minutes. Eight twenty-eight. If I wanted to be five minutes 'late,' I had seven minutes to kill. Across the street I could see a delicatessen, so I decided to pay a visit. In the refrigerated section there were little tubs of yogurt. I checked all of their expiration dates—there wasn't much time left. When yogurt has expired don't serve it to your loved ones. Here is a pretty little plastic tub with French words on it, printed in New Jersey, and inside is a scary dairy product that is turning against you. Don't open the tub. Back away from the tub. The tub wants to hurt you. Eight thirty-three. "Are you looking for something, buddy?"

"No, ah, thank you."

I crossed the street once again and searched the buttons outside the building entrance for 12A. "Hello."

"Hi, it's Michael."

"Come on up, 12th floor." The palms of my hands were like wet naps, which, of course, is why we wear jeans. I started breathing deeply. When I got off the elevator I noticed that one of the apartment doors was already open. I approached and sang "Hello..." Lauren came to the door immediately. "Hi, Michael...nice to see you again!" She extended her hand warmly.

"It's nice to see you, too."

If I tell you how breathtaking she looked you'll say 'Oh, that's just how he thinks he remembers she looked,' right? You're convinced that I would misrepresent the truth just to give this moment the titillating gratification those daytime soaps give you. Sorry, but turn off the TV—you're not in your room anymore. You're in Lauren's room with me; she is beautiful, and you share my astonishment and my anguish. A dancer. Long, dark hair, unbound, flowing over a pearl-colored, antique silk blouse. Underneath, a tiny black embroidered tank top. Her breasts are small and unsupported. Black leotards under a black silk mini wrap-skirt. Black, glove-soft, calf-height, high-heeled boots. How does a small person have this stature? The confidence of the shoulders, the neck. The lithe lyricism of the legs and arms. A piercing, yet open face. "Would you like to come in for a few minutes before we leave?"

"Sure." She bustled about the apartment finding little things to put in her small pearl bag. She introduced me to the cats, Theo and Scarlet.

What are cats for? How do they benefit us? Well, they did look right with Lauren. Exquisitely feline.

"So, what have you been up to? It seems like ages since we met, doesn't it?" It was nice of her to begin a conversation. But I didn't know what to say—I mean, I've only been up to one thing for a week. Man overboard! Will I be able to return to mid-thought one hundred sixty-eight hours later?

"Yeah, I can hardly believe it. Uh, well, I've mostly been working, and my partner and I went to Detroit this week for a presentation…yeah, we worked really hard this week." And, of course, I became a single-celled animal whose exclusive purpose in life was to find an emotional host—yourself—to which I could attach my twitching, needy microcosmic being…how was your week?

"Mine was exhausting, too. I taught five classes…and my company is rehearsing for a performance at BAM in early April—you should come!"

"That sounds great, I'd love to." My sister had taken me to see Twyla Tharp once years ago. I could see some more dance. I would like to see Lauren dance. I checked my watch. "Maybe we should get going," I suggested. "The reservation's for nine, and it's nine! Although it's just a ten-minute walk from here."

"I'll just get my coat."

Out on 72nd Street, dozens of the signs were still taped everywhere. "So you noticed these?" I said with a slightly uncomfortable smile.

"My friend and I counted forty-three," she said, with an easy smile and a squeeze of my hand. "And you said there were more?"

"Well, two more blocks' worth, all the way to Broadway. Actually, just over a hundred in all…but I'm feeling much better now, thank you. I was released from the clinic yesterday, and advised to just stay out of taxis for another four to five weeks."

"You poor thing. I'm glad you're feeling better. It did occur to me that you might be a little crazy…but I thought if we stayed on the major thoroughfares, and in well-lit places, I shouldn't have to worry." I laughed inside. Then I laughed out loud. Then I just stopped and gave her a hug.

"Don't worry, you're safe—they declawed me at the clinic while I was sedated." We both laughed. It was getting easier to be near her. What a beautiful planet. And upon it I had gone to a place where I had never been, and found something that I'd lost years before. How is that possible? Do you see the two of us now, walking hand-in-hand along Columbus Avenue, talking about how frustrating and yet how wonderful it is to dance in New York? Maybe you can tell me what I had for dinner, because I don't remember. Our eyes were dancing when we talked and it seemed only moments after sitting down that we were the last ones in the restaurant. I told the manager that I would close up, to send the staff home, give me the key—I would put the bags out on the sidewalk, pull down the gate and lock up. No I didn't. I asked for the check.

"What a nice dinner," Lauren said as we got up from the table. "I'm glad you took the trouble to 'find' me!"

"Me, too," I said. "I hope we'll get together again soon. You'll have to give me your number…" Out on the sidewalk, the night was slowing down. It was nearly one o'clock already! We walked slowly to the north, back in the direction of her building.

And then Lauren said, "Maybe we should pick up the Sunday *Times*, and a few things for breakfast."

And I said, "You're right. Breakfast is the most important meal of the day." All right, I have no idea what I said. I was stunned. God was allowing me to view a classified film clip of the Creation of the Universe—the fiery explosions and molten implosions that caused the formation of the stars and planets, the constellations and galaxies. God was sending me home with Lauren.

I can't take you up in the elevator with me, into Lauren's apartment. You have to stay down here, on the sidewalk. It was decades ago, anyway, and the person Lauren was apartment-sitting for moved out of the City fifteen years ago! I just can't take you to that moment fully, that's all I mean. Oh stop complaining, for Christ's sake, I'm just sitting here at my desk trying to make this right for everybody. There are a few things I can share with you, but I'll ask you to first close your eyes. Do it, close them. Okay, right, how can you read with your eyes closed? Close, instead, the windows to your peripheral awareness and only think about and feel this: Underneath the antique silk blouse, the little wrap, the leotards and boots, behind the curtain of black hair, was the body of a dancer. Small, sculpted, powerful, unselfconscious. And she, this beautiful woman, Lauren, whom I had met and lost and found only moments before, and whom I now lay beside, told me how beautiful *I* looked. Jesus.

The phrase 'making love' is strange to me. You make toast. You make an appointment. Nonetheless, the phrase is indispensable. We 'shared love' sounds like Hallmark gibberish. Never use the word 'fuck' when referring to this time with another person. Don't do it. Never say, "And then we fucked," or "I fucked her once." Say, "We once made love," or something more openly descriptive, such as, "We broke through the seemingly impenetrable shell of our physical and emotional selves and entered each other." (Though I can't imagine who the fuck would want that information). Use the word 'fuck' for other things, for it is a great word—it's like a Swiss Army knife, but with many more functions. Use it to describe how you're being treated by your employer. Use it when marveling at an extraordinary athletic achievement, or when narrowly averting a serious auto accident, or when slapping your forehead because you left your tackle box on the dock, or when you receive a registered letter, or when the yolk breaks in your pan, or when you realize that the ground is frozen on the day you wanted to plant tubers.

My euphoria finally gave way to sleep, and into a trance I fell with my arm around Lauren. Hours later I was awakened. Awakened by the sound of someone crying. It was still nearly dark in the room. Lauren was not by my side. I could see her silhouette, sitting on the edge of the bed, arms clutched around her knees, head bowed down, hair over her face, ribs heaving. What was wrong? "Lauren, what's wrong? Are you all right? What happened…why are you crying?" Lauren turned to face me, pushing the hair away from her face. Her eyes and nose were red, covered in tears. She was still sobbing.

"I'm sorry…I think it was too soon for this…too soon for me. It's not your fault…the man I was living with for eight years, it's only six weeks ago that we broke up. I'm still confused. I guess I'm not as 'over it' as I thought I was." I sat up and put my hand on her shoulder. I wanted so painfully to hold her, but she would not accept my touch. We talked quietly and I professed to understand what she must be going through. It was five in the morning.

"Is it something you could talk about? Would that help?"

"Michael, I think it's something I have to come to terms with myself—and I haven't done that yet."

"Would you feel more comfortable if I weren't here right now? If you could be alone?"

"Yes," she said. "I think I need to be alone…I'm sorry."

"No, no, it's all right," I said. I left the bed and stood up. I could feel the weight in the room lift as I put my clothes on. She put on a robe and faced me.

"I'm sorry," Lauren said again.

"It's all right. I don't want you to be unhappy, but I'd still like to see you again. This was an amazing night, especially after all that came before it. Can I call you in a couple of days…to see how you're feeling?"

"Yes, you can call me. As long as you don't lose the number." Good, a smile. A smile and a kiss on the cheek.

Minutes later I was standing on 72nd Street. Dawn's early light. Trucks delivering the newspapers. Trucks picking up the garbage. Signs on the light poles seeking the whereabouts of Lauren. I looked at all of this, and into my chest cavity, where only a small, dim refrigerator light could be seen. I walked home, sat on the edge of my bed and shook my head in disbelief. Then I lay me down to sleep. Of course, I couldn't wait more than two days before calling Lauren. I could think of nothing else. We had to take this somewhere. We had to recognize that something unique was unfolding, we should not prevent it from doing so, from blossoming into what it would become.

Lauren's voice was warm, but not near. It was across a bridge that she would not traverse. She was feeling better, much better. She had had a wonderful time, and I was a special person. She knew that she was not ready to see someone just now. It would be a mistake, at least right now, if we got together again. Oh, yes, I could call her once in a while. Yes, she would call me if she needed anything at all, but I shouldn't worry about her. Someone special would love to meet a man like me.

Sightings

Have you ever looked up at a cloud formation and seen the face of Gandalf? Or Santa? Or the head of a dragon? Me too. It's always kind of magical. And when the image disappears after a few moments, it's okay. It doesn't sting, it was just a fleeting moment, nothing more.

Those cloud formations aren't just in the sky, you know. They're in the way we view lots of things, as much with our imagination as with our eyes. Like that incredible person you once thought was The One. An overwhelming feeling. You remember falling hard for him or her, don't you? As if some version of destiny had brought you two together. And then, he or she disappointed you and was suddenly—or slowly—gone. Still, it wasn't really all for nothing, was it? Don't you look back affectionately on that moment, when your imagination could create a cloud formation resembling your soul mate? Of course you do. Or maybe you don't— maybe it's a wretched memory. I'm so sorry. Will you repeat this act of invention over and over again? Possibly. But don't shut the door, keep it open. Otherwise, may as well stop reading this and pick up something about, for example, the history of the railway system in America.

Today I went to Central Park for a stroll. Were you there? A mid-November day, the air crisp, slight breeze, the sun low but brilliant in the sky, temperature in the upper 50s. Thank God they don't allow parking for trailers and Airstreams—no bumper stickers saying WE CAMPED IN CENTRAL PARK! out there. Just a blissfully welcoming universe of paths and promenades, lakes and fountains, fields, forests, arbors, gardens, cafes, benches, statuary—created not by ancient rivers and spewing lava, but by humans. Well done, humans.

People are sitting on the south-facing benches with their jackets loosened, absorbing the sun. A beautiful Chinese woman is breastfeeding her baby while her mother peels an apple and her husband takes a photograph. So exquisite and painterly is this scene that these delicate

19

figures seem barely to touch the bench upon which they're seated.

Another couple quietly discusses some item from a newspaper. A woman gives roller-skating lessons to eight people who look like they'd rather be sitting on those benches. Runners and cyclists float silently by. A bare-chested old man whom I've come to recognize is meticulously washing his body with cloth and water from Evian bottles standing at his feet. A Hispanic couple is making out next to the fountain. Her left ear is rimmed with rings, her right thigh between his legs, his arms around her waist. They kiss, he whispers something, she smiles, they kiss. They seem so comfortable I'm surprised their skeletons can support them, that they don't just slump blissfully to the ground. Beautiful.

■   ■   ■

My mother and stepfather were supposed to fly from Rochester to New York City Friday afternoon for Mother's Day weekend, but Mom called in the morning and said Ben wasn't feeling well when he woke up. He had trouble walking from the bed to the dresser. He felt dizzy and disoriented. She canceled the flight and made an appointment for him to have X-Rays on Monday. She's saying Ben may have had a "small stroke." She's saying, "It's probably nothing serious, but we just want to be sure."

That's what she said when my father had his heart attack in Florida almost 30 years earlier. "It's nothing serious—Dad's going to be fine. He doesn't want you kids rushing to his bedside, it'll just embarrass and depress him. I'll call you and keep you informed." Three weeks later Dad was dead—the next, and last, time we saw him was in his casket. Now Mom is almost eighty and Ben's not "feeling well." If Ben goes Mom will be alone. She'll never move to New York. "I'm not leaving Rochester again. This is my home and this is where my routine is, and Ben will probably outlast me anyway!" The thought of Mom being alone empties me out. From this place, the very next thought is that of Mom not being around. Mom gone.

Mother's Day weekend, and I'm thinking about Mom not being in New York, not being here, on our beautiful planet. I wish my mind didn't go to these places. Damn it. Is your mother alive? Are you close to her?

I fight with my mother. She loves driving carpet tacks into my psyche. But what if she weren't here? Jesus. I'll order some flowers for Saturday delivery and call her on Sunday. She'll be taking care of Ben. She'll make sure he's dressed and drive him to church. Mom will be taking care of Ben, and I'll be writing a fucking thing about finding your soul mate. Thirty years with Dad, making sure his home ran smoothly, and the kids were all scrubbed and off to school. Almost twenty-five years with Ben—if they can just hang in there another seven months. And I'm writing this? To shed some light on something? As if I have a fucking clue. Jesus.

Later that summer we all came to Rochester for Mom's eightieth birthday. She wanted to make it a big party. "Our family and friends never get together like the old days. I wanted to do it now, for my birthday, instead of waiting for my wake. I thought we'd enjoy this more, don't you think, honey?"

"You did the right thing, Mom. We're definitely enjoying it more than your wake—it's a fantastic party!" And it was. There had to be sixty people. The really old ones—the few remaining. The widows and widowers. And the younger cousins, with their new families. And the single-for-the-second-or-third-timers. After dinner, I heard somebody clinking a glass. Ben was handed a microphone by the restaurant maitre d'. I was nervous, maybe a little uncomfortable. Ben's "small stroke" had left him frail and unable to speak evenly. I didn't want him to embarrass himself. Or was I thinking of *my* self? And then Ben spoke, in a steady voice.

"I want to thank everybody for coming tonight. Jeanne and I really appreciate it. I just want to say 'Happy Birthday' to my wife, and to thank her for being with me for twenty-five years, and for making them the best years of my life. I love you, Jeanne. Happy Birthday."

Ben's words entered me through the chest where they transformed into feelings and expanded like a stream after a cloudburst, overflowing its banks at the rims of my eyes. How fortunate for Ben to have found my mother. How fortunate for both of them. And now I can add Ben's words to this page. If they were the only words that stuck to any of these pages the book would still be complete. I'd have Ben sign your copy.

■ ■ ■

Many winters ago I was having dinner with a friend in a smoky little downtown bistro in the Village. We sat in the crowded front room, trying to get to the bottom of a bottle of Sancerre, when I felt something tapping on my shoulder. I turned around to see that it was Kate Moss! In the nano-moment prior to first spoken words, I thought to myself, 'Why did Kate Moss tap my shoulder? What was her reason for wanting to get my attention? Had she overheard me speaking about the decline of substance in popular culture? Is it possible she finds me interesting?' I was struck by the shape of her mouth and her immaculate complexion.

And then she said something so unexpected that Sancerre ran out of my gaping jaw. "Hi, I'm Kate."

"I'm Michael…nice to meet you."

"Sorry for eavesdropping, but what you were saying was so interesting…would you like to get together later and talk? Maybe see a movie?"

"Ha! Well, I promise I'm not that interesting—but, sure, I'd love to."

"Great! Let's chat before we leave this place…"

"Absolutely—enjoy your brunch!"

But Kate Moss didn't say any of that to me. She said, "Excuse me, could you remove your chair from my coat?" She didn't use any of her facial muscles when she spoke. The words just came from her mouth in one weary monotone.

"Oh, sorry, of course", I said. I turned around, facing my friend.

"It's a small room," he said, "the tables are really close. More wine?"

■　■　■

Walking south along Central Park Drive I approach an older couple, sitting with books in their laps. They're holding hands and look at me with a smile. They know I recognize what they have. They know it's a collector's item and they're proud—not boastful—to show it off. And it looks beautiful, with the afternoon sun glinting off of it, their love. I have some important questions for them, but I smile, nod and move on.

"Beautiful day."

"It sure is. Enjoy!"

There are many couples out for a walk this day, arm-in-arm. Some are pushing strollers. The babies asleep in the dreamy autumn atmosphere. I hear German spoken, and French, Spanish, Hebrew, and Mandarin (I think). What a great moment for them, here in America's greatest metropolis. They made love before coming down from their hotel rooms for breakfast and the bus tour, don't you think? I remember when my wife and I went to Paris for the first time, walking forever, taking that dinner cruise down the Seine, spotlights illuminating the ancient buildings along the river bank and a roving accordion player strolling from table to table, destroying American standards. We kissed and asked for more Champagne. It didn't really matter what was drifting by outside the window; the current was beneath our skin; we used our hearts for floatation. We were shipmates. We were soul mates. We were making love in Paris.

We're not married anymore. I'm alone, walking south along the Central Park Drive.

What Do Souls Look Like?

Probably any narrative involving the idea of a 'soul mate' should at least pause to contemplate the *soul*. What is it? Do we really have a soul? Or is it just a word we use to comfort ourselves about an 'afterlife'—a way of believing that there *is* an afterlife, and our 'spirit' never really dies, and we live forever and ever, amen?

Early in the previous century a physician from Massachusetts, Duncan MacDougall, attempted to prove that we do, in fact, have a physical soul. His method? Weighing the bodies of several dying persons shortly before their demise, then weighing them again immediately upon their death. Of the six bodies he weighed in—and out—one of them registered a weight loss of approximately 21 grams (about three-quarters of an ounce). The others did not show the same results, which he attributed to a faulty calibration of the scale. The reason for the weight loss? The corpse's 21-gram soul had left his body. This fascinating experiment was ridiculed by many in the scientific community (the sample size being rather small), though it did receive a great deal of press.

Most religions, and nearly all of the early philosophers refer to a soul or souls as an incorporeal though crucial part of human life—an entity both detached from yet integral to the human *being*. In virtually all Christian sects there is a belief that our souls will be judged by God once we have died, and God will decide whether we go to heaven or to hell—or in between—depending upon how we have lived our lives, how we have measured up against His Commandments. Better say your prayers!

In Jainism, every living being has a soul (Jīva), from plants to humans. There are liberated souls, which can rest in peace, so to speak, and non-liberated souls, which will have to repeat the birth and death cycles endlessly, presumably till they get it right. Karma.

From Hinduism to Judaism to Taoism and everywhere in between there is reference to and reverence for the soul, the soul's relationship to life, to god, the nature and purpose(s) of the soul, where it goes or doesn't go when we die. If you were born into one of the aforementioned religions and grew up in its teachings you would probably accept and understand the spiritual narrative of that religion. Maybe even question the legitimacy of all the others. (Sound familiar?) If you were born and raised in an agnostic underground compound, then liberated at the age of 18 and offered a complete menu of religious belief systems to choose from, you could probably live out the rest of your life just reading the collected canons, gospels, scriptures, parables, commandments, dogma and etcetera. And wonder to yourself, What the...? (Remarkably, some people actually choose to do that.)

So, back to the question: *Do* we have a soul? The answer is, Yes, we really do have a soul. It's light blue, and nearly spherical in shape, between three and four inches in diameter. (Mine is about three and three-eighths.) All souls are translucent and have a somewhat gelatinous texture. Even in good light, you can't see objects clearly behind them. Souls are virtually weightless—well, under normal conditions they're actually a bit lighter than air. Meaning that the average, unencumbered soul will hover a few feet off the ground.

And yet a soul's vertical coordinates can change dramatically. That's because souls are affected by emotional gravity, and levity. It's quite remarkable, really. If you see a soul at or barely above ground level, you might assume there is some weight, some gravity. Weight caused by an extract of emotional friction—also known as *soul freight*. This 'symptom' manifests itself due to the release of xenon, one of the noble gases that are heavier than oxygen. And if you see a soul drifting above the head— even rising up, like a blown bubble—you know that there is levity. It is caused by the release of neon, a gaseous byproduct of both the resting and ebullient emotional states. (Also one of the noble gases, neon is colorless, odorless and inert, but will display a blueish bioluminescence under these conditions.)

If you're standing by a still pond, or on a beach, at dusk, it's possible you'd see a number of souls floating, or rising above the heads of those nearby. Yes, you *can* see them anywhere—city streets, baseball stadiums, malls, though it's quite difficult due to the multiple visual distractions at all elevations. But in a tranquil 'still life' setting they just look delicate and beautiful in their state of levity. Conversely, a soul at ground-level, or even below (they have little density, so any surface is potential quicksand to the soul), is a depressing sight. Just look into the eyes of the owner of such a soul. Actually, look in the mirror, into your own eyes, and you will probably sense the position of your soul right now. Don't be afraid! I don't need to do it because I already know what I'll see looking back at me. I know my soul isn't floating above the ground. When I go into the subway this morning, I won't let your eyes meet mine. I'll avert my gaze. Don't worry, I don't think it's anything serious. Although today would not be a great day to die, I have to admit. That's a digression, sorry.

So if the soul is light blue, round, three to four inches in diameter and gelatinous, why have so few people seen it? Good question. Because of its translucence (the blown bubble image), it's very difficult to detect in daylight. And when it can be observed, closer to dusk, it may seem more like an optical illusion, fleeting, like the brief appearance of a rainbow after a shower. Or a shooting star. I'm guessing that it's easier to *feel* the soul than to see it. Whatever the case, for millennia people have talked about, written about the soul, sometimes referring to it as the *spirit*, which is nearly universal among indigenous American cultures. From the Ojibwe (who are credited with creating the dreamcatcher) to the Lakota Sioux, who believe in Wakan Tanka—the Great Spirit or Great Mystery—to the Shawnee, whose Great Spirit was female, indigenous peoples believed in a very direct relationship between all life on Earth and the Great Mystery beyond.

This we do know: the soul is created in the same way that the soul states are created—bio-electric wave patterns emanating from the brain, tempered by a combination of life experience and emotional stimuli. These waves are so sensitive to your feelings, your emotional state, there is a great deal of flux. Yet they're of such a low frequency they're barely detectable. Exponentially lower, for example, than the radio waves traveling between cell phones and base stations. Still, as previously suggested, the soul functions as a sort of barometer of the human emotional—some would say *spiritual*—condition. When we refer to a person's *aura* we're probably describing something about them that can't easily be seen but which can be *felt* or *sensed*. So subtle are these 'signals' that we might rush to judgment about an individual only to be proven wrong later—a too hasty interpretation of that aura.

So maybe that's another way of thinking about the soul. Fine. But let's move on. Now that we've settled the questions of whether we have a soul and what it looks like, what then is a *soul mate*? And why do we go looking for one? In the context we're examining here, we're not interested in the popular usage of the term, whose meaning has been reduced to the size of a heart emoji. Like the word awesome. *That's an awesome hat! Those jeans are awesome! This rosé is awesome! Everything's awesome.* Hey, everything's *not* fucking awesome. Sorry. Didn't mean to go off there. Although I have to say, those shoes you're wearing *are* pretty awesome. Anyway, back to soul mates. We're not talking about a trusted friend, nor your closest sibling, the one you can share your most intimate secrets with. Not an amazing lover, no matter how compelling those euphoric moments are. And definitely not either of your parents, however supportive they were during your formative years. God help us, we may not even be talking about your husband, or your wife. Hey, it's not my fault if you didn't marry your soul mate. It happens—look at the divorce rate!

We're talking about someone unique indeed: the individual who singularly contributes to the near completeness of your being by simultaneously engaging your senses, intellect and spirit in both a positive and negative manner, resulting in a kind of bio-electric feedback loop that is nurturing to each of your souls individually while giving birth to a third sphere whose makeup consists of new wave patterns—hopefully resulting in blueish bioluminescence—from your jointly-created universe. At the very least someone in whose presence your own soul could maintain a more constant state of levity. Maybe even soar.

In reality, even if we didn't have a soul we would probably still seek the companionship of someone who "contributes to our near completeness ...engaging (our) senses, intellect, and spirit..." Who wouldn't want that?

So there it is. We have a soul and it's light blue and nearly spherical. I hope yours is floating beautifully. And good luck with the search.

Going Back

(I'm certain it seems strange, but I can't allow myself to narrate this story as it actually happened, because it also involves someone else whose privacy and feelings must be protected. A sacred trust. But I'm grateful that my dear friend Michelle, an amazing actor, has agreed to assume my 'part' in this summer's tale. I have no doubt she has the emotional depth and experience to tell it fearlessly and from the heart. And that 'someone else...'—here she will be Jake, another close friend and successful actor. Thank you, Michelle, and thank you, Jake.)

I've known Jake for over eighteen years. We took acting classes together in New York when we were barely twenty. And we actually worked in the same restaurant for about three months—a trendy place near Lincoln Center that attracted a lot of theatre and television execs. What a bunch of phonies some of those guys were. Balding bean counters and talent reps who loved being able to say, "Why yes, I'm in the arts, too!" I don't know how many times I heard "You have incredible eyes—are you an actress?" Why no, my dream has always been to wait tables. But thank you for your flattering assumption.

I got out of there, but Jake stayed on a few months longer, I think until he landed a paying showcase, or some out-of-town summer thing. It was eighteen years ago for God's sake. Jake had sad eyes—maybe not sad, but seeming somehow to convey a deep sense of empathy. They had a twinkle in them, too. They still do! I think he had a bit of a crush on me but was somehow careful not to express it. Maybe he felt a little insecure and didn't want to put our friendship at risk by showing interest. He must have seen men coming on to me pretty much all the time. (It's been that way since I was thirteen, but I never let it turn me into a bitch. I had fun and I had great girlfriends, too, and we just knew how to make a scene. Nobody ever got hurt. Well maybe a couple of bruised hearts, but that's gonna happen, right?) I'm actually thankful he didn't go for it—we worked well together, we found it easy to talk, about 'the business,' our dreams, how long we'd give it before getting a 'real' job. And we laughed a lot—you can't want much more of a friend in a city like New York.

What an amazing time it was. People will say you're all grown up by the end of your teens—who and what you are is pretty much complete. But I'll tell you from experience, it's just starting. You have the chance to take events and opportunities and ideas and shape the rest of your life with them. It's not Driver's Ed anymore—you've got the wheel and there's no one else in the car. We were starting to get legitimate work (a great theatrical expression, *legitimate*—not to be confused with exotic dancing, I suppose, or commercials?). It was happening for both of us, and of course it pulled us away from the common thread of our New York lives—acting classes, the restaurant. We went from Off-Broadway to auditions and parts on the other coast. I would never wear an apron again (not counting "Frankie and Johnny," for which I was underpaid, by the way, but that was early on).

Though Jake and I never had the opportunity to work together in theatre or film we remained good friends. I'd see him several times a year at industry functions, of course, and we'd always take those moments to catch up. And it always felt so easy to fall right back into our rhythm and our humor. We've seen each other through our career lows and relationship highs and vice versa. I'd sometimes wished we'd had that little fling, wondered what it might have led to—Jake's such a great guy, and a pretty special person where it counts, where the camera doesn't see.

Things changed last summer. I was between projects—and between some other things as well—and had decided to spend most of June, July and August in East Hampton. My soul needed ocean air rushing through it, my heart needed to lose some weight. With a handful of friends around me, this would be a great season for just recharging. I had no idea that Jake was going to be in the Hamptons as well, until he showed up at a little dinner party at Kathleen's. Why did this feel like camp all of a sudden? All the years we'd known each other and I'd never seen him in a pair of shorts! I started talking his ear off immediately, and at the end of the evening I didn't want to say goodbye. I suggested my place for a last glass of wine. "I haven't had a chance to entertain yet—this will be my trial housewarming!"

"Sounds like a plan," he said. It turned out that Jake was renting less than a half-mile away, on Egypt Lane. I hardly gave it a thought.

We were still talking when the birds started their own conversations—a pre-dawn ritual I wasn't yet familiar with. I offered another refill, but Jake put his glass on the table, stood up and intercepted me at the fridge. He put his hand on my shoulder and gently turned me around. "And then he kissed me," as the song goes. I don't believe I've kissed a friend very many times in my life. It seems strange to say that and having said it, strange to even think it. All the history and knowledge, all the intellectual and emotional experience, and intimacy. And now a kiss. Eighteen years later. And there are no barriers to throw up in front of this kiss—or we are too exhausted to put them up—and so this kiss grows wild in a field no one is tending. I'd never thought that his lips might be soft, or that there might be something on the tip of his tongue other than a kind thought or some playfully wicked advice. But here it was, and it was changing my breathing. Jake pulled away for a moment and looked at me as if he'd had an epiphany. "Whatever happens, whatever this summer brings…nothing can get in the way of our friendship, Michelle—we can't let that happen."

"We won't," I said, "we'll never let that happen."

I led us upstairs to my bedroom and we undressed each other in the just before daylight. Why had I never imagined that the skin on his back might be smooth? Never imagined the touch of his hands on me? Well, why would I? Our sad eyes flooded with happiness as we looked at each other. We were smiling. A laugh escaped, I'm sure of it. And an "Oh my God."

Daylight took its place in the room, and the occasional vehicle could be heard outside. Off to work, off to market.

"I better go let Teddy out," Jake whispered, referring to his Yellow Lab. "He's a good boy, but he expected me home last night! I'm pretty sure he'll want to have a word."

"I'm pretty sure he'll want to have a poop!" We kissed, he put his clothes on slowly, and we kissed again. I shook my head, but the smile wouldn't come loose.

"Can I call you later? Do you have plans tonight?"

"They're not firm," I confessed.

"Maybe we could firm them up," he suggested with a clever glance. Oh God.

That's how the summer started. I felt my heart filling with helium and there wasn't any Off valve. Apparently, preparations were underway for a circumnavigation. My tender, pink heart, so achingly full, now barely tethered several hundred feet above the lawn. I could see my body down there, trying to wave me back, and Jake was there, too, shaking his head with an incredulous smile. And I could hear the distant voices of children on the beach, mingling with crashing waves and an occasional seagull. What a soft breeze was pushing me back and forth up here—I was ready to go, needed no provisions. I would follow the trades and land where I landed. Every ascension of this kind begins with the presumption of a glorious journey—you do not get here thinking about a forced landing.

I must tell you about Sunday brunch in August. I never go to brunch—it seems such a wasteful intrusion into perfectly beautiful daylight. Time better spent in the garden, on a bicycle, or being pummeled in the surf! But Jake insisted he was suffering eggs Benedict withdrawal and promised we'd have beach time long before the sun sank into the sea. Seeing him on his knees at my doorway was disturbing—well, fairly hilarious, actually— so I relented. And off we drove for a dockside repast on Three Mile Harbor. I felt like a tourist, sitting beside my gentle companion, watching the older folks being seated in their Sunday best for an endless afternoon. They weren't thinking about rushing off to the beach. And like them, I found myself savoring what was here on the table before us—quiet talk, soft breeze, lines slapping against masts, kids' footsteps on cedar planks, food and drink in a slow rhythm. Slow. The vignette was no longer a moving picture. Everything stopped…it became a painting, in which each object evoked the same feeling, throwing off light in the same muted trajectory.

"I guess we should go," I heard his voice speak from the painting, perhaps hours later.

"Yes, we should go." I drove, top-down, along Three Mile Harbor's winding route, as he pressed instructions into the sound system. And into my ears flowed a voluminous refrain from another time—Al Stewart's "Year of the Cat." His feminine, vulnerable voice proclaiming, *"Well the mornin' comes and you're still with her"*...Spanish guitar articulating the gorgeous counter-melody...lush strings filling the torso...the deliriously soulful saxophone solo breaking your heart and forcing a laugh for joy, while the wind swoops along your cheeks and the one seated beside you, whom you know so well, becomes, like you, transported to another place. A dirigible, inflated with emotion and propelled by magic, already passing through hemispheres never before attempted. We arrived in his driveway. I stopped, turned off the engine, sat motionless. I looked at my companion, touched his cheek and whispered, "That was nice."

"Yes," he said.

"We should go to the beach."

"Yes," he said. Then I kissed him beneath the high afternoon sun. I held his face close to me, to feel him while we kissed. This was the kiss. If I could hold this kiss in my hand I would take it around the world. I would show it to people of all cultures, speak of its amazing powers and try to explain how this kiss could be recreated under the proper climatic and sonic conditions. Teddy barked at the doorway, anxious to end all kissing and intercept a bit of affection for himself.

"Maybe we should go inside," he said.

"Yes," I said. He held me closely as we walked through the front door, both of us smiling at our vignette, whose unfolding moments we could almost foretell.

"Hello! Hello? Anybody home?" Teddy shot out the door behind us, housesitting duties over for now. Jake's guests were at the beach, of course. (I would like to belatedly thank them for that.) We walked slowly upstairs, to a sunlight-flooded room. He opened the curtains and windows wide so the breeze and distant surf could occupy the space with us, and we embraced. He lifted me onto the bed. We had never seen each other in this light before, and though the prickle of shyness I felt was real, we never took our eyes from each other. There was no other consciousness. Warm blood rushed through my body and my head became light. We belonged only to this moment. "Does this feel all right?" he whispered.

"Yes…yes, it does." No attachment or mooring. No other thing to cling to. Only this. Drifting in the room, our tide rising, eyes open, floating away.

You couldn't have realized that the world stood still just then. Over an hour was taken from your life, as all movement in the Universe ceased. Yet you never missed it, and when the day resumed the journey through its lifespan, you may even have felt, perhaps subconsciously, rejuvenated. One day you will thank us.

If I say that both Jake and I were free and unencumbered that summer, it would still require an asterisk, some clarification. He was ending a relationship that had been at the center of his life for many years. I think most of us know that feeling. Have you ever tried to remove a small tree from your backyard, and one last root would not give way to the shovel? No amount of pulling would loosen its grip. You have to take a break, go into the house for a beer, maybe check the mail. Then come back to the root with renewed strength and resolve. (I haven't actually done that, but it seems like a reasonable analogy.) Jake was taking a break. It's not that he lacked the resolve, but he'd given himself the summer before returning to the root. I understood this, of course, but at the same time I was not myself involved in such a task. Stuck in the ground? Hey, if you look up that's my pink heart floating past Montauk! And that's where it remained, through all the days of summer. No wonder I could run for miles without feeling exhausted—I was practically weightless.

■　■　■

Why is there always an element of melancholy associated with the final weekend of summer? Labor Day, but no labor. Laboring under the weight of the coming season? The season drifting away? Strong tide. Your hand is on the rope, but you can't hold it any longer…it's slipping, isn't it? A labor of love? Empty the refrigerator, empty the bottles. Empty your heart. Jake and I were talking a lot this weekend. I needed to be clear about what was happening to me, to my heart. I would be returning to the City the day after tomorrow, and I wanted to bring it with me, not leave it floating here, in a summer place. I wanted to know he felt this way, too, that he understood in the same way I did the uniqueness of what we had found together and the importance of transporting it carefully to its next destination. But Jake needed me to understand something else. That his business back there was unfinished—the root had yet to be removed, and this ground could not be covered again until it was.

Sunday night Ely Klein's annual lawn bash was 'the place to be.' Summer's last stand by the sea. Everything was so beautiful, so perfect, you almost had to laugh. A steel band playing on the upper tier of the pool deck, a path of lanterns all the way to the beach, preppie kids in white shirts passing mini salmon cakes and stems of champagne. Jake and I moved slowly through the happy celebrants, recognizing a few faces, stopping for refills and "Saluds!" to an incredible summer. Ely grabbed me by the sleeve and screamed for joy, "I'm so glad you're here, Michelle! This is amazing, isn't it? I wish this summer would never end—has there ever been one like it?!" Jake had the great fortune to be introduced to two older gentlemen—owners of a furnishings shop on Newtown Lane—one of whom I heard say, "The remarkable thing is that you don't really look like an actor. Harrison Ford looks like an actor." And thus, we were separated in the tide of festivity that swirled on the shore of this final summer night, tossed from one encounter to the next as the hours passed.

I cannot describe the smile on my face and the sadness in my heart that coexisted impossibly on this night, and I finally resolved to end the conflict. I had to leave. When I told Jake I needed to find my bed but that he should stay and not worry about me, real anger flashed across his face. Which filled me with dread. I led him away from the patio and onto a more private area of the lawn. "I'm just really tired and I can't stay here any longer…it's fine, I don't want you to worry about me."

"What are you doing?" he pleaded. "You've got the rest of your life to sleep, why not stay here and enjoy this party with me?"

"Honey, I don't think we're really here together anyway, do you? Now I'm just not up to partying any more, so let's talk in the morning, okay?"

"What are you talking about, Michelle?"

"I'm not talking about anything, Jake, so please don't make something more of it. I just need to go now." And then I left.

It was just a fifteen-minute walk north from Ely's estate to my cottage on David's Lane. I've never felt so grateful for the darkness. The conflict was gone—there was no smile on my face anymore. Somewhere, far out to sea, my heart was descending. Even now, thinking about this feeling causes me to ache inside. My empty torso...oh Jesus. You know this feeling, don't you? You've come home, alone for the first time, with the knowledge that it would be that way for an indefinite time to come. There will be no counterpoint to the respiration of your being in this space. Wherever you go, you will hear only the sound of yourself. No rustling of clothing in an upstairs closet. No footsteps moving along the hallway. No water running in a room in which you are not. I entered the house through the front door and went directly to the kitchen. I didn't turn any lights on. I sat on a stool by the butcher block counter, sat in the darkness, and heard only the hum of the refrigerator. Jesus. I started to cry.

All the emotion comes to our face when we cry. We empty our hearts through our eyes, through our tears. Empty our pain and sadness. I guess that's why we feel better afterward, because some of that pain and sadness have flowed out of us, although their source may remain. I knew where mine had come from and it wasn't from any words Jake had spoken this evening. He was kind as he is always kind. My sadness came from the knowledge that this season of my heart was ending. Something I'd foolishly believed would remain and grow inside me would soon, I realized, expire.

Suddenly the phone rang, sending a shock into the dark silence. "Hello."

"Honey, it's Jake...are you all right?"

"Yes, I'm fine," I said in a low voice.

"I'm back home now. There was no reason to be at the party without you."

"Why would you say that? All of our friends were there, saying 'Goodbye,' to each other and to the summer. It was lovely."

"Michelle, I said I couldn't be there without you…" I felt Jake's voice breaking, the way the coming of tears can affect the vocal cords and make it difficult to speak. "…and I need to be with you now."

"It's almost four in the morning, Jake…"

"It doesn't matter what time it is, does it? I can't allow the distance between us to increase by another hour. Please let me come over." I felt a hesitant warmth returning to my chest, sitting in the kitchen, in the dark, hearing this man whom I had come to love plead for my company on the precipice of summer's end.

"Come to the kitchen door, in the back. We'll have a glass of Champagne." I began to cry again. I don't understand why we cry sometimes when we feel joy. Why would our hearts require the expulsion of happiness? Maybe it's that certain emotions expand, like volatile substances when they're heated, and cannot be contained.

Only moments later Jake was at the kitchen door. I opened it, and he embraced me. I could feel him thinking, trying to understand what to say. "There are certain things we shouldn't talk about right now," I said. "I know you have things you need to do, that you have to go through. Right now, we should pour a glass of Champagne and raise it to the wonderful summer that's about to end."

"Yes, that's exactly what we should do," Jake agreed. "And I hope there's a worthy bottle in the fridge."

"Oh, there is," I promised. We talked, reliving many of the summer's highlights and surprises, like two people who've just seen the same movie: "Remember how…" "I loved it when…" And all those scenes came back so vividly, I didn't have to close my eyes to see them. In fact, it was remarkable to look into Jake's eyes and find them, these images, so momentous, yet no one else on Earth could see. Outside, the air was damp and light was returning to the sky. The birds were wide awake and demanding attention again with their noisy chatter. "Let's walk to the beach," I said. "I want to see if they've drained the ocean for winter yet."

"I think they wait a few more weeks for that, but we can check."

We walked slowly along the lane, southward, toward the Atlantic, in a hypnotic embrace. Passing moments, passing thoughts. Soon our feet were in the sand, and an orange globe was beginning to emerge from the eastern horizon line, far beyond the ocean. The air was thick and still, sensuous with the smells of the sea. My long hair was soaking wet from the dew. We walked toward the sun near the tide's edge for a short time, then Jake turned toward me and smiled and kissed me. The moisture on our lips and on our faces, the effect on our senses created by his touch, it overcame me. My heart was pounding and my breathing rapid as we poured over each other's skin. My God, he possessed so much of me. And do I feel my heart filling up again, rising above the sand toward the sky?

"We have to do this," he said, holding me closely.

"What?"

"We have to make love."

"But where? There's no place!" I whispered in frustration.

"Here. We'll do it here."

"We can't do it here! This is where people run. Where they walk their dogs, for God's sake!"

"Then over there, away from the water," he insisted, pointing toward the edge of the dune. "Come on."

Jake took my hand and we walked away from the breaking waves. "Here, we can lie down here."

"But it's still so close...people could see!" He put his arm around me and drew me closer, and kissed me again. I felt his hand beneath my sweatshirt, stroking the skin on my back gently. And then I felt his palm on my stomach, now embracing my breast, now touching my nipple. Oh God. My legs buckled as he pulled me to the sand, and now we lay facing each other, his hand on my buttock, now the inside of my thigh. I was lost, responding only to messages from the surface of my body.

I pulled his shirt out of his jeans and undid the buttons, rubbing my fingers across his chest. He sat up suddenly and removed the shirt, covering my middle with it. "Here, no one will see us now." I smiled. It didn't matter. As we kissed my fingers went to the button of his jeans and unbound them, and I held him in my hand. Down came my leotard and off the tip of my toes. I pulled his clothing to his knees and drew him closer to me, his pale, warm flesh against my belly, and on our sides, facing each other in this way, I guided him inside of me. We looked at each other, barely breathing now. He could see beyond me to the ocean's edge, notice if anyone was passing close by, but he didn't, he didn't look away from me. I kissed his nipple and he put his hand to the side of my face. Closer to shore, the rhythm of the waves slowed. They seemed to break on the sand every two minutes, then three minutes. "I love you," he whispered.

"I love you, too, darling, I love you so." We were speaking those words to each other for the first time.

But the drifting away is real. The line is slipping through your fingers, weeks before the autumnal equinox. And you have to loosen your grip, don't you? I didn't want to. I just didn't. But I did.

It's already winter now…we've even had a first snowfall, blanketing the streets. Still, unlike the dread my heart had conjured the night of Ely's party, it didn't all come crashing to an end. We're back in the city, Jake and I. He's found his footing again, he says, and I can sense that it's true. We said "I love you" before going to sleep last night. And I think it's okay that the days are getting shorter.

The Readers Speak

The following gathering took place at the Olive Garden restaurant on Sixth Avenue in Chelsea (sadly, now closed) on a Sunday afternoon in September. Those in attendance were people I'd given early chapters of this book with the hope of getting feedback, suggestions and additional input. All of the stories told here are true, at least to the extent that those speaking were telling the truth, because I recorded the entire 'session.'

"Hi...Hi folks. Could I have your attention. I'm Michael...and it looks like we're all here, so I'd first like to thank everyone for coming. And I'd also like to thank the manager of this Olive Garden, Mario, for letting us use the back dining room. It's between their lunch and dinner service, but I promised we'd order some appetizers and beverages, so please be my guest.

"I think you all know why we're here this afternoon, right? Last week I was handing out the first chapters of my book-in-progress, *The Soul Mate Expeditions*, on Sixth Avenue near Bryant Park. You're the ones who were kind enough to take them from me, agreed to read them and to meet here for an early shall we call it 'book club' discussion. And I really appreciate your being here.

"The basic premise of the book, an exploration of what it means to find the one special individual you might share your life with, your soul mate if you will, it's a pretty subjective thing, I have no doubt about that. What I'm hoping for is to get your feedback at this early stage, to make sure I haven't drifted too far from reality. That the ideas and stories being told actually resonate with others. And, selfishly, I hope to gain new insights by having you first readers respond before the critics rip me a new soul." *(Laughter, head nodding in the room)*

"The truth is, at a certain point you're just holding a book in your hands—any book—unable to do much more than ponder the ideas and stories put there by the writer for your reading pleasure, your intellectual and/or emotional stimulation, whatever. You can't manipulate the book to make it something it isn't. All you can do is open it up and pour out what's been prepared for you. So I want to do something about that, which is why we're here. I'll take your questions, or you may simply want to share a story or an observation with us—it can only help to broaden our understanding—mine anyway—of what we're trying to find...and remind us, I suspect, that we're not alone in this quest to find a soul mate. I only ask that you speak one at a time, and give your fellow readers an opportunity to speak, as well. Okay, who'd like to begin? There's an eager hand in the air—yes, go ahead, sir."

"Yeah, I have a question."

"Please speak up so we can all hear you, okay? And tell us your name, if you will."

"Right, my name is Todd."

"Hi, Todd. What's your question?"

"My question is, What makes you qualified to even talk about finding a soul mate? Aren't you just another guy who's been married and divorced, *twice*? I mean, do you even have a degree in psychology or relationships or something?"

"Okay, Todd, thank you. That's a pretty aggressive first question, don't you think? Did I say I was an expert on the subject of soul mates, or finding a soul mate? I don't think so. Do I have advanced degrees in the subjects at hand? No, I do not. Have I been married and divorced twice? Yes, Todd. And I hope there's nothing I've said here or written in those pages that would suggest I view myself as an authority. Intellectually and emotionally superior? Possibly. *(Laughter)* But an authority? No way. That's why I've asked you to join me today—I'm hoping to pick your brains...and souls. Imagine we're building a psychic bathyscaphe to explore the world in which our quest is taking place—physically, emotionally and spiritually. A vehicle made out of stories, observations and questions. Does that help at all, Todd?"

"I guess, in a way. But you didn't have to jump on me like that, for

Christ's sake. I mean, this is a discussion, right? Felt more like the so-called 'leader' humiliating a member of the group for the purpose of establishing his own superiority."

"I'm sorry, Todd. You're absolutely right. I think I just took a defensive posture when you came on so aggressively, questioning my credibility from word one. Please accept my apology."

"Okay. And I apologize, too. You seem like a decent guy—and there is something about your book that I can relate to, but I'm not sure what yet."

"Thanks, Todd, fair enough. Let's take another question and see where it leads. Yes, over there."

"Hi, I'm Teresa, from Bowling Green, Ohio."

"Hi, Teresa, what's your question?"

"Well, um, it's not really a question. It's about something that happened to me. Is that okay?"

"Of course, Teresa, please continue."

"Well I was sure I'd found my soul mate—his name is Jimmy—seven years ago, when we were still in high school."

"That's great, Teresa."

"I thought it was great, too. We had so much in common, so much fun together. But Jimmy said we were too young to just be exclusive together and not ever see other people and find out about things. It hurt me when he said that, but I thought I had to go along if he felt that way."

"I'm guessing you had no other choice at the time."

"Yes, but it hurt. Jimmy was the first person I ever made love to— when he was inside me it felt so perfect—not just physically, but in my heart, too. It was as if, during our lovemaking, I became something new that was the two of us as one. That probably sounds stupid, right?"

"No, no, of course it doesn't sound stupid."

"Anyway, then, when I learned that he was seeing other people, that he was actually seeing a close friend of mine—her name is Sheila—it was so hurtful to me. I imagined Jimmy and my friend making love together, lying naked beside each other and sharing the intimacy that I believed only we could have. I hurt so much inside with this thought." (*The room is silent.*)

"Did you continue to see Jimmy?"

"Yes, I did, for maybe a year longer."

"Wasn't it difficult, Teresa? I mean, you believed that the two of you belonged together, had so much to share, and now you were sharing Jimmy, compromising your most deeply held feelings. Did you believe that he would change?"

"Yes, I did, but it was very hard for me, and in the end I considered taking my life, I really did. On the one hand, I pretended to still care about my friend, so that I wouldn't appear small-minded, or threatened by her. At the same time I became more clinging with Jimmy, trying to please him more and more sexually, buying him little gifts…"

"What happened, Teresa? What finally changed the dynamic of this situation?"

"Well, it was spring of our senior year. Jimmy told me he was going down to Fort Lauderdale with his friends to celebrate for a few days, but how would I like to go out to dinner before they left. It sounded fine to me. He took me to a really romantic place just south of Toledo. And afterward, he asked me if I'd like to spend the night in a nice hotel as a going-away present for both of us. And of course, it was beautiful—we made love for hours before sneaking home at daybreak. I felt so close to him at that moment."

"I sense that something changed after that."

"Yes, it did." (Teresa struggles to hold back her tears.) "I found out that when Jimmy went to Florida with his friends…Sheila went with them."

"I'm sorry, Teresa."

"And six weeks later she told me she was pregnant with his baby, and that she was going to have it, no matter what." (Teresa requires a moment to collect herself.)

"What did you do, Teresa?"

"I didn't do anything. I felt hurt and betrayed and humiliated by the one person on Earth whom I loved, and whom I believed loved me. I went away to college—to Ohio University—and then I moved back to Bowling Green. Jimmy went to Detroit to work at the Ford plant. He didn't marry Sheila, but he sends her money. Sheila lives with her mom, who takes care of the little boy when Sheila's working at the Municipal Building. I don't see her at all—the thought of their son together, I still can't deal with it."

"That's a very moving story, Teresa. So what brought you to New York? And is there something you'd like to ask?"

"Well, I'm here on a five-day vacation with a friend of mine—we're seeing a couple of shows and doing some shopping. And I started reading the book that you're writing—I guess you don't remember me, but I took a set of the chapters you were handing out Tuesday on the corner of Sixth Avenue and 42nd Street, which is not far from our hotel."

"Gosh, I'm sorry I didn't recognize you right away...I handed out chapters to over a hundred people that day and..."

"Oh, that's okay. Anyway, I thought the book was pretty good, and you invited the readers to come to Olive Garden, to speak and comment—and here I am. And this is my question: Do you think there's just one person for us in the world? You use the expression 'soul mate'—do you think it's possible we could meet that person when we are young, and then it not work out, and that's it...it might never happen again?"

"Could I answer that, Michael?"

"Todd, if it's okay let me start since Teresa has directed her question to me."

"All right, sure."

"Sorry, Teresa. Anyway, I don't believe that that's the case. I think that oftentimes, when we're very young, as you were when you fell in love with Jimmy, we simply don't have the experience or the maturity to be in a relationship that involves the highest levels of physical and emotional intimacy, the mutual teaching and learning that makes a relationship grow and develop. How could you have, both of you were high school students! But now you have that experience to draw from. You've felt emotions and physical attraction that you want to feel again, but you realize that it must come with trust, and a sharing of values and interests, as well. You're young and beautiful—this should be a wonderful time for you!"

"So what do you think I should do?"

"Well, I think it would be good if you could forget about high school and Jimmy and Sheila and a time in your life that could become sort of a mental jail cell. But that cell door's not locked, so why not break out? Maybe you will meet your soul mate. Maybe you won't. But nothing should prevent you from having a brilliant journey as you travel through your lifetime. I mean, there's no Amazon delivery service for this stuff, Teresa. You have to go get it. I think you should consider leaving Bowling Green, for one thing."

"But where would I go?"

"Michael, you're freaking her out! That's not cool, especially since you're not an 'authority'—you said so yourself."

"Okay, Todd, point taken, I'm not an authority. But do you think taking a risk is too risky? I feel nobody should spend their life with their head buried in the ground—there'll be plenty of time for that when we're dead. I didn't suggest that Teresa run off and start cocktail waitressing in Atlantic City. I suggested she think about leaving Bowling Green. Move to Boston. Or Chicago. Maybe New York! A city where she might already have friends. A place that might put new experiences in front of her. New people in her world. That's all I'm saying, that's what I believe—and yes, I'm no expert. What do you think, Teresa? Does that make any sense?"

"Sure, I guess so."

"I don't want you to be afraid..."

"It's okay, I'll be fine."

"I know you will. I mean, look at you! This planet is lucky to have you on its surface. Just keep your eyes open—and your heart, too—okay?"

"I will. Thanks."

"And I just want to add that you're really nice looking and I'm sure lots of guys would be attracted to you."

"Um, thanks, Todd."

"Yes, thanks, Todd. Okay, who else? Yes, right here..."

"Yes, hi. I'm Daryl."

"Hi, Daryl...I have to say, you look familiar—did we speak when I was handing out the chapters?"

"No, I picked up the chapters on a bench in Bryant Park. Guess someone had just left them there. I'm actually a correspondent for CBS2 News in New York—I mostly cover human interest stories in the five boroughs. So it's possible you've seen me on the broadcast—at least I hope so!"

"Ahh, of course—Daryl Gordon! Well it's great to have you here. But please, I've promised those who came that what was said here would be in strictest confidence and their privacy would be assured, unless they'd given permission otherwise."

"Absolutely. And I will honor that promise. But I did find the stories, and the idea of this meeting in the back room of a restaurant, really fascinating. And I wonder if I might ask a question of the group?"

"Please, go right ahead."

"Okay, how many of you here truly believe that you have found, or will find, your soul mate?"

"That's a good question. So let's see a show of hands if your answer is Yes, okay? Show of hands…okay, I count 5…7—remember, believe you have found or *will* find your soul mate—there's 4 more. So 11 out of 15 if I count correctly. And what about you, Daryl? How would you answer?"

"I would have to say Yes…I have found my soul mate. So that's 12. Now I'm wondering about the ones who have not raised their hands. Their thoughts…"

"Okay, a hand has gone up at the table behind you—go ahead."

"Yes, I'm Jonathan, but you can call me Jon. Um, I just think the idea of finding 'the one' is so random. People fall in love, they break up. They get married, they get divorced. For those who raised their hands, god bless. For me, I'm a skeptic. I'm in my 40s and nothing so far. Maybe I messed up too many times when I was young, I don't know. Anyway, the mozzarella sticks are great, so thanks for that." *(Much laughter)*

"You're welcome, Jon, and thanks for sharing."

"Don't mean to sound like a reporter, but just one more thing, Michael."

"Go right ahead, Daryl."

"So much of the book seems just to be about this search for one's soul mate, but you offer almost nothing on the subject of sustaining and nurturing that relationship, keeping it strong, the staying together part—why is that?"

"That's interesting, I hadn't thought about it in that way. Maybe if I believed I knew more about sustaining a great relationship I'd have more to say or share. But don't you think there are things that can be inferred from the telling of a story, even if the story ends in failure? Even when the failure is merely the failure of the story to continue? For example, in reading about the author's obsession with finding someone whom he barely knows—Lauren—don't you think we're imagining ways in which we might have anticipated—and avoided—the surprise and disappointment he experiences at the end? What we might have done differently?"

"Actually, I think we'd all put up a few signs on the street if we thought we could have that much fun on our first date!" *(Spontaneous laughter undermines my argument.)*

"Well I can't argue with that, especially coming from someone who's found her soul mate. He must be pretty special, Daryl."

"Why would you assume my soul mate is a 'he,' Michael?"

"Ouch, I'm so sorry. And you're absolutely right—there's no reason I should assume that. Please accept my apology."

"I do. By the way, he *is* a he."

"Of course, and if you'll just pass me your fork I'll go ahead and stab myself. All right moving on, who else? Right here in front."

"I'm Amy, and I'm from New York..."

"I don't know if they can hear you in back, Amy, could you speak up?"

"Yes. So far it seems like most of the 'expeditions' end badly. Love lost or never found. Maybe I expected to be reading stories about great soul mates instead of failed romances. Which makes me wonder, Where are you going with this? Do you reach a conclusion, have an epiphany?"

"Hmm. Sounds like I'd better or you'll want your money back! Honestly, I don't think the book is going to suggest an answer or reach a conclusion about how to find your soul mate. I'm guessing there are just too many variables in our individual makeup. The things that define who we are. Whether we're thoughtful or selfish and a million other things, including a little bit of luck. But as long as we're open to possibilities, willing to give something of ourselves, then anything can happen—and the encounters that don't work out can still have their value as memories, maybe lessons. At least that's what I think. Did you ever have a beautiful romance that turned out to be something less? Something that, after first filling your heart, left you empty or disappointed?"

"Yes."

"Do you want to tell us a little bit about it?"

"I don't know if it would be interesting to you or anybody else. I mean, this is your book thing."

"Amy, if you were going to tell us about your favorite toy growing up, I'd suggest maybe sharing it with Todd."

"You suck, Michael."

"Sorry, Todd, that was a joke. But, Amy, if you have a story to share with us I'd be honored if you would."

"All right, here goes. A few years ago I went on vacation with a girlfriend from work—we went to Italy, to the Amalfi Coast. I had always wanted to see it because I have friends who'd honeymooned there. It's just beautiful. Sorrento, Positano, Capri…these ancient towns built into the cliffs and hillsides overlooking the Mediterranean—it's so romantic. Anyway, we rented a car and traveled up the coast, staying in a different village each night, shopping, sightseeing and taking the sun during the day."

"It sounds wonderful. A place to be in love."

"Exactly! And that's sort of what happened. On the second night, Liz—she's my friend—Liz and I were having dinner outdoors in a piazza in Sorrento. Two very nice, well-dressed Italian men approached our table and said 'Ciao!' and started making small talk, asking us if we were Americans, were we on vacation, was this our first time in Italy the Land of Romance, you get the idea."

"That sounds like fun."

"Oh, it was so crazy! I mean, Liz and I didn't take them seriously or anything. But we went along with it because they seemed like charming guys, and pretty harmless. Fabrizio—Fabi—and Sonny. Fabi owned a men's boutique in Rome, and Sonny was his buddy—he managed a club, also in Rome. They were on vacation, too. And of course, they offered to show us around the area, to help us avoid the worst of the tourist stops and restaurants—not to mention taking us to the best night spots! They also made it clear that they had their own accommodations, so we didn't need to be concerned."

"So far, I'm absolutely with you. You're on an adventure."

"We had such a good time! For four days and nights we saw and did everything—from museums to the ruins of Pompeii, olive groves and fishing villages, brilliant shopping and amazing little cafes. At night we danced and drank vino and Vin Santo—it really seemed magical!"

"And now you're the American representative for the Italian Tourist Board!"

"Well, at that time I could have been. On day two, I was starting to feel a connection between Fabi and myself. Our sense of humor was similar—and I know it sounds shallow, but I loved the fact that he touched me when he spoke. It created an unexpected closeness. American men don't do that. But there, it seemed so easy, and I have to admit that I responded to it—I liked being near him. I let his arm be around me…I reached for his hand… and when he kissed the back of mine, I laughed."

"So sweet…I can imagine how enchanting that must have felt!"

"One night we all had dinner together, and then went to a small club outside of Positano. The music was amazing—I just let myself go to another planet. It was after four in the morning when we even started talking about leaving. Sonny drove back, with Liz in the front and Fabi and me in the back seat, and the music still ringing in our ears when we reached our hotel. And just then, when we were about to get out of the car and say 'Buona notte' I turned to Fabi and asked him if he'd like to have a glass of wine with me on the balcony of my room—overlooking the Mediterranean, of course."

"Of course."

"And of course, he said 'Of course!' *(Laughter in the room)* It was so crazy, Michael. We sat together, in the perfect night air, with barely a sound in the universe beyond us. Fabi moved his chair close to mine and began massaging my neck with his right hand as we watched the stars and sipped wine. He said, 'You know, Bella, this is a very special night, because I feel that I know you a little better—you have such a wonderful enjoyment for life.' To be truthful, he could have said, 'You know, Bella, roses are red and pizza is made from dough,' it wouldn't have mattered. I was 'Bella' and I felt like the Princess of Positano."

"Did you give Fabi a special souvenir from his new American friend?" *(A few moans are heard.)*

"Why yes, Michael, I did. And Fabi gave me something to remember him by as well. *(Laughter)* What can I say? We made love right there on the balcony, just as the first light of the new day was breaking—I can't believe I'm even talking about this…"

"Well, you definitely have our undivided attention, Amy."

"He–he was very tender with me, but also very confident in what to do. It was the most vivid sexual experience of my life. And he thanked me, for making the most beautiful love to him."

"As he should! What happened then?"

"We were inseparable after that. Liz and Sonny were having a pretty good time, too, as a matter of fact, although not in the same way. Still, we did most everything together, the four of us. And at night I fell into Fabi's arms. God, it was like being in a dream. Their vacation was ending a few days before ours, but they asked us if we'd like to come back to Rome with them and finish our vacation in the city. They'd show us everything—and besides, Fabi said, you can't plan everything when you're on vacation! We couldn't have agreed with them more at that point. I think Fabi could have said, 'I must now travel to Tibet to purchase fabric—can you assist me?' I would have said 'Of course, my darling!'" *(Laughter & applause)*

"So off to Rome you went…"

"Five days in Rome. I know it was the most romantic experience of my life. Fabi had to spend time in his store but, believe me, he created his world around me during those days. Liz and I shared a hotel room, but I always went back to his apartment when the evening finally would end. We even had dinner at his parents' house one night—I thought that was a very sweet and intimate level for him to take our brief encounter, don't you think?"

"I agree, Amy. What were you saying to each other?"

"We were saying that nothing like this had ever happened to us before."

"So this felt like love…that Fabi could be the one…"

"Yes."

"Well please continue."

"We made love for three hours in his apartment before Liz and I had to fly back to America. I've never felt so free, yet so sexually connected. To this day I don't think I understand where that feeling came from. At the airport we could barely let go of each other. For Liz and Sonny, it seemed more like a great, fun friendship was ending—or being interrupted. They weren't torn about saying 'Goodbye.' But for Fabi and I, this was tragedy."

"But you would see each other again, no?"

"We promised to write and speak often—we would meet again soon, there was no doubt about that. And for weeks we did write, it must have been every other day. I don't even want to think about my phone bill! Luckily, I was able to call him from the office a couple times a week… but on the weekend it was ridiculous, the way time could just evaporate over the phone. Those per-minute rates they're always advertising for long distance? What I needed was a day rate! Fabi would tell me about work, and his friends, how quiet things had become since the end of summer. He talked of missing me, wishing he could show me other parts of Italy even more beautiful than the Mediterranean. And I told him that he had to come to New York first, and give me the chance to share my world with the same generosity he had shown."

"So who traveled where first?"

"Fabi made arrangements to fly to New York at the end of September. It would be perfect because we could see and do tons of things in the City, and the weather would still be nice enough to show him our beaches out east—which happen to be a lot prettier than the Mediterranean, by the way."

"Yes they really are. Sounds like a great plan."

"It was so exciting, Michael. The thought of taking this wonderful affair to another level. Not only that, Fabi was very excited to see the shops on Fifth and Madison Avenues, and in SoHo—I started to imagine him relocating to New York, having his own business here. My mind was leapfrogging."

"You know you've got us on the edge of our seats now, don't you, Amy? Was Fabi's visit all you'd dreamed it would be?"

"His flight from Rome was on Friday morning, and I would meet him at Kennedy, the Al Italia Terminal, at 2:00 p.m., I think it was. I hired a car and brought Champagne for the ride back to Manhattan. You know, I've never been married, Michael, but it almost felt like my wedding day—that's the anticipation I was overcome with, standing with all those families waiting for relatives to come through customs, and drivers holding handwritten signs with passengers' names."

"I'll bet you wondered 'Will he recognize me right away? Will I recognize him?'"

"Fabi never got off the plane, Michael. *(Amy holds back tears, the room is still.)* I searched every face as it came through the corridor. Then the people with little children walked out with all their bags and strollers. Then the older people who required wheelchairs and electric carts. I waited until the terminal was nearly empty. I was terrified that somehow I'd missed him—maybe he was looking for me in some other area of the terminal, or out on the sidewalk, so I had him paged. 'Paging Fabrizio Ponti, Fabrizio Ponti. Meet your party at Al Italia ticket counter.' No one responded to the page. In my haste I'd stupidly left my phone charging on the counter at home, so I had no way to call him. I didn't know his number and the airline had no record of his ever being ticketed. Finally, I went home, in tears."

"Oh God…was there any message on your phone?"

"Yes. *(Amy pauses)* He had called…from Italy, a few hours earlier. He said he hoped it hadn't been too late to reach me before I went to the airport, but something had come up and he would have to reschedule the trip. He would try to reach me later. I had been out of my apartment since mid-morning, so Fabi should have been halfway across the Atlantic at the time of his call. I thought, 'Why did he wait so long to try to contact me?' I was devastated, Michael."

"I'm so sorry, Amy. When did you next speak with Fabi?"

"We never spoke again. I called, twice, and left concerned messages on his phone. The calls were not returned. The next day, Saturday, I received a text…*a text!*….from Fabi, apologizing for disappointing me. There had been a family 'emergency' that prevented him from leaving the country. And beyond that, he realized that it was probably a very bad time to abandon his shop, with the busy season just starting up again. He would talk to me just as soon as things returned to normal. I knew what his message really said, though. It said, 'It's over, Amy. Our vacation was just that, and now it is time for reality.' I was so humiliated. Everyone in my life knew that he was coming, that Amy was being reunited with her lover. How wonderful it will be to meet him! I just… How could this happen? Was I so stupid to believe that a man would get on an airplane in Rome just to see me?"

"Of course you weren't stupid to believe that, Amy. Any one of us would have believed exactly as you did under the same circumstances. Therefore I ask you to forgive me for characterizing Fabrizio exactly as we now see him to be: a shallow piece of Roman merda."

"How can you say that, Michael? You don't know him."

"No matter what his side of that same story might be, Amy, you deserved to be shown more respect than he showed. He's a coward to not have spoken with you truthfully. He let the thousands of miles between New York and Rome shield him, knowing that he would never have to face you again. You are a beautiful, intelligent and giving woman whom he was fortunate ever to have met. He could have spoken to you about his fears, even about his ambivalence."

"I agree with you on this one, Michael—this guy was a shit. And Amy is beautiful."

"Thank you for your support, Todd. You know, Amy, I have a little story I could share with you, if you'd care to revisit the Amalfi Coast for a few moments. Would you?"

"I guess so, if it's not too sad."

"Well, it's not too sad. I mean, in the sense that no one is beaten and robbed and left for carrion birds…"

"Sounds like a real fairytale…"

"Everybody…would you like to hear another story that's not in the chapters?" *(Hands go up, all say 'Yes.')*

"Okay, here goes. But I must say, I've rarely told this story, due to the humiliating nature of its outcome…"

"Great."

"We breathlessly await the motion picture!"

"Todd, damnit, Todd…I probably deserved that. All right, here it is: Four years ago I went on a vacation to the Amalfi Coast…"

"Four years ago? That's when Liz and I went! What time of year were you there, Michael?"

"The third week in August—height of the season."

"We were there from around the 17th to the 22nd! We could have met!"

"Amy, you and Liz didn't travel to Italy to meet Americans—you went to have an adventure! It was in your eyes when those two Italian men approached you. Your eyes said, 'Maybe something exciting will happen.'"

"Did something exciting happen to you, Michael?"

"I went to Italy, to this very special land by the sea, because, like you, I had always heard how magical it was, this mix of natural beauty, antiquity and sophistication. I traveled by myself, though—none of my single friends were interested in making the trip, and I was not with anyone at the time. It seemed if I wanted to see this part of the world, I better just buy a ticket and fly."

"Could you believe how beautiful it was!?"

"I was blown away by it, Amy."

"So what happened?"

"Nothing. *Nothing* happened. I've seldom felt so lonely in my entire adulthood. I met a few American families. I met two young couples from Australia who had finished university and were now traveling the world together. Imagine how special that would be—making love to your sweetheart in every corner of the planet! But I was alone. I could speak no language other than English. I sat alone in restaurants, watching the happy couples and families, out on their holidays. Little kids riding on their dads' shoulders, clinging to their pant legs. The Italians are so ebullient— waving their arms, drawing in the air with their hands, kissing and bear-hugging. I felt like a lost soul, sitting there in the piazzas at a table for one, pretending to read a book, while a joyful stream of vacationing humanity passed all around me."

"Michael, this is so sad! I wish you had met Liz and I—we could have had a great time together."

"How nice you are, Amy. But let's not forget the amazing adventure that you were on at this very time. Think about this: One afternoon I decided to take the sun by the pool at my hotel in Positano. It was simply a beautiful day and an atmosphere that, frankly, I'm not accustomed to. The pool deck overlooked the sea, an exquisite bar to one side, marble tables and lounge chairs all around, fit waiters in short, white jackets serving cocktails and antipasti from the menu. Flamenco music played softly from speakers at the bar...I almost felt comfortable! (*Low laughter in the room*) Finding a chaise near the pool, the white jackets immediately flew to my side with towels and cushions, expressing their desire to know if there was anything I required. Pinot Grigio and olives! The poolside conversations were hushed and intimate, but I heard English spoken right beside me. Four attractive American women, apparently unaccompanied, lay outstretched on the neighboring chaises."

"There you go, Michael! Did you introduce yourself?"

"Yes, Amy. And I made love to each of them, sequentially, from nearest to furthest from me, right there by the pool." *(Robust laughter)*

"You're a liar!"

"Yes, Todd, you are correct again, I am a liar. I did not make love to the beautiful American women. Instead, I made a fool of myself. Finding a harmless moment in their conversation I said, 'Where in the States are you ladies from?' I knew that in asking this question they would hear—comprehend—that I, too, was an American. It would be their opening, their opportunity to include me in the conversation, ask where I was from, invite me to join them for dinner, or something."

"What did they say, Michael?"

"One of them said they were from Minneapolis, Amy. And then they went back to talking among themselves. I felt as if I'd been reduced to a one-celled animal. I could not be seen on my lounge chair without a high-powered microscope. Or maybe I had leprosy. I checked my face for telltale lesions."

"That's not funny, Michael. My mother has leprosy."

"Sorry, Todd, that was insensitive of me."

"Just kidding. But you should be careful of people's feelings—sometimes I don't think you really hear what you're saying."

"Jesus, Todd, between you and Daryl I think I walked into the wrong book club! But I'm glad you're here anyway and I do appreciate your support. I was simply trying to illustrate the agony I felt at this moment."

"What happened next, Michael?"

"I spent several hours by the pool, Amy. I spoke to no one. I drank a couple glasses of wine. I lay on my stomach. I lay on my back. Later, I went to my room. The housekeeper was there, so I had her take my picture on the balcony, overlooking the Mediterranean. Alone. I went shopping by myself. I had dinner by myself in a great restaurant—I sat beside a young couple whom I believed were staring at me, looking for lesions. During dessert they made love on the table. I pretended not to look. Then I asked for the check. Then I went back to my room and I tried to masturbate, but I couldn't because I was so unhappy and so pissed at myself that I couldn't think of a fucking reason to get an erection. Then I started thinking about all of my dear friends back in New York, and my wonderful home by the beach in Amagansett, and the restaurants where all I had to do was walk in the door for the love to flow—handshakes, hugs, kisses and a glass of wine. Amy, the very next day—four days into my seventeen-day vacation to Italy—I took the train back to Rome, hopped a taxi to the airport, and flew back to New York City. Boarding that plane was the happiest moment of my vacation."

"Michael, that's the saddest thing I've ever heard!"

"But Amy, you just told me the saddest story—the one that happened to you, in exactly the same place!"

"Well, yes..."

"My only point in telling you this was that my vacation was empty. All I got from it was an understanding of what I needed. And a realization that I couldn't pretend it was there when it was not. But your vacation was filled with something joyful—even if it was fleeting. Wouldn't it be sad if you'd never met those men, had the chance to inhale that moment?"

"Yes, I guess it would. Anyway, now I'm seeing a guy from New Jersey!"

"But at least he's a primate, right?"

"That's not very nice."

"Sorry, of course he's a primate! Well, I wonder if anyone else would like to share a story, or ask a question? Okay, there in the middle..."

"Hi, my name is José Sanchez."

"Hi, José, thank you for being here. What did you want to say?"

"Okay. I am from Columbia and I work in the kitchen of a restaurant on Amsterdam Avenue. I work six days from five o'clock until three in the morning. Two of my cousins work there, too."

"That's a hard schedule, José."

"I know people who work seven days, and sometimes two shifts. By the way, I want to thank you for handing me the pages from your book. I enjoyed reading them."

"I'm happy to hear that. Somehow, it doesn't seem that you would have a lot of time to be searching for true love. What did you feel, reading this?" (*I'm holding up the stapled chapters.*)

"You know, much of it made me smile—this looking all over the place for someone to love. I have a wife, but she is in Columbia with our three children. They are living in the home of her mother."

"That has to be difficult…"

"Yes. I haven't seen her in six months, but we write to each other. There is not very much money where I come from, and there are no jobs. So I work here and send money back to Columbia. She can't afford to come here with our children, and there would be no place for them—I live with my cousins and two other Columbians in a small apartment in Brooklyn."

"What will you do, José?"

"I will work here in the restaurant for one more year, and then return to my country. We will try to get the papers to come back and live in America—there are people in Bogota who have helped some of our friends."

"So your soul mate is living on another continent…"

"Yes, it is true. And I only wanted to say one thing about this book…"

"Please, José."

"I think it takes sacrifice, to hold and to keep the thing that you love, I think it takes sacrifice. In my religion, you make a sacrifice to God so that you might receive God's blessing. And for my wife, I make a sacrifice so that she and our children will eat and be taken care of, and so that one day we will be together again, and maybe that day will be a better one. In your pages, I do not find the people who will make this sacrifice—except your mother! Maybe they feel they do not have to. Maybe they feel that it all just happens suddenly, like magic. But I believe it is important to sacrifice. To put food on the table for someone you love…to clothe your children… That's what I wanted to say."

"So the story of me putting up the posters—it's not what you would call 'sacrifice.'"

"Yes. Even though they are funny stories."

"I'm humbled by the truth of your words, José. Maybe you're pointing to the difference between fantasy and a deeper spiritual reality when it comes to relationships."

"I hope I wasn't judging you because I still liked reading it, don't get me wrong. Yet I could never place myself in your position, to be able to pursue this dream that you have."

"Because you must work in a kitchen, far from your homeland, just to make money to feed the family you left behind. Why is that? Can anyone comment on that?" *(Readers shift uncomfortably in their seats.)*

"You don't really have to ask. I am grateful to be here and to have an opportunity, in spite of the sacrifice. One day my children will come to this country, and maybe they will own the restaurant their father works in! In the meantime, don't worry. I will go home for Christmas soon and we will make love constantly."

"That sounds like a good vacation plan, José. Maybe you would be so kind as to bring a chapter back for me."

"I am sorry, but I don't expect to have much free time. At least not as much as you seem to!" *(Laughter, again at my expense, fills the room.)*

"Of course, José, I understand completely. Well look, everybody, I see the Olive Garden folks are starting to set tables for the dinner crowd so I guess we should wrap things up for now. I'm just so grateful to you for coming and sharing your thoughts, even though not everyone had a chance to speak. Todd, I see your hand is up again, but you've already spoken several times."

"Yea, but nobody's said anything about the ridiculous blue spheres. I mean, are you kidding with that? I doubt that anyone on the planet has ever seen a little blue spongy translucent sphere floating—*or sinking.*"

"So, what are you saying, Todd?"

"I'm saying your book jumps all over the place, from break-up story to pure fantasy and seems to arrive nowhere in its quote-unquote 'expedition.'"

"So you think just because no one else has seen a soul that means they don't exist? Would you describe yourself as a literalist?"

"Jesus. You're right, we should wrap this up. Thanks for the informative group therapy."

"You're being pretty hard on Todd, Michael. In fact, you're expecting from all of us a great suspension of disbelief with this story about the blue balls."

"Fair enough, Sting, and I am sorry that Todd and I have seemed to be at odds on a few things. I never meant to question anyone's personal beliefs here. But to your other point, what's the problem with my description of the soul?"

"But you just made it up! It's just floating there like your own little thought bubble."

"Don't you believe that our psyches manifest their unique condition or state through barely detectable wave patterns created in the brain under emotional stimuli from internal and external sources?"

"How the hell would I know—I'm an agnostic. Even if it were plausible—and I'm not certain of that by any means—one wouldn't simply ingest it as fact. Why do you think there are so many religions, and philosophies, and theories, and answer-seeking devices? Not to mention therapists."

"Maybe because people are afraid to face the obvious."

"The little blue spheres?"

"Well, the idea of the little blue spheres."

"Oh, the *idea* of the spheres! So it's become a notion all of a sudden."

"Hey, I like the translucent blue spheres, Michael. I believe in them!"

"Thank you, Amy."

"If you started a religion based on the blue spheres, and giving them levity, I'd sign right up!"

"God, I hope you wouldn't do that. But maybe Sting is right. Maybe even Todd is right. They're just a notion. Just a way of talking about the soul."

"Are you saying we don't have a soul? 'Cause I don't want to hear that. Please don't say that."

"Sting, why don't you answer Amy. Do we have a soul?"

"Yes, we do, Amy."

"Well, what does it look like, then?"

"Right. Ah, I think it's light blue and translucent. You can't see objects behind it clearly. The soul responds to messages from the human psyche that affect its gravity, or its levity. Observing it carefully is one way of knowing how you feel inside. You know you're feeling pretty good when your soul is floating somewhere above the frost line. At least that's what Michael would like to believe. And so would I."

"Thanks, Sting."

"You're welcome, Amy."

"Okay, I have to ask Sting something."

"Go right ahead, Todd."

"Sting, why are you even here?"

"Obviously for the mozzarella sticks. *(Burst of laughter)* Seriously, I didn't receive the chapters on the street—they were handed to me by my assistant who read them and thought I might find them entertaining. Which I did. She's gone back to London, but I'm here in New York for a few weeks. So here we all are, aren't we?"

"Michael?"

"Yes, hi there."

"Uh, I'm Daniel—everybody calls me Dan—anyway I'm just wondering if you're going to hold another discussion? Will your readers get to comment again?"

"I hadn't thought about it, Dan, but, sure, that's possible. If those of you who came today would like to leave your names and contact info with me, I'll send you details when available. Hopefully, the book will be further along by then. *(Murmurs of approval in the room)* Well, again, thank you for coming."

(All) "Thank you, Michael!" *(Spontaneous applause. I'm lifted above the heads of the readers and carried from the restaurant to the street.)*

Veronique

It was almost ten years ago when Tara left me. I don't blame her for leaving. She was so young when we met and then married. In the beginning, it was beautiful and exciting and fun, of course. Then things cooled. Then the light dimmed and expired. I'm certain I'd been far too consumed with career and business difficulties to give all that needed to be given, emotionally and physically. And Tara needed to see the world and to experience herself in it, with or without me. At the time, it was easier for her to imagine it without me than to see us, or me, changing substantially. We just decided to put "a little space between us," and that space turned into ten years, ten light-years. We didn't know how to talk. We couldn't put feelings—anger, pain, need—into words. Maybe it was just easier to let it all slide away. But I'll tell you this: If you love somebody, don't set them free until you've let them see your soul as clearly as they can see your face. Better open your mouth quick.

On our final day of cohabitation, she said, "I'll always love you, Michael."

"Me, too," I whispered as we embraced, while from within me the remains of my spirit discharged.

Regarding the impact zone of a separation—it's not just next to the heart. There's a ripple effect. Like lava flowing slowly away from the source, into the tree line, the valley, everything in its path. And that separation—it spreads to your relatives and friends. Business associates. The ladies at the dry cleaner. Toughest was my daughter, Kim, who loved Tara and now saw her dad failing again, bringing disappointment again.

In the aftermath of this separation, I had as many as one brilliant idea—an idea that would bring Kim and I closer together by doing something we'd never done before. "How would you like to go to Paris and St. Tropez with me this summer, Kim?"

"Are you serious, Dad?"

"Absolutely. Hanging around me in the city might not be so much fun without Tara—but seeing some new places together, that could be great. What do you say?"

"It sounds fantastic! But I'll need some new clothes if we're going to Paris, don't you think?"

"I'm sure you're right."

Six weeks later, early in August, at the peak of the European holidays, we were airborne out of JFK on our way to Paris. The single dad and the beautiful teenage daughter. In fact, I didn't even feel single. I only felt like Dad, because this was for Kim. Well, for Kim and I. Well, for me.

Upon arrival at L'hotel La Villa in mid-morning, Dad needed a little nap. But beautiful Kim needed to explore Paris. ('Grownups' swear they would never, ever wish to be teenagers again, but they're lying—from their balding skulls to their softening bellies to their receding gums—they're lying! Of course we'd love to be young again, but so what? We don't have a fucking choice anyway.) So into the streets of Paris skipped beautiful Kim, on her beautiful American legs, map of the Left Bank in hand. And off to bed crawled Dad, paternal joy comforting his aching back. A few hours later it was a luscious sleep from which I was awakened by knocking at the door and Kim's excited voice. "Dad! Dad! Wake up! You've been asleep for hours and I'm hungry! Come on!"

"All right, honey. Just give me a few minutes and I'll meet you at the front desk."

Kim's excitement was palpable, and infectious. I couldn't stop smiling, just listening to her talk about her tour de Paris. "I crossed over that river (the Seine) on a bridge and walked around and then crossed over on another bridge and people were painting, it was so...*French*...and some guy came up to me and asked me if I was American and then he proposed to me, can you believe it?! I don't think French men really know what love is, Dad. Where should we eat?"

"Well, I'm pretty new here, too. What do you say we get a recommendation from our concierge?" The young lady at the desk was lovely, and very engaging.

"A restaurant for you and your daughter? But she cannot be your daughter…you are too young! She ees your girlfriend, no?" Is it necessary to discuss the effect of the French accent, as rendered in English by une demoiselle, on the American male primate? I was immediately disabled. An electrical current flowed through dormant parts of my body.

"Oh, she is definitely my daughter, because I have a clear memory of being present at her birth—but thank you for your flattering assumption. This is Kim…and I'm Michael." Kim rolled her eyes in mock disbelief. She hated watching her father being single.

"So good to meet you, Kim…I am Veronique," offered our charming concierge, extending her hand. "Do you enjoy your veesit to Paree?" Kim was smitten. Here was a new friend, after only three hours in this magical city, so far from home in every respect.

"I love it here—it's such a beautiful city. Someday I want to live in Paris!"

"And where 'ave you come from?" Veronique asked.

"From just across the ocean—New York City," I volunteered.

"Ah, but I love New York Ceety! I would leeve zere eef I could een a meenit!" Kim was astonished at this notion. Why would a Parisian want to live in New York? "But New York ees so exciting, so full of energy…Paree ees lovely to look at, but Paree ees asleep!"

Veronique informed us that our dining choices would be somewhat limited since much of the city was closed for the summer holiday. Restaurateurs and shopkeepers had locked their doors and gone to the sea. Still, she was able to guide us to a few of her favorite bistros and cafes—places that "real Parisians" frequented, unlike the tourist hordes moving along Boulevard St. Germain. On our final day in Paris, I asked Kim how she would feel if we invited Veronique to join us for dinner; fortunately, she thought it was a wonderful idea. Unfortunately, Veronique graciously declined, saying that she was required to be at the desk until late at night, and then again in the morning, what with the hotel struggling to rotate a smaller, summer staff, but thank you so much for theenking of me, eet would 'ave been so much fun. The following morning Kim and I met in the lobby, packed and ready to fly off to the Mediterranean for the second part of our father-daughter adventure. Veronique took our picture in front of La Villa. And then I took a picture of Kim and Veronique in a happy embrace.

"I'm sorry to see you leave—eet weel be so boring weesout you!"

"Well, we had such a wonderful time," I said, "Thank you for helping us find our way around the city. Everything was fantastic, wasn't it Kim?"

"It was beautiful, Veronique, thank you so much for everything. And if you're ever in New York, you have to come and see us, okay?"

"I would love that, merci!" And off to St. Tropez we flew—a sunny week during which daughter would receive proposals from one German and one Italian, and an offer to see North Africa from two American students on a summer trust fund adventure.

"Why can't I, Dad? It's a chance to see another country! It'll be totally safe! You met Max and Richie—they're great guys. What could happen?"

"Kim, you're seventeen and I'm responsible for you. Next time you'll come back with a girlfriend, and you'll be a little older, and you'll be able to go where you want to."

"That's not fair, Dad." I cannot tell you how happy I was to be flying west, over the Atlantic, back to New York City, with Kim in coach beside me, watching *Groundhog Day* on the little screen. So desperate was I to be not parenting for a while. God bless America and her beautiful American daughters, storming the coastlines on their beautiful American legs.

A few days later the photos came back—two sets of everything. Kim on the footbridge. Kim on the Bateaux Parisiens. Kim in front of la tour Eiffel…in front of L'Arc de Triomphe, inside Cafe des Fleures (hey, we were tourists). Kim sur la plage in St. Tropez. Kim on the Carousel. Kim and Dad, in front of La Villa. Kim and Veronique, in front of La Villa. Veronique. How pretty she is, with her warm, ready smile, embracing Kim. I liked that she liked New York—that she didn't seem to be infected with that condescension toward Americans so many Parisians are fond of displaying. Even on our shores. I wondered what might have happened had she been able to join us for dinner. Nothing, of course. But it was my brain so I could imagine anything I wanted. In our animated conversation, we would have discovered that she and Kim had much in common. They loved music and dance. They both were passionate about fitness and worked out nearly every day. They wanted to travel, and explore new worlds.

"Maybe you will come to visit us someday. It would be wonderful to return your kindness and show you around our city."

"Oh, I would love zat so much!"

I decided to mail this photo to Veronique. Why not? It had made me smile, it might make her smile. What could she think? *I hate dees photo... eet ees stupeed! Phut!* No. She would open the envelope, pull out the photo, and smile. And if not...?

September 5

Dear Veronique,

The pictures from our vacation came back, and this one of you and Kim reminded me of what a wonderful time we had during our few days in Paris—made even more special thanks to your very personal restaurant selections!

Hope you had some time to enjoy yourself before the summer ended. Kim sends her best, too, and can't wait to return to Paris!

Thanks again for everything. All the best —

Michael

Easy. Not a big deal. Four stamps. Gone.

⬛　⬛　⬛

"Michael, phone for you."

"Did you get a name?"

"No. She sounds French, though—maybe it's 557-LIPPS returning your call."

"Very funny... Hello, this is Michael."

64

"'Ello, Michael, eet ees Veronique calling you from Paree!"

"Oh my God! It's so great to hear your voice—how are you?!"

"I am fine, sank you. I am seeing 'ere at La Villa and I am looking at a happy photograph of Kim and me that makes me smile, so I decide to call you and say Hi. And how are you?"

"Back at my desk, as you've discovered. But everything's fine. And just got better—hearing your voice makes me think of Paris again...we had such a nice time."

"Well you and your daughter are so sweet to me, making eet easier to be working. So I sank you for sending me a photo to remind me."

We spoke for a few moments longer. No, her summer hadn't been lost entirely—she, too, had traveled south at the end of August, to her parents' home between Nice and Cannes. I wondered if she was planning a trip to the U. S. any time soon. Maybe sometime next year, hopefully in the summer. It was easy talking with Veronique. Why? She didn't know about my two failed marriages. She didn't know how I felt about myself. I could invent an idealized version of Michael for the benefit of someone I'd probably never see again. Have you ever done that? Have you ever met someone so far removed from your daily existence that you felt you could be an entirely different individual in their presence? Or, like yourself, but unburdened, relieved of all that discomfits you. It's an amazing feeling, isn't it? And don't you wish you could hold onto that sense of self, and carry it with you everywhere? Show it to your ex. Model it at the office. Hold it up to your mother. In truth, we just want to be that person, unencumbered by the severe judgments we pass upon ourselves for our failures, real or perceived. I'm going to try to remember this—maybe you should, too. I mean, you're not a bad person. In fact, you're a decent person, trying to figure it out, reading this helpful volume in the hope of gaining new insight into the meaning of your existence, the essence of your being, and how this understanding might lead you closer to the discovery of the one individual who could join you, enrich and magnify you, on your journey through eternity. Is that what you think? Are you out of your mind? Well, maybe it'll all work out. But for the moment, I'm thinking about Veronique. I thanked her for calling and told her I hoped we'd have a chance to speak again soon. She wished me a happy and successful autumn and said to give Kim a hug for her.

Didn't that feel good? A shot of masculinity returning to my uncertain body. Thank you. Whoever you are, whatever it's about, Thank you. How incredible I felt for the rest of the day. I decided to contribute all of my net worth to the International Red Cross. Then I changed my mind and gave $10 to a homeless man selling *Street News* on the corner of 23rd and Sixth. Two weeks later I received a note from Veronique, thanking me again for the photo, saying how much she'd enjoyed speaking over the phone, wishing it had been possible for her to join Kim and I for dinner, describing the changing weather in Paris, and her own desire to change jobs—maybe seek a position in hotel management, perhaps outside of France. She hoped I was well, and Kim, too. After reading her words for the tenth time it was too late to call Paris, what with the six-hour time difference...

...But I called the hotel at 10:00 a.m. New York time the following day. It was her day off. I called at 10:00 a.m. again a day later, and found her at the front desk. Veronique and I spoke like old acquaintances for forty-five minutes, interrupted from time to time by her concierge duties. I overheard her speaking French, German and English to various guests seeking vital information about Paris. When we were finished, had hung up the phones, I sat at my desk and thought about this beautiful woman sitting at a hotel desk across the Atlantic Ocean. In my imagination, I placed her by my side in New York City, walking in the Village. We held hands, our conversation was animated. She pointed to things in shop windows that caught her fancy—an antique necklace, a hanger-wire sculpture, an Italian lamp. I protested that the lamp was too modern looking—it would be old in a minute. She poked my arm and said I was too in love with traditional things. Then I pulled her around to face me and said, "I think it's important for me to kiss you now." And we kissed right there on the sidewalk, on Bleecker Street, as the gay and straight worlds walked by, smiling at this French-American kiss.

"Michael. Michael...Come in, Michael. Dan is on the phone and he wants to know if lunch is still on."

"What? Dan? Oh, right, yes, it's still on—ask him where he wants to meet and I'll be there at one."

The following day I sent her a postcard displaying an aerial photo of the Statue of Liberty.

> *Dear Veronique,*
>
> *I don't know if anyone has ever thanked you personally for the Statue of Liberty, but I would like to take the opportunity now. It looks great in the Harbor, and everyone loves it! Also, enjoyed speaking with you yesterday and I'll look forward to the next time. Is there an address where you would prefer receiving postcards from the States? Be well, and enjoy the season...*
>
> *Yours from New York —*
>
> *Michael*

In mid-October, I started thinking about the Island. The one where Tara and I had honeymooned, and where we had subsequently vacationed nine times over a period of five years—the five years of our marriage. With the frigid weather approaching how could I deny myself this annual pleasure just because Tara had left me in the spring? I knew lots of people there, and they weren't just *our* friends. I decided to take the 5 days after Thanksgiving. Low key time. Not too long.

"Just one ticket, Michael?" my travel agent asked, as if to correct me. "Yes, Julie, just one ticket—Tara and I aren't together anymore, I don't know if you knew that..."

"I'm sorry, Michael, I had no idea..."

"It's all right—we're still great friends. But I really need a vacation, and it should be to a place I love..."

"Well, you know so many people down there—I'm sure you'll have a great time, and you'll meet new people, too." And thus I was booked.

When do you know something is wrong? When there is no one sitting beside you in the back of the taxi en route to the airport, you start to know it. Inside the terminal, at your gate, standing alone, among approximately one hundred fifty couples, and many of their children—many of them loud. The sense of wrongness is stronger. You pick up a newspaper and a book—maybe a Demille or le Carré or some rock star autobio—and begin to create the intimate, insulated space which you will be occupying for the next 5 days. "Headphones, sir?"

"Okay, thank you. By the way, what is the movie?"

"*The Return of Lassie*—do you still want headphones?"

"Sure, yes, thank you."

"Another cocktail, sir?"

"Yes, thank you." At the airport in St. Maarten you board a small twin-engine plane for the twelve-minute flight to the small island. There are only couples on this plane, and they are all deeply in love. And they will begin making love upon arrival at their villas, or their hotel rooms. Some will make love while waiting in line to rent their Mokes. Others will make love in their Mokes while exiting the airport. But I will pretend to continue reading the *Times* as I wait in line, ignoring the sunny fornication going on all around me.

When do you know something is wrong? When the maitre d' says, "Ahh, Monsieur Michael! 'Ow wonderful to see you! And where ees beautiful Tara?"

"So good to see you, Georges. I'm afraid Tara and I are not together anymore, but we remain close friends and I know she sends her love."

"Mon Dieu! Zees cannot be! So you are dining alone? Seet anywhere you like…oh ees so sad!"

When there is more room than necessary in your king-size bed to contain the single, sleepless body lying beneath the open window from which can be heard the muffled crunching of waves against the soft sands of la plage upon which you would walk arm-in-arm with someone no longer accompanying you beneath a canopy of galaxies with the expectation that this will be forever. That's when you know something is wrong.

Are you on a vacation like that right now? Alone for the first time in years, trying to recapture remembered pleasures in a place that was so personal, so special for so long? Get the hell out of there. Put the fucking book down and call your travel agent. Pack up your shit—put the wet bathing suit in a plastic bag. Take a shower, get the salt off your body. Tell everyone there's an emergency at your office and it's vital that you return and handle it. Careers are at stake. Homes are at stake. Lives could be lost. You've got to go, but you'll be back later in the winter. Love you. Kiss, kiss. Save a place on the beach for me. Au revoir, mes amis!

But you probably already knew this, didn't you? When you were separated, you knew to take that first vacation with a good friend, right? And you had a great time! You laughed, read passages aloud from each other's books, pointed out great looking bodies on the beach, swam across the bay every day, enjoyed a little nightlife—even met some Portuguese tourists from the cruise ship in the harbor. Why didn't you tell *me*? Why would you allow me to go through this emasculating experience without saying a thing? Just so you'd have the pleasure of reading about it later, right here, in these pages? You make me sick with your selfishness!

I called my travel agent to make departure arrangements, with three of five nights remaining on my 'vacation.' "Why are you leaving so soon, Michael? Is the weather terrible?" Yes, yes, that's it, Julie. There's a cloud formation in my chest cavity and it's not moving, must be part of a larger system, some kind of inversion—I'll come back another time, after the Trades have blown it out of here.

The flight back to New York was tomorrow. I wished I had someone to talk with, but there was no one. How would I pass the next twenty-four hours? All the sand had been removed from the beach, the water emptied out of Baie St. Jean, and the horizon line, where the sea had always met the sky, had been eradicated. I was hungry, but couldn't again bear to be seated alone in some tranquil jardin, listening to the sexuality of Bob Marley, jammin', jammin', jammin' till the break of dawn, watching young lovers feeding each other, pretending to read my stupid airport 'thriller.' I strolled to the local grocery and purchased a cooked chicken, Camembert, a baguette, olives and a bottle of Sancerre. And as I ate and drank on the patio outside of my room, I noticed the water returning to the baie. If you are lonely, and your heart is aching, it's very important to eat something.

Sitting on the patio, drinking wine, staring past the emerald sea, I became aware once again of how beautiful this place is. I felt that I could stay... because I knew that I was leaving. For that reason, I felt ridiculous. Feeling ridiculous has always been therapeutic for me—arrival at the acceptance of illogic. So, in this frame of mind, and with a fresh appreciation for my surroundings, and for my absurdity, I wished very much to share my thoughts and feelings with someone. I decided to call Veronique in Paris. It would be like exposing myself to her—no pretense, no clever cards, just a call from a lonely American on a French Island with his chest cavity carved out and any mystery about him undone, and how are you, by the way? I'm embarrassed just thinking about not knowing what I was thinking. "Hello, Veronique?"

"Ees eet you, Michael!"

"Yes, it is me—how have you been?"

"I 'ave been fine, but I 'ave been meesing your voice! Do you call me from your office?"

"No, not my office. I'm actually calling you from St. Barth, an island in the French West Indies—have you ever been here?"

"No, never, but I 'ear eet ees beautiful. I did not know you were going on vacance again...eet must feel great to be een a warm place—I envy you!"

I told Veronique why I had come to the island and the circumstances under which I had visited so many times before. I told her that I'd been having a miserable time, that I had been lonely and never should have traveled without a friend—maybe never should have come here at all. I told her I was ending my vacation early, leaving tomorrow, but that I'd just wanted to call her and show her how stupid a 'stupid American tourist' can be. And also that I just wanted to hear her voice.

"But I am 'appy to 'ear your voice, too, Michael. I am sorry zat you are not 'aving so much fun—I can't believe you would come back to your honeymoon place alone! I 'ate to say—but eet ees pretty funny, no?" If you are a self-acknowledged idiot, there is little risk in making a phone call like this. I started laughing. I knew I'd never make love again. I would purchase a loom and make rugs for the rest of my life. I would study with old Pakistani women, memorizing the rapid movements of their gnarled fingers. I would begin slowly, with simple patterns, geometric forms repeated at intervals. Years later, I would weave colorful flowers and interlocking vines, animals with spotted skins, birds with elaborate plumage and, finally, portraits of the Presidents.

"I 'ave an idea, Michael, eef you weel leesen to me."

"Of course I will, Veronique."

"Instead of dees vacationing alone stuff, why don't you come to Paree for New Year? It weel be so much fun 'ere zen, and I 'ave a friend who works in a wonderful restaurant where we can 'ave a great New Year's feast wees many nice people. What do you say? Do you already 'ave some plans?"

"Well, no, I mean, Kim and I will spend Christmas together, but then I, ah, have nothing special…"

"Zen I want you to say 'Yes,' you weel come to Paree…"

"Veronique…Veronique, I'm afraid you're just feeling sorry for me because of the pathetic story I've told you about my island vacation. I mean, I don't want your pity…"

"Do you mean zat you would not want to come and veesit me, Michael?"

"No, no, I don't mean that at all! I would love to see you again, Veronique."

"Zen why not New Year, when eet weel be so much fun in Paree, and I weel 'ave some time off from zee 'otel?" I fell silent. Warm water was rushing around my heart, some of it reaching my eyes. I could see her mouth close to the phone, thousands of miles away, her lips still, waiting for the next sound, which was supposed to be the sound of my voice, which was choked up beneath my heart. "Michael? Michael, are you okay?"

"Yes."

"What deed you say?"

71

"Yes, yes I'd love to come to Paris to be with you for New Year's."

"Yes?! You weel come?"

"Yes, and I can't wait to see you again, Veronique."

"Oh me too, Michael."

"What if I left New York on, say, the twenty-ninth…and stayed in Paris till the second…would that be too much? Would you have time to spend together?"

"Yes, and I weel make time. You weel meet wonderful people, and I'll show you Paree as Parisians see eet!"

"It sounds wonderful, Veronique—I can't possibly imagine a better way to spend the New Year…Why does it feel like I know you so well?"

"I don't know—I feel zat way, too. Eet ees crazy, no? But eet's great!"

"Look, I better go now, but I'll call you again the day after tomorrow, when I'm back in New York, okay? Maybe you could see if there is a modest hotel where I could stay—but not La Villa, okay?"

"I weel find somesing, don't worry. Now enjoy the rest of your vacance, and don't be lonely, okay? Au revoir, Michael."

"Goodbye, Veronique. Merci beaucoup."

I could stop right now, couldn't I? My chest refilled with affirmation and hope, my heart bouncing like a buoy in la baie. And you would know this feeling, and nod your smiling head in recognition of its shallow gratification…

I now looked forward to being back in New York. And to the weeks of planning for my New Year's journey to Paris. A rendezvous. Rendezvous: an appointment between two or more persons to meet at a certain time or place. Flights must be booked. Schedules cleared (as if I had anything else planned). There were clothes to buy, and gifts, too. I wondered what we would do. If we only walked the streets of Paris, ate brilliant food, drank good wine, and talked, it would be perfect. On New Year's Eve we should certainly kiss. It's the most wonderful time of the year, is it not? In every store window I saw something for Veronique. Is this necklace too romantic? Is this sweater too plain? What if she hates scarves? How would I manage to shop for Kim, as well? Or Mom? Actually, I wasn't thinking of either, lost in my reveries. *'What are you doing for New Year's, Michael?'* *'Oh, New Year's, yeah, well, uh, a lovely woman I met briefly this summer when I was in France with Kim has invited me to join her in Paris for New Year's, and so I'm going to fly over there the night of the 29th and spend the most enchanting four days of my life in the company of someone I hardly know. What are you doing?'*

My efficiency in the office dropped precipitously—if I didn't own the company I probably would have let myself go. *'I know it's Christmastime, Michael, and believe me, it hurts to have to do this now, but you're just not performing up to par—Friday will be your last day here. Be sure to give your copy of the bathroom key to Marsha before you leave.'* Luckily, my mood was so effervescent that things sailed along pretty well anyway. In fact, I considered giving myself a raise.

It's wrong that soundtracks can only be heard in the movies, don't you think? I think this chapter should have a soundtrack, so here's what you should begin to hear playing just below the surface of your consciousness as you continue reading: Everything from Stan Getz's "The Bossa Nova Years," including his collaborations with Astrud Gilberto. When we arrive in Paris, you'll be listening to Edith Piaf, and moved by the ruby-hued plaintiveness which her voice evokes. In lobbies and dining rooms, passing antique shops and cafes, also hear Louis Armstrong, Yves Montand, Miles Davis, Depeche Mode, Billie Holiday and Andres Segovia. This soundtrack is not available in any store—it's only playing in your head. And you paid *nothing!* Just don't try to change the music.

Veronique had found a charming room for me in an ancient little place called, appropriately, L'Hotel de Paris, only a dozen blocks or so from La Villa, where she would still be working when I arrived. I would taxi from de Gaulle, check into the hotel and rest a little, and Veronique would come get me for lunch. Easy. In spite of the simplicity of this plan, however, in New York, in my apartment, packing and preparing for the trip on departure day, I was losing my grip. Wrapping Christmas gifts, I even questioned the wrapping paper—was it too childish? The little snowmen on the paper? Jesus! I ran out to get some tissue and beautiful rice paper. I love this necklace—I hope she thinks it's okay. Will this sweater fit her? It *has* to fit—she's tiny, it's meant to be big. How can she not love this antique perfume bottle? But what if she hates Chanel? Shut up and wrap it! I hated all of my clothes. I wear these things all year, but now I hate them. This is an American shirt! Why am I even bringing a tie? I don't wear ties! But maybe we're going someplace where they require ties. No pants, no shoes, no underwear—just ties. Shut up and pack it! Jesus. Passport. Tickets. Go, grab the stuff and leave.

"Where to, sir?"

"Kennedy Airport, please, the TWA terminal."

"Ahhh, so you're going away?"

"Yes, but now I must take a little sleep—could you please wake me when we get to the airport?"

"Si, yes, boss."

I didn't want to talk to the driver. I wanted to stay inside my dream, listen to my soundtrack, bring the image of Veronique to life on the inside of my eyelids, imagine what it would be like meeting her at the hotel for the first time. I mean, aren't you curious about that? Think how the hell I felt! "'Eadphones, Monsieur?"

"Yes, thank you. By the way, what is the movie?"

"Eet ees *Green Card*, wees Gerard Depardieu. Do you steel weesh to 'ave zee 'eadphones?"

"Oui, merci."

"Somesing to dreenk, Monsieur?"

"Oui...un verre de vin blanc, si vous plait."

"Voila."

"Merci."

The hotel was so unaffected, so unglamorous, I would be astounded to learn that they advertised, that they even had a brochure, even permitted non-French persons to stay there. Yet I felt welcomed. "'Ow many nights, Monsieur?"

"Trois...three." I loved the place. I loved ma petite chambre—so old and worn, yet spotless, like Aunt Jewel's house—even a crucifix on the wall above the bed! I phoned Veronique at La Villa and let her know that I'd arrived and was at the hotel. "Welcome to Paree, Michael! I am excited to see you—ees your room okay? And 'ow do you feel after your long flight?"

"I feel great—very happy to be here, and excited to see you, too… and the room is fine, perfect, thank you."

"Well I weel come for you een just two hours, eef zat ees okay, as soon as I feeneesh 'ere, zen maybe you would like to take some lunch weez me, no?"

"Absolutely, anywhere you like." I undressed to take a nap before Veronique arrived. I thought I would be too excited to sleep, but I slept, soundly. Other than Veronique, not a person in the world knew where I was at this moment. Not my daughter, not my travel agent, not my secretary. In the 'grown-up' world there are few occasions when you cannot be tracked down, and quickly, for some reason or other—a business or personal emergency, the death of an uncle… But here I was, in this tiny chamber, so quiet, so lost in an extraordinarily private moment, drifting far, far away from my port of disembarkation. Never Never Land. Seldom Ever Land. I can fly. I can sleep.

One hour later, the wakeup call: "Il est treize heures, Monsieur." "Merci." Time to shower and dress. Time to get ready to greet someone I hadn't seen since August, had never even had coffee with. I wish you were with me, to help break the ice, make the first meeting less—awkward. But it was all those years ago, and you're just reading this now. In fact, maybe you're reading this twenty years from now, so you couldn't possibly be of assistance. But would you have if you could? You should think about that. I was looking at myself in the mirror when she called. I don't know how I looked, but I saw happiness in my eyes. I smiled. "I am 'ere een zee lobby, Michael."

"Don't move, I'll come right down!" I whispered 'Thank you' to the quiet room, grabbed my coat, and the bag of gifts, and I left ma chambre.

Do you want to know how she looked, standing there in the lobby in front of the little elevator, waiting for me as the door slid open? I'm sorry, but

I don't remember what she was wearing. I only remember that she was beautiful. That she was smiling. That there was happiness in her eyes. "Hello, Veronique."

"Bonjour, Michael! Eet ees so good to see you again!" We kissed on both cheeks, that's what you do. Then we looked at each other.

"This is pretty amazing, I must tell you," I said.

"Yes, and I am so 'appy zat you 'ave come." You know that we embraced now, don't you? Well, I will tell you that there is water in my eyes as I write this. We held each other for less than a minute. "I wonder what this is?" I whispered.

"Maybe we weel start to find out over lunch, what do you seenk?" I smiled.

"What a good idea—but first you must open your presents!"

"Oh, Michael, what deed you do? You should not 'ave done zees! It ees too much—you are so crazy!" She held up the sweater against her torso like a little girl. "Oh eet ees so beautiful!" She lifted her hair and insisted I fasten the necklace for her. "'Ow do you 'ave such wonderful taste—eet ees so pretty, I love eet, Michael!" Even the perfume seemed to be right. "Ah, Chanel! One of zee few sings we French do well!" she proclaimed, opening the bottle, dabbing her wrist and extending it to my nose. "Do you like eet?" Why, yes. In fact, it's giving me an incredible appetite.

Have you ever presented a gift to someone—something that you thought very hard about giving—and detected in their response, just beneath the "Thank you—you shouldn't have!" that the thing was wrong, wasn't the correct 'fit,' that, if the recipient could, they would return it for store credit immediately? That's not what was happening here. Veronique was in a fairy tale, and she made me feel I was its creator. That was her gift to me, and I'm going to keep it forever.

"Are you 'ungry, Michael?"

"Yes, I could definitely eat something, how about you?"

"I am starving! Come on, I know a leettle place close by where zey 'ave wonderful crepes and soups and good wine too." We left the boxes and wrappings at the hotel desk and walked outside. Veronique took my hand and led me to I don't know where—a tiny street with narrow book and fabric shops, all as ancient as Paris itself, and a small stone structure with a sign above its wooden door, Gascogne. "Dees ees eet!" Inside there were no more than ten tables resting on the well-worn stone floor, a mix of wood chairs and simple benches, an open oven behind a sturdy bar, and only a few couples, lingering over espressos and glasses of wine.

"'Alo, Veronique, bonjour!" called the friendly face behind the bar.

"Bonjour, Alain!" my companion replied, "Ça va?"

"Ça va bien, merci."

"Alain, je present Michael, mon ami de New York Ceety. Michael, Alain."

"Enchanté, Monsieur. Parlez vous Francaise?"

"Ahh, non, je suis desolee."

"Okay, zen eet ees good to meet you, Michael—welcome to Paree, to Gascogne!"

"Merci. It's great to be here…it's a wonderful place you have."

"Merci…eet ees small but very friendly I 'ope. You must seet and 'ave some wine and somesing to eat, yes?"

"Ah, oui—Michael 'ave just arrived today, we must feed 'eem well!"

It was 9:30 p.m. New York time, and we were just sitting for lunch. Well, time had stopped, actually—somewhere over the Atlantic, I believe. Bowls of soup thick with vegetables and sticky cheese came to the table, along with a baguette and a dark bottle from Bordeaux. I could see a light snow falling through the tiny window to the street, but inside, the room was toasting from the oven's steady flame. We touched glasses. "To a 'appy New Year, okay?"

"Yes, to a happy New Year, in a place where I have never been before—where I never imagined being before."

"I 'ope you are 'appy zat you 'ave come to Paree, Michael, not even knowing who ees Veronique!"

"But why does it seem as though we know each other well somehow? I am very happy I came to Paris, maybe just to answer that question."

"Maybe we are brusser and seester and have only now just found each other!"

"Impossible—I would never give my sister that necklace."

"You would not love your seester, Michael?" she asked mischievously.

"Of course, just like a brother."

"Ah well, I already 'ave a brusser—and zat ees enough." Veronique placed her hand on mine and looked at me playfully.

"Look! It's snowing, but it feels warmer than the Caribbean in here. Why is that?"

"Maybe you are seetting too close to zee fire." She laughed and took a sip of wine.

"Maybe I'm not sitting close enough to the fire." I shook my head in disbelief, at myself, at this.

"What are you seenking?"

"I'm thinking I want you to tell me all about yourself."

"I'm theeking you are crazy."

"I'm serious—I want to know everything, and you can start with your birth. Ready? Go."

"Okay, but zen you must tell me everysing, too."

It wasn't the food bombarding our senses with a myriad of flavors and impressions, sumptuous as Gascogne's brief menu was. It was the stories, of two lives, being served across a heavy wooden table, each course, each flavor more interesting than the last. The room emptied, and by five Alain announced that he had to go out, for bread, before the start of evening's dinner service, but we shouldn't move, he would be right back. "Before I go I weel open anuzzer bottle for you, and trust zat you weel know what to do—now don't be afraid by yourselves!" As he flipped over the fermé sign and bolted out the door Veronique called out, "Don't worry, Alain, we weel take special care of your customers!" I looked around Gascogne, and Gascogne was empty. I turned my eyes toward Veronique and got up from the chair. "Where are you going, Michael?"

Picking up the bottle I said, "I must take your order—our kitchen is very busy just now. Wine, Mademoiselle?"

"Oui, Monsieur."

"And something to start?"

"Mmm...peut-etre."

"And what might that be?" I asked, pouring the wine.

"Ahh, je voudrais…"

"Perhaps I could recommend something," I said, leaning closer to my customer. She put her hand on my arm and smiled.

"And what would you recommend, Monsieur?"

"Have you tried our spécialité du chef?"

"Et qu'est-ce que c'est?"

"You may have a sample before you order if you like."

"Oui, s'il vous plaît." I leaned closer and her lips parted so slightly, and then I kissed her. For a few seconds there was tentativeness, but our lips did not separate. And then she touched the side of my cheek with her palm, her eyes closed, and I felt the tip of her tongue on my own. As our kiss deepened several days passed. Breathing became unnecessary, our respiratory systems taking sustenance from one another. Finally, we parted, looking at each other breathlessly. Her mouth was moist, her face flushed. "What do you think?" I asked. She smiled.

"Eef dere ees any left een zee keetchen I weel 'ave some. Eef not, I must leave."

"Ahh but I know we have not run out—I'll bring you more." I kissed her again, putting my arms around her, pulling our bodies close together. Some coincidental alignment of events in the solar system had allowed us to create a tiny, ancient restaurant in Paris, to light a fire in its oven, and to be its only customers. Are we able to assert any control over the circumstances that might unfold from such an alignment? Can the events be linked, one to the other? Or are they like meteoroids, passing close to each other in trajectories of different origin, en route to destinations that cannot be foretold, till one or the other enters the atmosphere of a planet and is drawn to its surface? I am holding Veronique, and I am trying to hold these events together.

Alain returned from the now darkened street, where the snow continued to fall. I had forgotten about outside. That there was an outside. That the tiny universe formed by the walls of the restaurant actually existed within a much larger universe that included, but was not limited to, the street outside the door, the other interconnected streets and boulevards, the city of Paris itself, France and all of Europe, the other continents, and the oceans, of course, and New York City. "I see zat you 'ave been 'elping yourselves—I 'ope zee service was not a deesappointment!"

"On zee contrary, Alain, everysing 'as been perfect. Don't you agree, Michael?" Yes, I think. I think too much. Yes, everything has been perfect, and I think that I will not think any further.

"'Ere, 'ave zee baguette—I must join zee keetchen and prepare for dinner. For you, Michael, I weel put on some musique to make you feel at home. Do you like James Taylor, eh?"

"But right now, I *am* at home," I said, smiling at Veronique. And besides, James Taylor wasn't on my soundtrack. "Do you have Edith Piaf?"

"Mais oui! Edith Piaf eet weel be!" proclaimed Alain with a laugh as he disappeared into the kitchen.

"What a beautiful night in the universe," I said to the woman sitting beside me.

"Yes, eet certainly ees," she whispered, squeezing my hand.

Couples began to enter this universe, dusting snow from their shoulders, shaking their caps, extending salutations to Alain, who greeted all as family members. Crepes went into the oven, hot bowls came from the kitchen, bottles came off the shelves. "Why is someone so beautiful and charming as you sitting here with an American tonight?"

"But before tonight I am alone, too, Michael."

"But you are so..."

"I am...so...pretty?"

"Well..."

"What does zat mean? I 'ad to t'row out my boyfriend four months ago. And 'ee ees a French man!"

"But why?"

"'Ee want to leeve weeth me...and 'ee want to make love to my girlfriend, too. Zat ees not okay for me—I am not such a modern girl!" For the first time, I could see something else in Veronique's eyes, adding complexity to the warmth and playfulness: the sadness. And I felt I knew her now on another level. "And so now I am seeing wees a nice man from outer space, I mean, New York Ceety. Zat ees my real Christmas present dees year, Michael—so—Merci!" She touched her glass against mine.

"You've made me feel very special—I'm lucky to have met you at the moment I did."

"But we must blame Kim, too!" she laughed.

"Yes, to Kim. To you. To our Happy New Year."

"You must be exhausted, Michael. Look what time eet ees! We cannot be zee last ones to leave 'ere—Alain weel sink we are 'omeless!"

"I no longer require sleep, Veronique. But maybe you're right, we should probably go." We rose carefully from the table and accepted strong bear hugs from Alain, who warned me that we'd better return to Gascogne before I returned to the States. I promised. Kisses to Veronique, bundle up, then out onto the street, into the other universe. We walked slowly, our arms locked around each other. "I must get to zee Metro, Michael—my apartment ees quite far from 'ere, een Chateauneuf—zee suburbs, as you say." I thought for a moment about this. But I didn't allow myself to think too much.

"Veronique, the hotel is just a few blocks away—although I'm sure I could never find it. Without you, that is. Please stay the night. I'll sleep in the bathtub, I promise." She laughed and hit me in the chest.

"You are a crazy man!"

"Please. Don't go away."

"My God. Okay, but we must be careful—promise!"

"I will be in the bathtub, and I will stay there until you wish to take a bath."

"Michael, stop! I weel keel you!"

"You will kiss me!" I demanded, turning toward her.

"No, I weel keel you—but first I weel kees you." And so we keesed right zere, a snowy baiser on zee rue. And in this crazy moment, I felt like the Almighty. An incredible feeling, wheeling all that Almighty Power, just walking to a small hotel in Paris with a wonderful companion, ignoring all the saints and sinners, devils and demons, whom I hadn't bothered to inform of My whereabouts. A lot of people still thought I was Everywhere, being the Supreme Being, and all. But I was in Paris. Still wonder why your prayers weren't answered for a few days? Sorry. But I want you to know that I did forgive you for everything. I was in such a Goddamn great mood.

An old-fashioned skeleton key unlocked the door to chambre sept. And inside the door was the shopping bag with Veronique's gifts. "Look, they brought your presents up to the room! Did you tell them you'd be staying here tonight, tell me the truth?"

"You are so bad!" she said, giving me another push in the chest. "Eet ees such a petite chambre, Michael. Are you sure you are 'appy 'ere?"

"It has everything I could possibly need, Veronique. But are *you* comfortable here?"

"Yes, I am. I am very comfortable near you, Michael." I removed her coat, and mine, and threw them onto the tiny sofa.

"I'm so happy you're here with me, and not on the train." I stood before her, taking her shoulders in my hands. I brushed a lock of light brown hair away from her eyes and touched her lips with the back of my fingers. She kissed them, keeping her gaze on my eyes. I moved my hand to the side of her face, and beneath her hair to the back of the neck, gently pulling her head closer to me, her lips to mine. We stood like that for many moments in the quiet, petite chambre. I became so warm I feared my clothing would burst into flames spontaneously. My hand was on the small of her back and we rocked hypnotically back and forth in a slow waltz. Removing my lips from hers I whispered, "This would be an appropriate time for me to step into the bathtub."

"Eet would be an appropriate time for you to not talk," she replied with a smile, and a kiss. "Eef you weel excuse me, Monsieur, I weel go eento zee bathroom for a moment. Weel you be okay?"

"Absolutement." She picked up the shopping bag, shut the door to the bath behind her and soon I could hear the sound of running water.

And humming. I think it was an Edith Piaf song. I turned on the television and flipped the channels, but there wasn't much. A round-table talk show, in French. Click. A game show, in French. Click. Some kind of French hospital soap. Click. An old "Kojak" segment, dubbed in French. I stared as the bald detective shouted at the bad men in French, while his lips formed words in English. Off. I walked to the window and parted the heavy velvet curtains. A beautiful sight, we're happy tonight, the streets are silenced in snowfall.

The door to the bath opened. "Voila! 'Ow do you like my nightgown?" Veronique wore only her new sweater, which barely reached her thigh.

"Why… it's beautiful. And you smell…amazing." I was crumbling.

"Eet's zee perfume zat you gave me! Do you like?" She leaned closer to me, turning her head slightly so that I could inhale her neck, which I immediately kissed.

"Mmm. It's you, it's perfect."

"Sank you, for your wonderful geefts—now eet ees your turn een zee bath." I dutifully closed the door behind me, washed myself, brushed my teeth, looked in the mirror and shook my smiling head. *Tell me your name again.' 'Michael.' 'Right. Michael The Almighty.' 'Yes.'*

When I emerged from the bathroom, Veronique was in bed, peeking out from beneath the covers. "Belle nuit," I whispered.

"Oui." I turned out the lamps and came to the side of the bed. Turning back the covers I eased onto the mattress, fully clothed, shoes and all.

"And what do you seenk you are doing!?" Veronique protested.

"We must be careful," I intoned with mock seriousness, "I promised you that I would, and I am being careful." She could barely stop laughing.

"You are from outer space! Eet ees unacceptable to wear zat een zee bed. Now take eet off or I weel keel you!" She pushed me out of the bed.

"Okay, okay! You don't have to be so rough!" I removed my clothing, but for the boxers, and asked permission to return to the bed.

"Oui, Monsieur, you may return. But no more jokes!" I obeyed her and slid under the covers, laying on my side to face the girl in the new sweater. I saw in the dim light that she was smiling in this exploding moment in chambre sept, outside of which the snow was falling down on at least one street in Paris.

When we finished making love it was New Year's eve on the Left Bank and December 30th on the Upper West Side. 3:20 a.m. and 9:20 p.m. For someone who did not want to fall asleep, I embraced sleep passionately, in the arms of someone with whom I had recently had lunch for the first time. But when I awoke, many hours later, I was alone in the bed. Sunshine attempted entry to the room through a slit between the curtains. Water was running in the bathroom. And then it was not. "Hello! Veronique!" I called from the mattress. She opened the door, still dripping, wrapped in a towel.

"Bonne année, my beautiful Michael! And 'ow do you feel dees wonderful morning?"

"I feel amazing, and it is New Year's Eve!" I said, climbing out of the bed to greet her, to hold her. "And why are you up and out of our beautiful bed so early?"

"So early! Eet ees apres-midi! I 'ave to work for a few hours dees afternoon, but first I 'ave to go 'ome to get clothes. And after my work I go home again to dress for New Year's Eve!" Veronique gave me explicit directions via the Paris Métro to a restaurant on the Right Bank, about 6 miles from my hotel, where we and her friends would be meeting for dinner at 10 p.m. "You weel be fine, yes?"

"Yes, of course, but will you be okay with all that?"

"Yes, I weel be fine. I 'ave just 'ad the most wonderful night in my memory, and I will 'old that memory weeth me today, until I can see you again. Am I crazy? Ees zat okay?"

"Yes, that is a good idea. I loved last night. And we will love tonight, Veronique." We kissed again, and out the door she went, with a big smile and an "à bientôt!" I stood for a while, thinking about how I came to be here, thinking I should take a shower, have breakfast. Someone would know where eggs were being served.

■　■　■

I allowed myself 40 minutes to get to the restaurant. Boarded a train at 9:25 and thought 'This isn't hard—I'm finding my own way in Paris!' All the passengers were dressed for a celebration, oblivious to the cold and snow. We all could have made a toast right there! At 9:34 the train pulled into the third station. Doors opened. But they did not close again. Passengers began looking at each other. Then an announcement came reverberating off the tile walls from the station PA system. The announcement was, of course, in French. Even if you were French, you couldn't have translated. Just the burst of an electronically garbled voice announcing… what? The announcement was repeated, and concerned riders began shifting in their seats, murmuring amongst themselves. Had someone understood? A few people began to leave the train. Again, the transmission over the intercom. And now, more people exiting the car. It was now nearly 9:50. And I was thinking 'Shit! What the hell's going on? What should I do?'

To anyone nearby I pleaded loudly, "Uh, parlez vous Anglais? Le train… What is le problem!?"

And someone answered, "Ah, le train ees feeneeshed ce soir! Zee men zay go on strike! Phutt! No more train!" And now I thought, 'Oh Christ, it's New Year's Eve and the Metro's gone on strike, I'm on the train, in an unknown station somewhere under Paris and it's almost 10 o'clock!' I instinctively followed my fellow sheep off the platform, up the stairs and out onto Boulevard Rue de Rivoli, where thousands of freezing, frustrated Parisians were now contemplating new ideas for their New Year's celebrations, and fighting for the nonexistent taxis. What could Veronique possibly be imagining now? I shuddered at the thought. She would call the hotel, but they could not help her. She was in a restaurant, sitting not beside me, wearing a beautiful necklace, explaining that I must be en route. I prayed. 'Please Almighty, i realize i am the least impressive of Your lowest creations. In this pathetic context, nonetheless, i beg, if You could take just the briefest moment from Your Own New Year's preparations and deliver me from this chaos, amen.'

I didn't really expect God to transport me to the restaurant, so I jumped into the middle of the boulevard, stood between the two lanes of oncoming traffic and waved my arms wildly. Cars flew by me recklessly, and in the glinting light I could see shocked expressions on the faces of the drivers. *"What the fuck?!"* How would they say that in French? Finally, I saw a taxi light approaching and moved directly into its oncoming lane, holding up my palm as if it were a sign: Arretez! It worked. The driver attempted a panic stop and I stepped aside to avoid bodily harm. I didn't wait for a discussion, just opened the passenger door, jumped in and handed the driver the little piece of paper that had the words Les Routiers Rue Marx Dormoy written in Veronique's hand. "Merci, Monsieur," I gasped, "Le Metro…eet ees on strike! This restaurant, s'il vous plait." The driver appeared to be horribly inconvenienced by my desperate act—which had made me his passenger against his will. But I ignored this fact and continued to babble on about being incredibly late, lost in the streets of Paris, deeply concerned about my friend, a single woman who would think I had been killed, and if only you can find this restaurant I weel teep you weeth many francs, Monsieur! I detected a slight smile in the rearview. I think my pathetic display of desperation was beginning to appeal to his sense of humor.

"We weel find zee place, Monsieur." He clicked on his car phone and began talking, I imagine to 'base.' I heard the words "Les Routiers." then static, then words, then static, then my driver saying, "Oui…oui…oui…oui…merci, bientot." Click.

Ten minutes later we pulled up to an awning in front of an ancient townhouse with twinkling candles in the windows. The meter required thirty-five francs. I handed the driver a fifty note and said, "Merci, Monsieur!" waving that no change was required.

"Merci beaucoup, Monsieur—et Bon Année!"

I ran inside Les Routiers and into the festive dining room just twenty minutes before midnight. It was filled with happy voices, popping corks and clinking glasses as I searched for Veronique's table. She spotted me first, jumped up from the table, threw her arms around me. "Oh I am so 'appy to see you! I got so worried because we 'ear about zee Metro strike, and I could not even get 'ere until a 'alf hour ago—ma mère 'ad to drive me, can you believe!?" I was so relieved and so excited at the same time.

"Well we are here, thank God, and you look beautiful! Bon Année, Veronique! My train just stopped in the fucking middle of Paris! I walked around for an hour…no one would take pity on a tragic American searching on foot for a woman with beautiful hair."

"Oh, crazy Michael! 'Ere, I weel kees you and make eet better."

And there I was, moments before New Year's in Paris. It seemed many of the evening's guests had arrived late for the same reason. The chef promised the kitchen would remain open, therefore, until after midnight. All would be served! Veronique introduced me to her attractive young friends, who graciously switched from French to English in an effort to include me in their happy chatter. Which almost immediately turned to the obligatory countdown to the New Year. "…six!…cinq!…quatre!…trois!… deux!…Bon Année!!!" All jumped up from our seats, to kiss-kiss and accept big hugs, and to sing a song that I had never heard before. I felt a pang of sadness inside of me just then, even embraced in this merriment, because it was New Year's, and I was distant from my home, the home of my diffused cultural origins, the home that maybe wondered where I was. Veronique found my eyes and put her arms around me. "I know zat you 'ave come to a strange place, Michael, and I 'ope zat eet ees 'appy for you."

Her openness and warmth brought me back to Les Routiers, and I smiled. "I haven't come to Paris. I've come to *Veronique*, and I am very happy to be here. And the first thing I want to do in this new year is thank you." And I kissed her. The way new lovers kiss. Veronique's friends applauded playfully. I acknowledged with faux modesty. She punched me in the chest.

We all left the restaurant around 2:30…and, of course, the trains were not running. Nor were taxis to be found at that hour. So Veronique and I walked the nearly 6 miles back to the hotel. Yes, at moments we staggered a bit. It's possible we needed to pee between parked cars along the way. We even stopped at a tiny bar where singing could be heard from behind steamy windows—and inside we went, the ancient room packed with people hoisting glasses, swaying to what sounded like wartime barroom ballads, sheet music and all. What else to do but order another round and sing along? By the time we arrived at the hotel it was daylight. We crawled into bed. And woke up in time for dinner. Finished dinner in time to return to the bed in chambre sept. In time for a long embrace before my departure from Paris, my flight back to New York City, and Veronique's return to the front desk at La Villa.

■ ■ ■

In the weeks that followed, Veronique and I remained close, as close as cards and calls could allow. It became clear to me over time that she was unhappy in Paris, with the routine of her life, with the hotel—she even seemed bored with her own friends...and her family. Paradoxically, she began to sound like any young person wanting to escape from small-town life. Imagine that, living in Paris! But it doesn't matter where you live, does it? It's not the town, or city, big or small. It's about how you feel there, how you feel about yourself. Or so I tell myself.

In February I invited Veronique to come to New York—arranged the tickets, she would stay with me, I would attempt to create for her some version of the magical experience she'd so generously given to me. But the petite beauty I met at JFK's Air France Terminal was not the luminous spirit I'd held in Paris. Veronique was in a terrible mood, even as we embraced. The airline had lost her bag. It had never made it onto the plane. It would probably be at the baggage claim office by tomorrow, late afternoon.

I could have given a shit. We were together—the bag would show up eventually. But something was off and there would not be a full recovery in a New York minute, or a New York week. Even after recovering her lost bag at the airport the following day. Yes, we had happy dinners together, spent time with my friends, and with each other. And yes, we made love...I wouldn't forget that. Yet nearly every conversation returned to Veronique's longing for something other than what she had. "Eet ees so boring for me at zee 'otel...zere ees nussing for me to learn anymore...I don't like zee 'otel business anyway, eet goes nowhere...I 'ate Paree and zee fucking Parisians—zey are such chauvinists...my friends, zey do not want anysing from zere lives..." It was difficult to hear these things and I felt incapable of offering comfort or an idea for turning everything around. I also felt ashamed that I'd been unable to create an enchanting time for Veronique. Should we have taken a carriage ride in the park? A Circle Line tour around Manhattan? Some of the things I'd asked myself in the weeks that followed.

Have you ever awakened in the middle of a amazing dream and tried desperately to fall back asleep, to return to the dream? When I took Veronique to the airport for her return flight we held each other for a long time. We talked about how wonderful it had been being together again, about trying to arrange a return visit soon. It never happened. There were letters, and calls…becoming less frequent as the weeks passed. She even apologized in one note for being so "negative" during her stay in New York, which would not have happened "'ad zey not lost my suitcase!" That was in late February, 1991. I haven't seen Veronique since. It feels awful, really shitty, getting to the end of this story—I should have stopped it at Charles de Gaulle Airport, where I was still in the dream. I apologize.

The Previous Chapter

Much of the previous chapter was written on the island of St. Barth, at the Hotel Emeraude Plage (sadly, destroyed by Hurricane Irma). *This* chapter is about a brief encounter that took place during the writing of that chapter. Perhaps you'd like to enjoy a glass of vin blanc or rosé as you read. Maybe with a baguette, brie, some sliced pear. It's a light read, I assure you, nearly weightless. In fact, I'll be pleased if the words adhere to the page.

I'm actually seated in the exact place where the previous chapter was written—at a small table on my patio, facing the water's edge of Bay St. Jean, a mere forty feet of white sand separating my knees from the lapping waves. Here, while writing that chapter, I have, from time to time, glanced up to reach for a word or a thought, and found in my field of vision an attractive young couple, lying upon their chaises directly in front of me at a distance no greater than thirteen paces. They are staying in the room adjacent to mine. I am alone, writing a chapter about one of the lost loves of my life, and these two lovers are posed before a liquid turquoise backdrop, reading books by John Grisham and Stephen King respectively.

Occasionally, when I'm attempting to summon my muse, *or any* muse, I catch a glimpse of one or the other of these lovers glancing above their volumes at me. This has gone on for five days in a row and, frankly, it is both disconcerting and entertaining to me. From time to time they get up and go to their room. To make Mai Tai's or French 75's? Perhaps. But I doubt it. I think they go to their room to remove their swimwear and make tender yet wildly passionate love away from the intense scrutiny of the sun. So, while they're making love, I sit alone and recall the beautiful times I once shared with Tara on this very island. Staring at my laptop, typing away, with an erection no more than twelve inches beneath my keypad, while my neighbors are next door, as noted in the previous sentence, having a rum drink and fornicating until it's time to go back in the sun. Okay wait, now they're taking a shower and saying, "That was great, I love you, baby," then ready to come out for more sun and reading and wondering what the guy with the computer is doing on his fucking patio. Are you enjoying your rosé and brie sandwich? I hope so. And I wish you would stop judging me.

Over the course of these five days, I've come to like this couple. We've bonded. We nod and say Hello when we pass each other on our respective beach walks. But only today did we really speak. I had to walk by their chaises on the way to lunch with friends at La Plage, and I said, "How are you today?"

And they each said, in their own words, of course, "Fine. How are you?" They sounded French.

I said, "Great, thanks. It's just so beautiful here, isn't it?"

And that was our opening. "We love it here, it's fantastic," she said.

"Everyone is so friendly," he said. "And it seems really safe!"

"Yes," I replied, "It's definitely a very safe island. Have you been before?"

"It's our first time," she said.

"But we would definitely come back," he added, "and what about you?"

"Well I love it, too. I actually honeymooned here years ago—but even though we're not together anymore, I still come back. I have friends on the island now, so we get together a bit." And then she went for it:

"You seem to have quite a project going while you're here." And so I went for it, too:

"Well, I'm actually trying to write a book." I could just as well have said, "Well, I'm actually recording the followup to my multi-platinum selling debut album," that's how excited their response seemed. They sat upright on their lounges immediately.

"Oh really?" he quizzed. "That's great! What's it about?"

"I'm almost embarrassed to say—but it's really about the struggle to find the one, true love of your life. And here I am, sitting before you two every day, writing away, thinking, Maybe they've found the one! Strange, eh? My name is Michael, by the way."

"I'm Vasko, and this is my wife, Marie-France."

"Very nice to meet you. Are you *from* France?"

"We're both from Montreal, actually," Marie-France said.

"Well, you seem like a really great couple, so I hope I'm not invading your privacy here at the beach."

"Absolutely not!" Vasko reassured.

"You know, ours is a very special story—we could tell you, if you like," Marie-France volunteered."

"Yes, it's a great story," Vasko confirmed.

"I'd love to hear about you two. Especially since I was thinking I might write something about how strange it was writing about the search for true love, while sitting alone on a patio facing two lovers, on a beach where I once spent my honeymoon. Is that strange?"

"Yes. But it's kind of funny, no?"

"We'll find out, Vasko. Maybe the sun is just melting my brain away. So how did you two meet?"

"Vasko, you tell it," Marie-France deferred.

"Okay, but you just fill in anywhere you want to. Before we actually met, we had spoken on the phone over business matters for probably four years. Maybe six or seven times a month we would speak. Her company was actually a client of mine."

"Yes, my company was a distributor of independent film properties in Canada, and Vasko's is a film dubbing company."

"We dub English language films and television programs in French, preparing them for distribution in French-speaking markets."

"So you spoke, but never met, for four years?"

"Yes, but I always loved the sound of her voice, and speaking with her."

"Then how did you finally come to meet each other?"

"There was a problem with one of the films," Marie-France inserted. "And then we had to speak a lot," Vasko finished.

"The film was *The Piano*—do you know it?" she asked.

"Yes, a wonderful movie."

"Exactly. But there was difficulty in getting it exactly right in French. Without boring you with details, Vasko and I had to speak a lot about that one."

"But after a couple of weeks it was all good, the problems were solved. And I asked Marie-France if she would have lunch with me, to celebrate."

"A fine business gesture," I acknowledged.

"And yet this, to us at the time, was going to be like a date," Marie-France clarified. "Because, after all these years, we were finally going to meet."

"At the time, I was living with my girlfriend, with whom I had a two-year-old son. The relationship was not good at that point—we were together for the most part because of our child."

"And I was practically living with my boyfriend—who happened to be my boss—and his two teenage daughters."

"What lovely lunch dates you two must have been," I marveled.

"To be honest with you, Michael, it was amazing. We talked for four hours—as if we were on the phone with each other, but now there was an additional connection. A genuine attraction."

"This seems pretty complicated—the boss, *his* daughters, Vasko's girlfriend, *their* son—what could be next? Phone sex?"

"Actually, he called me the next day and told me he was in love with me," Marie-France recalled.

"Holy shit, Vasko!" I threw at him. "That's a pretty big leap!"

"It was December the 7th, 1995," she said, shaking her head with a smile.

"I just knew that she was the one, Michael. We both had been with other people, but this was it, I knew it."

"I told him to slow down! I was about to go to Florida for three weeks on vacation with my boyfriend and his daughters—there was no time to think about this!"

"And did you go to Florida, Marie-France?"

"Oh, yes. But I brought my girlfriend's calling card with me so I could talk with Vasko." They both laughed at the thought of this.

"Our phone bill was $460.00!" Vasko proclaimed proudly.

"I don't even want to ask how you and your boyfriend—your *boss*—got along."

"It was not so good, I can tell you."

"And here's something pretty amazing," Vasko added. "Three and a half weeks after she returned from Florida, we moved in with each other."

"Jesus!"

"My lease was up, and it seemed like the best thing to do was to end what was not right, and to begin what felt completely right, to both of us."

"And how did the 'boss' take this, Marie-France?"

"I work for a competitor now. More money, better benefits."

"And you've been talking happily ever after."

"We were married six months after moving in together. And we still love talking!" Vasko swore. "Our friends think we are crazy."

"In fact, after two weeks here, it will be very hard to go back to work, and to speak on the phone a couple of times a day," Marie-France lamented.

"Well I love your story, and I feel lucky to have met you."

"You know, Michael, we had made up our own story about you when we first saw you take the room," Vasko volunteered with a smile, which spread to Marie-France's face. "We thought you were married to the big girl who came to the room with you."

"Who?" I asked, incredulously.

"The woman who helped carry bags with you. But then we realized that she works for the hotel."

"Oh right, Camille! She checked me in that day, helped me get set up. She's very nice."

"Well, the next day, when we saw you alone on the patio, with your computer, we knew you were by yourself."

That's when I'd begun writing the previous chapter.

Holiday Cheer

It's cold outside, baby. But we're rubbing each other's hands and I feel a glow coming on. Over the river we go, through the mall, along the avenue—pointing at fantasy window displays, laughing at the little ones, their rosy faces mesmerized by lights, colors, the sounds of a million wishes, from video games to electric trains. Skating together in matching sweaters, barely aware of another presence on our icy stage. It's the most wonderful time of the year, no doubt.

Actually, I'm pretty much solo for the holidays again this year. Not looking for sympathy—it'll still be good. My daughter's coming to New York for a few days, which I'm excited about. We're so much closer now that she's all grown up and doesn't have to listen to advice and speeches from me. And my folks are coming in from Rochester. Mom will rearrange the apartment and tell me to eat more greens. She'll bring some underwear and socks. She's eighty for Christ's sake. Friends will be getting together, too—movies, dinners, a few parties. Yay.

But there's another holiday reality, isn't there? I can see it in your faces— okay, *our* faces—on the street, in the bistros. Searching. Longing for someone special to be with, to draw closer, to help quiet our racing hearts in the throes of this obligatory cheerfulness. There's more pressure just now, do you feel it? And it's not just the finding-the-right-gift thing. It's in the air, in the stores, on the radio, on television, live from Rockefeller Center. Everybody's holding hands. Guys reaching under their girlfriends' sweaters. Why isn't it me? Or you? Do you think for a minute I'd be sitting here, writing this, if my lover was in this room with me? Of course not. I'd say 'Let's take a walk in Central Park and watch the skaters!' We'd have a hot pretzel from a hot pretzel cart. Then I'd have to use the restroom at Tavern On The Green, and after I'd suggest we have a glass of wine at the big circular bar. Then we'd walk along Columbus Avenue and look in the shop windows. Then we'd peek into this little Swedish boutique and I'd buy her a pair of mittens. Then we'd get coffee and a cookie at The Muffins Café and talk about what to plan for the 1st. Should we go to the Islands? Or maybe stay close to home for a few days, get a fire going, put the pillows on the floor...

But, as previously noted and with the exception of the aforementioned family visits, I'm alone for the holidays this year, so never mind. I mean, it's not like I've been singled out to be alone. Show of hands—how many of you out there will be alone for the holidays this year? Okay, 6...7... wow, I see that just over 18 million hands have gone up. So we're not alone. Reassuring.

Maybe the love of your life is in the room with you right now, even as you read these words. If so, I must say it's a pleasure to be with you. How radiant and happy you look. Do you think you might be soul mates? Do you think you'll be together till the end of time, over and around the obstacles, but always flowing downstream, on one current? Put the book down and think about that person. 17 seconds, good enough. Okay done. Isn't it astonishing what you've found? There must be something very special inside you to have noticed each other, to have recognized what it might become, then brought each other to this room. Why are you even reading this? Maybe you're reminded of how things once were, before you'd discovered each other, and it helps you count your blessings. I don't care—I'm just happy to feel your unaffected joy and peace. Here, get up for a minute, I'll hang a string of tiny lights around you!

But maybe that's not the love of your life in the room with you right now. Maybe it's someone you're uncertain of, even after all this time 'together.' Someone who's always seemed slightly guarded, not telling you something, not sharing something.

Is everything all right?
Everything's fine, why?

Oh, I don't know—you just seem a little…distant.
Don't be ridiculous, I'm just reading…are you okay?
Uh-huh. Hey, why don't we see what's playing at the movies?
Maybe another time, I'm not really feeling it right now.

Does it feel like that too much of the time? And now you're reading this and, in a way, the secret's out, isn't it? I mean, the individual we're talking about is sitting right there, in the same room, and you're reading *this!* What are we investing in here, anyway? The *possibility* that this may be the one and patience is all that's called for? That it's *you*—you haven't yet fully understood what your lover's 'needs' are, and you've got to give it time. You can't just walk away from another one. And anyway, everyone thinks you two are so great together, so lucky that you met, and you *do* have a lot in common, so many of the same friends. Sure, it would be lovely if you found it easier to talk, to share each other's feelings. On the other hand, it *is* the holidays, there's a lot of pressure and tension—it'll be easier when they're over.

But I must tell you, I'm not really enjoying being in the room with you two, and changing the music wouldn't make a difference, believe me. Still, here we are. Your lover's sitting right there, and you're reading this—which means you're trapped. With me! Out of respect for the fact that you've invested your good money in this book, or out of respect for the judgment of the person who gave it to you, I will now tell you what to do: It's time to lower the bucket into the well. If it comes up empty, *Goodfuckingbye!* Now close the book—no, wait till I finish this thought (not much more to go, promise). It's time to talk, and you know that deep down—so don't give me any shit about waiting a week or two and seeing how things are going. It's time to talk *now*. In a few moments you'll put the book down. You know that you need and deserve someone who will *want* to look into your eyes and understand *you* and what you are feeling. Who will want to hold your little heart very carefully in their hands, because it is a *privilege* to hold a beautiful heart like yours. Who will want to give you the few things that you desire, because you give so selflessly, so effortlessly. You don't need any guarded, brooding bullshit in your life. *Life* has plenty of that as it is. What if you have only five decades left to live? Or four, or three? You don't know—how can you know? And you, you've spent too much of your precious life in neutral, wondering if you looked all right, wondering if people thought you were too 'normal,' or too intellectual, too geeky, too boring, too whatever. Fuck it—that's it!

Now I don't want you to freak out on this person—remember, he or she has no idea what we're discussing here. Just realize that something is about to happen and that you're going to be fine, whatever it is. But that which is *not* happening is no longer acceptable—unless you have recently lost your job, and all of your possessions in a four-alarm fire caused by a gas explosion in the basement of your building. If that's the case, feel free to hang out for a couple weeks. All right, now start it with something like this: "Honey, we need to talk about something for a few minutes…I think things could be so much better between us—and should be—and I want us to think about how we can make that happen." Hey, maybe not those words. Okay, maybe start with the first five words, then take it from there. *Honey, we need to talk.* A little scary, right? It's going to be a lot less scary knowing exactly what's in the well. And if the bucket comes up empty, don't panic—you'll still feel better. And besides, I'll be downstairs on the sidewalk—maybe we'll catch a movie, or go see the decorations on Fifth Avenue. Now close the book.

■　■　■

"Hi there. Everything all right?"

"Excuse me…do I know you?"

"I'm Michael. I wrote the book you were just reading."

"You what?"

"I'm sorry. Were you just reading a book in an apartment upstairs?"

"Uh, yes, but…"

"Were you at the part where the author—me—suggested that if your relationship wasn't all it should be you should close the book and talk with him about it?"

"Yes, but…but how would you know what was going on…that I was even in there…that I would leave the apartment? This is freaking me out."

"Well, honestly, I didn't *know* what would happen.I just promised I'd be here if things didn't go well. So…how did it go? Did you two speak?"

"Yes. We spoke. But I'm not sure I should be speaking with you. This is crazy."

"I understand. Well l can certainly just say goodnight and wish you a happy holiday then—I apologize if I've upset you."

"When you said I deserved someone who would hold my heart carefully because it was a privilege to hold a heart like mine…I started to cry, because that's what I want. That's what everyone wants. So, yes, we spoke."

"And…"

"I guess I could use your expression: the bucket came up empty…or pretty close. He said he wasn't ready to go that deep. He thought we were "having fun" and everything was good and what was my problem. And I said that after a year together I thought we should be talking about more than where we were having dinner or what we were doing on the weekend. He just looked at me like I was from another galaxy. A deafening silence led to the "Maybe we should take a break" part…and here I am. Weirdly talking to you."

"Wow, that's tough. How do you feel now?"

"Like my bucket is empty…actually, like shit."

"Damn. Not liberated…free to start fresh? Even a little?"

"Maybe, a little. But still a little more like shit."

"I, yea, of course, sure you do. Look, I said maybe we could see a movie, or the decorations on Fifth Avenue if you wanted."

"I—I don't think so. But thanks. I'm not really in much of a holiday mood right now. And I don't even know you, Michael."

"Okay, well you know my name is Michael. And you know a lot more about me than most people do—you're reading the book! By the way, I haven't even finished *writing* it, so how is it you were reading that chapter?"

"A friend of mine gave me an envelope with a few chapters, typed and copied—he said the writer was passing them out on Sixth Avenue a few weeks ago…and maybe I'd find it interesting. So that was you?"

"I guess it was. I–I was hoping to get some early feedback before writing any more. Maybe a fear of failure, not sure. Well, uh, what do you think of what you've read so far?"

"I like parts of it okay. And some of it hits a little close to home at this point for me, so I don't know if I can be objective. Everybody's looking for their 'soul mate' blah blah, but there's no answer—you can't will it into happening. So there you are, wherever you are. Right?"

"I guess I'm not sure. I'll have to read the book when I finish it and find out."

"Very funny."

"Hey, I don't even know your name."

"It's Mabel. And it's nice to meet you, Michael."

"You're my first Mabel…it's nice to meet you, too."

"It was my great grandmother's name. Mom wanted to keep it alive in the family."

"She did good! Did your grandma have red hair, too? Hey, I get that you might not be in the mood for holiday windows just now, Mabel, but how about coffee or a glass of wine? There's a great little café half a block from here on Perry Street and I'd love to hear more of your thoughts, um, on the book."

"God, you're stubborn."

The Bus Tour

This feels a bit ridiculous, in a way. Chartering a double-decker Big Apple bus just to take those readers on a short tour of Manhattan—not to see the famous landmarks, but to look for 'love' on the sidewalks, benches and bus stops. Even saying it sounds kind of stupid. But I felt I learned so much from our gathering at the Olive Garden, maybe this would be an, um, interesting way to see and learn more, through all of our observations. And I can steal their thoughts yet again! Hey, it cost me two thousand to rent this bus for 2 hours. I don't have that kind of money to throw around, so I should get something out of the experiment, right? Don't answer that.

Almost everyone from our previous meeting RSVP'd for today, with a couple of plus-ones, so I'm pretty excited about this. I told them to meet first at the Brooklyn Diner on 57th for coffee, then come as a group and meet me at the bus in front of The Plaza at 9:30. With the clock running, I couldn't afford stragglers. It's a perfect Saturday in early December, sunny and bracing but not frigid, and the city's all decked out for Christmas. And here they come. Shit. Okay, positive thoughts.

"Hey everybody! So glad you could join me for a tour of our great city on this beautiful day—I think it's gonna be fantastic!" Greetings are exchanged and I can see some puzzled looks on a few faces, and some smiles, too. I'm sure most have shown up out of sheer curiosity, plus a free bus tour of Manhattan doesn't hurt. "All right, there should be enough seats for us all on the upper deck, so I'd like you to proceed directly up the steps and take a seat. It's a steep, narrow stairwell, so go carefully. That's it, take the railing. Hey, Daniel…Jon…Daryl—wow, you're back!"

"This sounded just too crazy to not come check it out, Michael—had to see for my self."

"Remember, I've assured all of these readers complete confidentiality with regard to their thoughts and stories, unless permission is otherwise granted. I'm sorry to remind you, but…"

"Don't worry, my friend, we all spoke at the diner. They're fine with my being here and reporting whatever I like. And you'll notice there's no camera crew with me, so don't be concerned."

"Okay, I have to trust you, so welcome aboard." Oh Jesus, and here's my nemesis. "Todd, good to see you again."

"Wouldn't miss it for the world, Mr. Soul Mate Man." God save this ship.

"Teresa? I–I didn't have you on the list…I assumed you were back in Bowling Green."

"Well I didn't come back to New York just for this, Michael. I actually have a job interview with a public relations firm on Thursday, so I thought I'd come a couple days early and join your tour, and reconnect with your readers."

"That's just amazing, Teresa. I'm really thrilled you're with us today— and I hope you get the job. They'd be lucky to have you."

"Thanks…fingers crossed!"

I welcome the rest of the passengers on board, including Amy, who's brought her good friend Liz, José, who leaves for Columbia in two weeks to join his family for Christmas, and Sting, who said he's in the city to do some shopping and wanted to see where I was "going to take this little mystery tour." Also, he brought his assistant, Angela. And, surprise, Mabel showed up, with a girlfriend, Teri.

"Mabel! Um…" We have a brief hug and I immediately feel nervous. As you know, Mabel has red hair.

"You did mention this to me, Michael, in case you forgot. I thought it would be a good opportunity to see just how crazy you are. And look at all the chaperones I'll have! Oh, this is my friend, Teri."

"Nice to meet you, Teri. Hey, I'm really happy you're here and I hope you enjoy the ride. And feel free to jump into the conversation, okay?"

"Sure. But I'm mostly here to look and listen."

"Your choice. Welcome aboard."

A few minutes later we're all on the upper deck of the Big Apple bus, occupying no more than half the seats. It's 9:45 a.m. and I need to have the bus back at The Plaza by noon. (The company is giving me a 'complimentary' extra half-hour to board and then disembark. So generous.) I take the tour guide's microphone—one button for the upper deck, another to talk to the driver, Flo. Yikes. Here we go, and where we stop nobody...

"Hi again, everybody!'

All, sort of in unison... "Hi, Michael."

"Thanks again so much for being here today. I really do appreciate it. Actually, it was Dan who'd asked at the Olive Garden if you readers would be invited to meet again, and I didn't know at the time. But here we are, though I didn't pass out any new chapters to read. I do want to suggest that when anyone speaks you raise your voice so we can all hear you above the street noise. I'll be the only one with the mic. Sorry about that!"

"So why are we doing this, Michael?"

"Well, Amy, I was thinking that sometimes you can get a better perspective on things if there's a little distance, a different view from where you would normally observe them. Did you ever notice that?"

"I guess so."

"In this case, the different perspective is the upper deck of this bus. At least it's a beautiful day, so it should be fun finding out. Okay, so as you know, we're going to take a tour of Manhattan—but not the standard tour they give to students from Japan or Kansas. We're not looking for landmarks, although we'll certainly see a few—we're looking for insights. Living exhibits that might jar our senses, probe our emotions, even cause a revelation. Pretty exciting idea, right?"

"That's a pretty big assumption, Michael."

"Todd, really? Already? Why would you want to take the tour if you're not open to making a positive experience out of it?"

"Hey, I'm just here to be a voice of reason, in case your bus runs off course. Isn't that a positive?"

"How about this: let's not look for reasons this is a bad idea. Let's look for things, including our conversation, that could make it interesting... even enlightening. Are you good with that?"

"Sure. But if I see something, I say something."

"Actually, that's the idea. So look over there—what do you see?"

"It's the fountain in front of The Plaza."

"Yes, it's the fountain, and it's covered in evergreens and sparkly lights for the holidays. I mean the couple sitting by the fountain."

"What about them?"

"Well you tell me, what about them? Anything at all you notice that'll get us started?"

"Fine. They're not sitting very close together."

"Maybe they're *not* a couple."

"Well they *look* like they're a couple, but they're just not talking or something. Maybe they had a fight."

"That's a pretty big assumption, Todd. It's just two people sitting by the fountain on a beautiful day, taking in the world."

"There's no joy in their faces. He's looking away, but not at anything in particular. She's staring down at her coffee cup. Something's wrong."

"Well that happens, doesn't it? The not talking."

"Yes. But it sucks, it's a waste."

"Do they remind you of something?"

"If he's searching for the words, that's one thing. But feelings are usually not that hard to identify. What's hard is searching for the words to *hide* the real feelings because you're afraid to share the truth—that you've lied to someone, or that you're insecure, or even that you've fallen out of love. Once you start looking for the words that aren't the feelings, you're screwed. The whole thing is screwed."

"Did you do that once?" No answer. "Todd, did you ever experience that?"

"Yes. Years ago."

"Has anyone else experienced that?" A few hands go up, including Mabel's.

"Were you able to start talking, Todd?"

"Talking? Sure. But nothing I said was actually what I felt. I was falling in love with someone, Alisha, and afraid that she would back away if I told her, or showed her. So I pretended that I didn't care, that it was just for fun."

"Then what?"

"She told me we shouldn't see each other anymore. That we were better as friends. And I assumed that's how she felt, which proved to me that I was right not to show her that I loved her."

"Lucky for you, right?"

"I ran into her at a party thrown by an old classmate of ours a few months ago. Alisha now has two kids and a great husband. Looked amazing. She joked about always finding me so attractive, and being disappointed that I didn't respond to her. I looked at her in disbelief. To be honest I almost choked up. I just said, 'Oh stop it! I always *adored* you, Alisha!' with a little laugh. Do you know how I felt at that moment, Mr. Soul Mate Man? I fucking died inside. The little game I'd played years ago, to protect my feelings, protect myself from being hurt—now I was alone, having a cocktail with someone special who never knew how I felt. Christ."

"Todd, even if you'd spoken honestly with Alisha way back then it doesn't mean you and she would have ended up together. And now, at least, you've got some understanding of yourself, and how you'd handle things in the future. A lot of people don't ever get that far."

"I don't know."

"Hey, how would you like to write down your instructions for that couple—then we'll make a paper plane and fly it on a rescue mission."

"Right. And it'll turn out they're brother and sister, commiserating because he just lost his job at the firm."

"Ha! You're probably right. Okay, let's get out of here. (*I press the other mic button: 'Driver, you can take us down 5th now.' 'Roger that, and you can call me Flo.' 'Roger, Flo.'*) Todd, I really appreciate your sharing that story with us—I can't write this alone, you've made that clear."

"All right, I'm with you." Extends his hand to me, amidst cheering and shouts of 'Todd! Todd!' What a brat.

"So we're on our way, my friends. And Todd has actually shown us what we're here to do—we're looking for clues. If we don't have much luck by the time we get to the Village, we'll stop for pizza and head back. Hey, that's sweet, isn't it? On your right, the promenade at Rockefeller Center."

"You mean the giant Christmas tree?"

"I actually meant the couple on that bench over there, Teresa. Though the tree's always amazing. (*'Stop here please, Flo.' 'Roger.'*) I think they're looking at some photos. Nothing too dramatic, I guess."

"Yeah, but they remind me of something, Michael."

"What's that, Dan?"

"I met a girl once on one of those benches years ago."

"Sounds romantic. Was it a chance encounter?"

"No, it was a rendezvous, sort of—the place where we had agreed to meet."

"And was it a beautiful day, like today?"

"Yeah. But it was spring. And it's not such a good memory. It's actually something I'm ashamed of."

"Is it something we could learn from?"

"Probably not. You people probably aren't that stupid."

"Don't underestimate us, Danny."

"Sting makes a good point, Dan. We probably *are* or have been that stupid."

"Michael, just look at the evidence: sixteen adults on top of a bus looking for soul mate sightings? The only thing stupider would be taking this bus through a car wash right now. We're lucky pedestrians aren't hurling water balloons at us from the sidewalk. You should tell your story, Dan."

"Todd, could…"

"Should I, Michael? Maybe it would actually make me feel better, sort of like a confession."

"Sure, go for it, Dan."

"Okay. Ten years ago I was supervising a Parks Department landscaping and maintenance crew assigned to Central Park."

"Big responsibility."

"Right. The Park is huge. And I was the one who had to staff the place for every season. And in the summer—which is the growing season—we needed more people, for lawn maintenance, pruning, trash pickup and so forth. So that spring I posted a summer employment notice on Cornell University's Ag School bulletin board. Within a week I had a dozen kids signed up and ready to start in mid-June. But two weeks after all the positions were filled I got a letter from a girl, Kathy, who says she was an English major looking for a physical, outdoor experience for the summer.

Her letter was long and beautifully written, almost poetic. I could tell how much she wanted a totally new experience. She made it very clear that to compensate for a lack of horticultural knowledge she would work hard and pay attention."

"I'm sure her letter was unlike what you'd see from the usual summer applicants."

"Completely. And very intriguing. Still, I had no positions open to offer. But instead of sending her a form 'rejection' letter, I decided to call her, and tell her that unfortunately all of the positions had been filled, that I'd been impressed with her enthusiasm and, if she would like, I'd keep her in mind should any of the new hires drop out before the summer season began."

"A sensitive way to handle it, Dan."

"Well, the thing is, we just kept talking. I loved the sound of her voice—so young and innocent sounding, yet she was really articulate and self-assured. So adult, somehow. Jeez, I'm embarrassed to even be talking about this. She was curious about working in Central Park and dreamed of living in New York City someday. I told her that she would certainly make her dream come true. After fifteen minutes or so we said 'Goodbye.'"

"So, I'm wondering about the bench…"

"Yeah. Well, a few days later I got a card from Kathy saying how much she had enjoyed speaking with me, and finding it surprising that a connection could be made in just a simple phone conversation, hoping that one of the summer positions would open up and that I would continue to keep her in mind if it did."

"Uh-huh…"

"I know. So here I am, this Parks Department guy in his late thirties feeling a vibe from some Cornell co-ed. I mean, I'm an educated man and all, but I was single—it was a very powerful feeling."

"I get it, Dan. Therefore you…"

"Well, I sent a little note back saying 'Thank you for your note, it was great hearing from you, I'll definitely keep you in mind,' etcetera, etcetera. And, of course, I enclosed a Central Park T-shirt as a souvenir."

"How thoughtful."

"I know. Sorry. Anyway, so Kathy *calls me up*—she'd gotten the

Department number and figured out how to reach me! 'I just wanted to thank you so much for the great T-shirt!' she said. Next thing you know she tells me that she has to come to New York the following week to do some research at the library, and she's staying with a friend up near Columbia, and wouldn't it be fun to meet for lunch or a cup of coffee. So I said, 'Sure, it would be nice to finally put a face with the voice!' And that's when I suggested that we meet right there, in front of that beautiful garden, by the benches. And I also suggested that we send each other any old snapshot, so we'd know who to look for. Makes sense, right?"

"Perfect sense, Dan."

"So I sent Kathy a stupid picture of myself standing next to the biggest Elm trunk on Central Park South, and a few days later I received a card from her, expressing excitement about meeting me."

"And did she also send a photo?"

"You could say that. It was a picture of her taking a picture of something. In other words, the camera was in front of her face in the photo."

"In other words, her face was obscured."

"Correct."

"Yet the meeting was arranged."

"Yes."

"And you were somewhat concerned."

"Yes. But I was also cautiously optimistic—I'm about to meet a young woman whom I've really enjoyed speaking with. The plan was to meet right there at one o'clock, maybe sit for a few minutes and chat, then decide on a place for lunch. It turned out to be just a beautiful day. God. So I arrived early and kind of walked around the courtyard gardens, always keeping an eye out for Kathy at the Fifth Avenue end of the promenade. And then I thought I spotted her—a young woman with extremely long brown hair, wearing one of those Granny dresses, just sort of looking around. So I approached her, and she saw me. 'Danny?' she said a little uncertainly. And I said, 'That's right, and you're Kathy?' 'I am. It's so nice to meet you at last!' And she extended her hand to me. 'It's so good to meet you, too!' I said. 'Why don't we sit down for a few minutes and then we'll think about getting some lunch?'"

"So far this sounds like a very nice encounter."

"I was so not attracted to her, Michael. God help me. This nice young woman with pimples all over her face and big glasses and sort of a dumpy figure. I felt like the shit of the world. I *was* the shit of the world."

"Anyone have any thoughts on Dan's story before he continues? Yes, Liz?"

"I vote we throw Dan under the bus."

"Wow, okay, Liz, I'm not sure Amy filled you in on what we were doing at our previous get-together, but the idea is pretty much to hear about real experiences people have had, whether good or bad. And maybe find a lesson or insight along the way. Dan did warn us it wasn't going to be a flattering tale, did he not? So I think we have an obligation to let him continue and to listen to what he has to say. What do you say, Todd?"

"I'm embarrassed for Dan, but you're right, he should continue. I'm kind of ashamed to say that his sad tale makes me smile. Does that make me a bad person?"

"Don't worry about it, Todd, you're already a bad person. Just kidding."

"Eat me."

"Sorry. All right, Dan, we're not going to be judgmental here…please proceed."

"Okay, so we sat and talked for a while. I asked her about school, what sort of research she was doing in the City, etcetera. The truth is, she came into town just to meet *me!* And now I'm sitting there feeling like I've got a carpenter ant in my shorts but I can't move for two hours. I told her how things were going in the Park—that we were pretty busy with the spring cleanup, and getting ready for summer, and, unfortunately, no positions had opened up."

"And did you suggest someplace for lunch?"

"I thought the Boathouse Cafe would be nice."

"Did she enjoy herself?"

"I guess so. But you know, nothing was clicking. She had to be disappointed. I mean, I wasn't checking my watch or anything, but I just remember settling up the bill, and saying how wonderful it had been to meet her, and wishing her the best no matter what she found for the summer. Clearly, I was not leaving room for a 'next step.' She asked me if I had time to walk in the Park for a while after lunch, and I said that, unfortunately, I had to supervise the emergency removal of a big tree limb over near the zoo, and I was already late. I gave her a little hug and said I hoped we'd have a chance to speak again before she had to return to Cornell. That's pretty much it. I never spoke with her again."

"Well, it's not really our business to comment on your story, Dan—unless that's what you'd like."

"You don't have to—I'll comment on it. It's great to follow your dream, or your fantasy, but if there's someone else involved you have to be careful. I was so hopped up about meeting Kathy, and then so disappointed, that my selfishness prevented me from even offering her my friendship—something she might have appreciated. Especially after laying so much on the line. Can we tell the driver to move on?"

"Sure. (*'Okay, we're ready to go, Flo.' 'Roger.'*) I don't think it's easy to share the stories in which we're not necessarily the good guys. So thanks for digging down, Dan."

"Yeah, it's okay."

"Well let's keep going and see what we see."

"Hey, there's St. Patrick's Cathedral! Should we stop and light a candle?"

"Maybe another time, Amy—but do say a little prayer for this bus as we pass by." That gets a laugh...probably inappropriate.

"Hi, I'm Bob."

"Hey, Bob. What's up?"

"Well, I think we got on the wrong bus here—I guess I had the headphones on when you gave your little speech a while back. Sorry."

"That's all right, Bob—I guess I assumed you were one of our readers' guests—do you want to be let off?"

"That's okay. Even though my boy and I just wanted to see some sights while my wife and daughter are shopping, this seems like it'll be all right. Do you mind if we stay?"

"I don't mind at all. But what about the young man?"

"Tommy? He'd rather be with his friends anyway, what do you say, son?"

"It's cool with me, Dad."

"How old are you, Tommy?"

"Fourteen. But I'm fully developed." Smart ass gets a laugh, his father cringes…ugh.

"We have no doubt. So it's not like this will be totally uninteresting to you—this whole discussion of relationships, and finding, um, the right one?"

"It's better than taking stupid pictures of a giant church, or those smelly carriages."

"Well, you're both welcome to be on board with us."

"So, I have a comment on the man's story, is that all right?"

"Sure, Tommy, what's your comment?"

"I don't think he handled it so bad. He didn't call her a pig or anything. And they were both meeting for the first time, just for the purpose of finding out if there would be some attraction or whatever. Isn't that right?"

"Yes, but."

"So what if the girl gets there and she's thinking, 'Here's this almost middle-aged balding guy in a green Parks Department outfit that I thought I wanted to meet, and he can barely talk to me, but I guess I can live through one lunch'? What if that's what she's thinking, while he thinks he broke her heart? I mean, did you ever hear from her again?"

"No, but."

"Anyway, that's all I was thinking—that maybe you're being a little hard on yourself."

"You know, I had more hair at the time that I met her."

"Whatever."

"In any event, thank you for your observation, Tommy. You remind us that each story has at least two sides, and there may be no one who alone can tell their story fully."

"Michael, someone's waving at you from the sidewalk!"

"Good God, that's Ivy! Ivy, hi there!" (*'Flo, stop here for a minute please!' 'Copy that.'*)

"Hey, Michael! How *are* you?"

"I'm fine, Ivy! How are *you?* Are those your kids?"

"Yes. This is Jonnie, she's five, and Tess is the little one—she's three. And I'm fine, thank you!"

"You look amazing. I didn't even know you were married!"

"I'm not. But André and I have lived together for the last eight years, so we might as well be."

"Are you still dancing?"

"Mostly teaching, but I perform with a few companies now and then. And I'm with the kids, of course, right girls?"

"Mommy's the best dancer in the world!"

"She certainly is, Tess. And what does André do, Ivy?"

"He's a documentary filmmaker, Michael—the best in the world! And what are you up too? I don't remember you wanting to give bus tours of New York! Do you repeat everything in Spanish, too?"

"Ha! You must be Ivy's evil twin. Actually, I'm writing a book about finding your soul mate, or something like that, and this is a little field trip with some awesome volunteer readers. And look who I ran into—a beautiful woman who wasn't my soul mate!"

"Well thank God I'm *somebody's!*"

"Okay, I need to keep this bus moving. It's fantastic seeing you, Ivy."

"You too, Michael. Good luck with your book."

"Thanks, Ivy. Take special care—and you too, kids.

"Bye, Michael!" So fearless—I'm not surprised. We all wave goodbye to Ivy and the kids. *('We're good to go, Flo.' 'Roger.')* Our bus heads south from the Public Library.

"She's beautiful, Michael. How long have you known each other?"

"Yes, she is, Mabel. I think we met 11 or 12 years ago. It seems like ages now. Jesus."

"Did you go out with her?"

"Maybe three times, Teresa. But I had such a big crush on her, this pretty, freckle-faced, Midwestern girl who'd come to New York to dance. Her spirit was so free, there was happiness in her eyes, and such determination."

"How did you two meet?"

"It was very unusual—we actually met in the subway. In the morning, on my way to work."

"I didn't think anybody met anybody in the subway."

"Right, that's generally true. Most people go into some kind of trance

112

when they hit the platform, just to create a little privacy. But on this particular morning I saw Ivy standing on the platform, not very far from me. She was wearing a sleeveless summer dress, and sandals, her hair tied back and still falling way beyond shoulder length. And she seemed just so open, so unguarded, like she wasn't always expecting the worst."

"So you hit on her."

"Thank you for your blunt characterization, Todd. Yes, I approached her and asked if she'd like to get a room. Christ!"

"Todd, shut up and let Michael tell us about meeting Ivy."

"Don't tell me to shut up, Jon!"

"All right, fuck off!"

"Guys! Please. This isn't a fucking prison bus. Can we just enjoy the afternoon?"

"So what happened, Michael?"

"Well, when the train pulled into the 72nd Street station, Ivy and I got on in different parts of the same car. I mean, I didn't want her to think I was stalking her or anything. So she was seated at the end of the car, and I was standing somewhere in the middle. And I had to get off in one stop, at Times Square. As she sat, she gazed around the car. I admit that I was staring at her, so when she glanced in my direction our eyes met. And she actually smiled. She actually smiled at me!"

"How old were you at the time, Michael?"

"Twenty-five? Twenty-six?"

"Wow, okay."

"So now I was sweating profusely. The train is approaching 42nd Street, I've made eye contact with this beautiful woman, and I have to get off and go to work, and if I don't do or say something, it's over. Simple as that. I will never see her on this planet again."

"I'm proud of you, my friend. Bless you."

"Thank you, José. As the train pulled into the station I walked toward her, stood in front of where she was seated and just blurted it out: 'I know this is crazy and nobody says Hello to someone in the subway but I noticed you and you seem, ah, like someone I wish I could meet, and now I've said something so there you are, and I have to leave the train but I was wondering if you'd like to have lunch sometime.'

"Body of Christ."

"And she said, 'Sure, that might be nice.' And I said, 'If you write your number down I could call you later.' And she said, 'Okay,' and she pulled a little note pad from her bag and wrote her number, ripped the page off and handed it to me. 'My name is Ivy, by the way.' And I said, 'Thanks, Ivy. It's great to meet you. And I'll call later!' Just as the doors of the train were opening and I was walking out, she shouted back to me, 'I don't even know your name!' And I shouted back, 'It's Michael!'"

"And that was the beginning of your beautiful relationship with Ivy."

"Well, like I said, I think we only went out three or four times. Including the lunch."

"What was so amazing, then, Michael?"

"I guess it was amazing to me how unlike each other we were. So much of what I was then needed unbottling—*I* was the guarded one. And here was the free-spirited Ivy, confident of her path, her emotions, comfortable with her body. The first night we were together we made love! And for Ivy, I could tell immediately that it was a purely physical experience. She liked me, but that's where it ended. And she knew it so quickly. I'm sure she also sensed that I wished it could be more. But it wasn't there for her. We became friends. I came to watch her perform. She loved being in the company of artists—others with flight patterns similar to her own. I think I privately wished I could fit in with them. Me, the young business guy. The tight-ass, who let go for a moment and met a dancer in the subway. Shit. Sometimes I wonder if I'm still that same…idiot."

"Who could doubt that you are?"

"Todd… Never mind."

"Michael, Ivy could never have made you happy. Ultimately, her free spirit would have made you crazy! But it's still a lovely story, and look what a wonderful friend she remains, even after all these years. There's a song in there somewhere."

"Thank you, Sting."

"Maybe something by Spandau Ballet."

"I kind of hope not."

"'This much is true-ue.'"

"Stop!"

"Hey, what's that?"

"What's what, Bob?"

"That funny looking building over there. Look."

"That's the Flatiron Building, Bob. But we're not really on a landmarks tour today, if you'll remember."

"Yeah, well, I wish I could make some kind of contribution since we're here anyway. How 'bout if the slices are my treat when we get downtown?"

"That's not at all necessary, Bob. We're happy to have you with us."

"This is so typical. My wife's off doin' her thing, I'm doin' mine, next thing you know we're in totally different worlds. Right, Tommy?"

"You guys still eat together, Dad."

"Yeah, but what else? See that young guy over there? Pushing the baby stroller?"

"What about him?"

"Where's his wife? It's a beautiful Saturday and he's out pushin' the baby around and where's she?"

"Maybe she's been with the kid all week, Dad, and she gets a little break on Saturday. Maybe she's visiting her Mom and it's a break for both of them if he takes the kid out for a few hours. No big deal."

"Yeah, I guess you're right. But I'm just thinking, these people are out looking all over the place for their one true love, right?"

"On a bus?"

"I guess so. Anyway, I find my one true love seventeen years ago—your mother—and now I hardly ever see her. Pretty strange, right?"

"It doesn't seem so strange, Dad, but you're freaking me out. You still love Mom, don't you?"

"Of course I do, Tommy. I've loved your mother since the first time we went out."

"Do you ever think about how much you love her, Bob?"

"Not really, Michael."

"But she loves you just as much, right, Dad?"

"I believe so, son. I hope so."

"I can't imagine you two ever not together."

"I can't either. But I have to admit, the thought scares me. I wouldn't know how to live without this woman that I'm hardly ever with."

"When's the last time you told her you love her, Bob?"

"The last time? I guess on our anniversary. Almost ten months ago. that's too long, right?"

"Dad, she *knows* how you feel."

"But look at all these unhappy people, Tommy—no offense, folks."

"It's all right, Bob."

"It would kill me to have to start looking all over again for something I already found. It would kill me. I'm going to tell her I love her tonight."

"Well don't say it out of the blue, Dad—she'll think something's wrong!"

"What are you folks doing tonight, Bob?"

"We're going to have dinner at some Chinese place she picked out, then all see a show together."

"Then what?"

"We'll go to the hotel and hit the hay, I guess. The kids'll watch some television for a couple hours before going to sleep, right, Tommy?

"No doubt."

"Then Bob, why don't you take your wife—"

"Janet."

"Why don't you take Janet to the Oak Room for a little nightcap?"

"Do it, Dad. Put a little move on Mom tonight. We'll be okay."

"You know, Bob, we're probably all looking for what you and Janet found all those years ago. It's not so bad to tell her how you feel once in a while. I would give anything to have someone I loved tell me once in a while."

"You will, Teresa, I'm certain of it."

"You can't be, Michael, but thanks for the kind words. I'm just talking about Bob, and what he has at his fingertips right now. And what he shouldn't forget to do."

"She's right. I think I'd like to get off the bus now, if it's all right with you. Are you ready, Tommy? I want to pick out something for your mother."

"I don't want to watch you shop, Dad. I'd rather stay here."

"He'll be all right, Bob. We'll watch out for him, but we're due back at The Plaza by noon, okay?"

"I'll be there."

('Could we stop here for a moment please?' 'Copy that.')

"Goodbye, everybody. Thanks for the tour and good luck to you all! See you later, son."

"Cool. Good luck shopping. And don't worry, Mom loves you."

"And I love you, son." A fatherly hug and Bob exits the bus. *('Okay, ready to go.' 'Roger.')*

"Wait! Wait! Can we get on the bus here?!" Two women on the sidewalk are waving frantically to get my attention. *('Not yet, Flo, sorry!' 'Copy that.')*

"I'm, I'm sorry, Miss, but this isn't really a tour bus."

"Right. Just another big, red, double-decker bus with an 'I Love New York' sign on the side and a lot of people on top. Let me guess, it's an emergency vehicle."

"Actually, it's a charter. And we're sort of people-watching today, as opposed to sightseeing. And I'm writing a book and this is part of the research, so…"

"Hey, we're just here for the weekend and when we saw your bus it seemed like a nice thing to do, sit up in the sun and take in the sights. Sorry."

"Please, you don't have to apologize."

"Let the ladies on, Michael. Stop playing 'author' for a minute and go with the flow."

"I suppose you're right, Todd. Does anybody have a problem with…" Of course, pretty much a thumbs-up from everyone. "Ladies, you're welcome to join us—it's a beautiful day to see whatever there is to see."

"That's very kind, but you don't have to do that—we can catch a real tour bus."

"No, really. Step inside and come up—there are two seats together right here."

"Are you sure?"

"Positive."

"How much is the ride?"

"No charge, he's paying."

"Sting's right, it's on me."

"And people say there are no bargains left in the City!" The ladies climb aboard. ('Okay, we're ready, Flo.' 'Roger.')

"Welcome, ladies. I'm Michael, and these are some friends who've joined me on this little outing."

"Hi, everyone. I'm Ginny."

"And I'm Corinne."

"So what brings you to New York?"

"Well, we both teach high school in Wilmington, Delaware. In fact, we both attended that same high school fifteen years ago. Anyway, Corinne just left her husband three weeks ago and we thought it would be a good idea to just have a little 'sister' weekend in the City, you know?"

"My God, that's pretty serious. Do you have any kids, Corinne?"

"A little boy. He's fine, though—he's with my mom for the weekend. I really don't want to talk about it right now, if you don't mind. I'm just taking a little break from all of that."

"Sure. Although I'm a bit embarrassed to say that this book I'm attempting to write, it's sort of about trying to find the true love of your life—your soul mate. And that's what we're talking about up here, getting another perspective—I don't know if that would make you uncomfortable, Corinne."

"Oh man, can you believe it, Corinne? You leave the shithead, try to clear your own head for a moment and end up in a mobile therapy session on top of a bus in New York City."

"Maybe later just for fun I could jump off the Empire State Building."

"The World Trade Center is taller."

"Todd, what the hell?"

"Sorry."

"It's all right, Ginny. He's not in my life anymore, and sitting on top of a bus in the sunshine is a million times better than where I was sitting a few weeks ago."

"Really, if you're uncomfortable we'll stop and let you off—it's not a problem."

"Thank you, I'm fine. It's actually kind of funny, isn't it? I mean, whether you do or do not believe in karma, or coincidence, or supreme irony—this is pretty crazy. So we'll just take the ride and see where it goes.

Then maybe we can get a little drinkypoo, right, Gin?"

"A lovely idea, sister."

"So tell us a little bit about your book, Michael."

"I don't know—at this moment I imagine it would seem somewhat trivial to you, with what you must be going through."

"Well, whatever I'm going through is not going to make me jaded—I won't let it do that. I still like men. Although at the moment, not quite as much as my dear Ginny. Most of us want to be with someone special, and I hope that I will again someday."

"Corinne, forgive me, my name is José."

"Nice to meet you, José."

"If you don't mind, what happened to your marriage—you are such a beautiful woman, and so well spoken."

"That's so sweet, José. Nothing happened all at once—it happened over a period of time. We were talking less and less, and then my husband started drinking more and more, and becoming rough with me. It frightened me, and he wouldn't agree to get help. I was raised to do the best I can, and then to change things if they're not right. That's what I did."

"You are very courageous. A man must never raise his hand to a woman. Why do you believe this change took place in him?"

"I think it was hard for him to accept that my career was going better than his own. And I'm just a teacher!"

"*And* the Assistant Principal, Corinne, don't forget that."

"That's not such a big deal, Gin. Anyway, Bill's been selling insurance for ten years. I know he wanted to have his own agency by now, but it never came together for him. He works for the 'good hands' people and he's tired of it. He sits with his whiskey, sees me loving my job, and my child, and his response is resentment and reclusion. It turns to anger, and sometimes it turns pretty ugly. That's it. Now I want to hear about this man's book!"

"Wow, that's pretty deep, Corinne. Well, the book, as I mentioned, is generally about the search for someone very special, hopefully a soul mate. It presumes, therefore, that there might actually be such a person. So I guess on some level I'm attempting to examine my own life, as well as the people in and around it, and look for anecdotal evidence that there may have been contact with a soul mate, or failure to recognize that there had been, or that there never has been but might still be, or never could be because of the absence of cognition, which is frequently confused with fantasy. Does that make any sense?"

"You sound ridiculous, Michael."

"For once, Todd, I'm sure you're right."

"No you don't, Michael. A bit naive, perhaps. But you're talking about things that everyone wants to find. I'm certain it's better that you're not trying to give a lesson, though—the subject is a bit nebulous. People are sometimes hurt most by the one whom they believed was their so-called soul mate. I think it's good that you're not becoming cynical. At least you don't seem to be."

"That's kind of you, Corinne."

"Michael, did you know that a planetary system not entirely unlike our own was discovered recently forty-four light-years away from Earth? The first time in all the hundreds of years of the science of astronomy that any such multiple planetary system had been detected around a single star?"

"No, I did not know that, Jon."

"Yes, it was discovered and yet *none* of the planets can be seen, even with the most powerful telescopes.

"Then how do they know they're out there?"

"Their existence has been inferred in two different studies that took place independently of each other, one in San Francisco and the other concurrently in Cambridge, Mass. and Boulder, Colorado. Each study detected and measured the planets' gravitational effects by observing the resultant reflex motions on the host star. The planets are *there* because the star behaves as it would *only* if they were."

"That's incredible."

"Isn't it? Truthfully, astronomers believed that there must be other solar systems similar to our own. But now they've found one. So, with two hundred billion stars in our solar system alone, and between 100 and 200 billion galaxies beyond this one, just imagine what might be out there."

"There could be a duplicate Earth!"

"That's right, young man. And your soul mate could be a thousand light-years away!"

"You're killing me, Jonathan. Twenty minutes ago you sort of seemed to be along for the ride. Now you're drawing my tiny brain into an inextricable orbit around your sphere of reasoning. Are you an astronomer by profession?"

"No, I'm actually a tax attorney, but astronomy has been a fascination of mine since I was a kid. And all I'm saying is this: even an exact science— astronomy—advances by speculation. Think of all the avenues available in your search for a soul mate: analytical reasoning, emotion, habit and habitat, physical attraction, geography, spirituality…that seems very inexact to me."

"So given your deep interest in the universe, I'm kind of surprised you never commented on the blue spheres and the bio-electric wave patterns emanating from the brain…"

"Well, I just described the discovery of planets that have never been seen but whose presence has been concretely inferred by the subtle movements of the sun around which they rotate. So why would I question the existence of blue spheres, or some variation thereof?"

"Wow, you guys have both left the Earth's atmosphere. Could we return to street level, please?"

"Good point, Angela. Thanks for steering us back. And thanks for the side excursion, Jon—really some provocative thoughts."

"No problem."

"Okay everybody, as you can see we've just turned onto 14th Street. We're heading to Sixth Avenue, where we'll turn right and make our way uptown again. I think we're pretty much on schedule, even with the stops, since it's just after eleven. All good."

"Hey, there's the Guitar Center! I wanna get off here!"

"No way we can let you off, Tommy—I promised your Dad that you'd be with us. Remember, you said you'd rather stay on the bus than go shopping with him. I'm sure he'll take you to the Guitar Center later if you want."

"Aw, man. Whatever."

"Michael, look out there at that couple!"

"What couple, Ginny?"

"The guy with the guitar and the girl—both dressed in black, both with combat boots, both with nose rings. Heading to that guitar place. Do you think *they're* a couple of soul mates?!"

"Well…"

"Maybe more like bandmates."

"That makes sense, Tommy. But they're walking arm-in-arm, so who knows?"

"I hate it when couples dress the same—it's so geeky."

"What do you mean, Amy?"

"You know, when they're both jogging or cycling and they're both wearing matching Day-Glo yellow parkas, like 'She's my property,' or, 'In case my husband gets lost he's wearing the same yellow parka as me.' Like, now you're in a relationship and there goes your individuality. You're a couple now. It's just not my thing, that's all."

"I get it, Amy. And kind of agree."

"Well hold on a minute, guys."

"Do you have a thought on this, Sting?"

"Yea. Back to those kids. You know, they're just kids, maybe 16, 17, maybe trying to be rock stars. I know, I know, sorry. But that's an age when most people are trying to get their fucking identity figured out. Trying to plant their flag in the big human pile. That's why kids start bands, or join rugby teams, or chess clubs, whatever. And why you gotta cut 'em some slack. They'll find their place eventually—that's all I'm saying."

"I hadn't thought of that, and it's true. I still don't like seeing couples in matching outfits!"

"We might even see those two at the Grammy's someday!"

"Or bagging groceries at Trader Joe's, in matching t-shirts."

"Nice, Todd…Jesus!"

"What?"

"Okay everybody, you can see we're heading up Sixth Avenue now. Anyone have any thoughts to share about the tour so far? Yes, Dan?"

"Well, this has been interesting, for sure. And I'm glad you gave me the chance to expose myself with that story. But honestly, I'm not sure it's realistic to think we'd identify soul mates from the upper deck of a bus, Michael. So I don't know what we've really learned—except from Jon, about the 200 billion galaxies. I haven't felt so insignificant since before I was born!" Dan gets a big laugh—especially from Jon—deserved, I have to say.

"I'm certain you were a very impressive embryo, Dan." Also a good laugh, thank you. "But for me, the conversation, thoughts and stories have been really interesting. So I'd say definitely worth the ride, and we've got twenty minutes still to go, give or take. Anyone else?"

"Hey, I've got a crazy idea—almost as crazy as this whole thing."

"Go for it, Teri." Mabel looks nervous.

"Why don't we just ask the couples—at least one—if they're soul mates? Just shout it out from the bus? That might be fun!"

"Um…I'm a little uncertain about that, Teri. I mean, invading their privacy and all."

"I think it's a great idea! Show of hands…" Todd's killing me. Majority of hands go up. Shit. "See!"

"All right, I see the vote. Look, here's what we'll do: when we get to Bryant Park we'll pull over. Couples entering or leaving the park might not mind a little distraction. Good?" Heads nod approval. I hit the button. (*'Flo, could we please pull over at Bryant Park?' 'Roger that.'*) "And if anyone has to use the restroom, there's a facility right across the park."

Thirteen minutes later we pull over to the curb, on the west side of Bryant Park. The sun is shining brilliantly, temperature in the upper 30's and there are actually quite a few couples strolling in and out of the park and seated on benches. Maybe this will lead to something?

"I'm gonna use the john."

"Tommy, can it wait a half hour, when we get back to the Plaza?"

"Not really."

"Well you can't wander off alone—the restrooms are near 42nd Street and we made a promise to your dad."

"I'll go with him, Michael. I could do a little business myself."

"Fine, Jon, I guess. Anybody else?" A few hands go up. "Okay, we'll be right here, but come right back, please. We're heading uptown again in ten minutes." (*Can you open the door, Flo? We have a few passengers getting off to use the facilities.' 'Copy that.'*) Within seconds everyone moves to the right side of the bus, craning to see whoever's walking by below. It's a little unsettling, to have lost control, or whatever it was I had.

"Michael, this is where you were passing out the chapters weeks ago, isn't it?"

"That's right, Teresa—a little closer to 42nd Street."

"Back where we started. Perfect!"

"Correct, Todd—but hopefully not repeating ourselves."

"Excuse me! Hello there, you two!" Of course, Teri first… "I have a quick question!" A middle-aged couple holding hands, looks up, nonplussed.

"We're just on holiday, miss, so we probably can't help you with directions." A good answer from Mr. Whomever.

"No, my question is, are you two soul mates? A forever and ever couple? We're doing some research and taking a poll."

"We've been together for 3 months, honey. So far, so good!" Nice follow-up from Ms. Whomever.

"Do you think it will last, your relationship?"

"Hopefully at least till Sunday—we have tickets to *Hamilton*." They laugh and continue walking. We're all laughing at this crazy exchange.

"Well good luck to you both!" Teri shouts.

"You too, honey!"

"Guys, I don't know if this…" Dan cuts me off, calling out to another couple exiting the park—they can't be more than twenty-somethings.

"Hello, hello there you two!" They look up, then at each other, obviously confused.

"Can I ask you a question real quick?" They stop walking.

"Um, okay."

"Thanks. Crazy question: Are you soul mates? Do you think you might be soul mates? We're doing some research for a book. Would be really helpful if you could answer." They smile at each other and she answers.

"It's possible. I hope so."

"Meaning, you could be the only ones—the perfect match—for each other for all time?"

"Not sure about 'all time,' but 60 or 70 years would be great. Does that help?" Brings a laugh and some applause from the upper deck.

"Yea, that's great. Thanks and all the best!"

"You're welcome!" They walk on…this is crazy. There are now at least a dozen people staring at the bus from the sidewalk, a few trying to board. Our driver lets them know it's a charter. I need to pull this together.

"Hey everybody, could I have your attention for a second? I know this is pretty entertaining, but I don't think it's really the way to get at the heart of our subject. We can't expect a full response to a deep question from people on the sidewalk we don't know!"

"That may be true, Michael, but this is your idea and your charter—you suggested things might at least be inferred, if not fully understood, from our conversations. So what's the alternative? Learn the history of Bryant Park?" I hate that Sting is so smart. They're agreeing with him of course. Shit.

"I guess you're right. Or not wrong anyway. How about 7 more minutes…then when the others return from the facilities we'll continue on?"

"Fine. Allow me to address the people gathered below." Of which there are now two dozen. This should be, um, interesting. "Hello, good people of New York and beyond. So nice to see you on a beautiful winter's day in this great city. We're doing some research for a documentary and we'd like to ask a straightforward question—would that be all right?" Most respond affirmatively and seem at least curious. "The question is for you couples, and here it is: Are you with your soul mate? Is he or she The One who means the most to you…who will be by your side perhaps forever? Anyone? You, sir, you raised your hand quickly."

"Yes. Uh, I'm with my sister. We've met for lunch. But my soul mate, my wife, is back at our apartment in Brooklyn with our new baby. Is that what you wanted to know?"

"Yes, that's wonderful! And where did you and your wife meet?"

"We met in high school, in St. Paul, Minnesota, but we never went out then. Not until we reconnected at the 10th year reunion and discovered we were both living and working in New York."

"So then you knew…"

"Not quite. But we agreed it would be nice to meet for lunch in the city and catch up some more."

"And then it clicked…"

"Well remember, we're from Minnesota. We're a little slower out there." Sting laughs, as do the others. "But we catch up. After a few more lunches, and dinners, I think we realized there was a lot in common. A lot we could share that we didn't find so easily in a city like this, as great as it is."

"So then, the lightning bolt…"

"Okay, we discovered there was an attraction, too. A physical attraction. And that kind of sealed it I think."

"Would you like to elaborate?"

"Um, not really. But I'm sure you all have great imaginations." Many smiles, on and off the bus.

"Brilliant, thank you…"

"Thomas. And this is my sister, Marie." She waves awkwardly. "And my wife is Darlene."

"Have a lovely day, Thomas, and Marie. And give our very best to Darlene and your baby…"

"April."

"We're all looking forward to April right now. Okay, more soul mates? You folks, right there." Sting points to an attractive couple, perhaps in their 30s—a tall, striking black man in a fitted overcoat and a beautiful Asian woman in a pale blue knitted sweater coat and thick scarf wrapped around her neck and shoulders. "I think you had your hand up, sir."

"So you're writing a book about soul mates?"

"No, *he's* writing the book—this is your author, Michael." So embarrassing. I raise my hand and shrug.

"So, Michael, I'm Michael, too. And this is Suki." She smiles modestly. "Just curious, man. How in God's name do you expect to learn anything about soul mates riding around on top of a tour bus? Gotta be something else goin' on here." Oh shit. I have no idea how to answer this.

"It's, um…thanks for asking that, Michael. I think…"

"If I may, Michael, let me try to answer Michael's question."

"Uh, sure…" Once again, no control. Jesus.

"Michael, Suki, I don't think Michael believes that he, or we, will learn anything definitive about soul mates, or what that might even mean. The hope is that we'll simply observe people—couples—from a different perspective, talk with them if possible, and have a conversation about what we see, or think we see. Something we actually do every day, without even thinking about it. Does that clarify things a bit?" I want to hate Sting.

"Not really, but I guess we'll take it."

"Good enough. So what about you two? Think you could answer the question? Suki?"

"I believe I could answer your question. But I won't, because it's very personal for me, something that should remain inside and be shared with only one other person." Suki looks at Michael and he gives a faint smile, his eyes on her face, unblinking. Possibly the truest words I've heard spoken today.

"And you, Michael?"

"I have nothing to add. Like you said, maybe you'll have a conversation about what you've observed and reach your conclusions. So, let me ask you, Why are *you* doing this, taking this bus tour?"

"That's an easy one. It's a beautiful day in New York. He's paying for the ride. And I got to meet you two. All for free!"

"Can't argue with that. Good luck, everybody—hope to see you all in paradise!" With that, Michael and Suki turn and walk into the park…and I see Tommy, Jon and the others making their way back to the bus. Thank God.

"Okay, fellow passengers, the rest of our group is returning from their bathroom break and it's about 11:45. So I do want to keep moving to make the scheduled arrival time and meet up with Tommy's dad. That was pretty great, by the way—thank you for insisting and introducing us to some interesting people. Don't you think?" There's applause and cheers, mostly for Teri and Sting I'm certain. I hit the button: (*'We're ready to move on, Flo, thanks.' 'Copy that.'*) I turn to the folks on the sidewalk. "Thanks, everybody—have a great day and a wonderful holiday!" From above and below, waving, peace signs and good wishes. For the next 10 minutes I have no announcements to make. The passengers are chatting among themselves and commenting on various tourists and shoppers now flooding the sidewalks. Suddenly Tommy jumps up and points.

"Hey, that's Radio City! That's where we're seeing the show tonight!"

"The world-famous Christmas Spectacular—you and the family will love it, Tommy!"

"I wanna meet a Rockette!"

"Maybe if you ask Santa, Tommy," Liz suggests playfully.

"Hey, I met a Rockette once," Todd adds.

"Did you think she was your soul mate, Todd?" I'm thinking Liz is going to torture him.

"It didn't get that far. I was just behind her in line to get a hot dog in the park."

"Did she just say, 'Hi, I'm a Rockette?'"

"No, she did not say that. She was wearing very short shorts and I noticed that she had very amazing legs, and when she sort of looked around I said, 'Hey, are you a dancer by any chance?' And she said, 'Well, I'm a Rockette,' then turned around to face the hot dog guy. That's it."

"What you should have said is, 'What a coincidence, I'm a Rockette scientist!'" At that point we pretty much all lose it, including Todd. What a soul mate expedition this has turned out to be. As we steer onto Central Park South, the musty scent of horse-drawn carriages fills the air. Maybe 15 of them, parallel-parked across the street halfway to The Plaza.

And suddenly we're there, just two minutes behind schedule. I can see Bob, waiting by the curb with a Zara shopping bag in one hand. Good move, Bob! And someone in a red Big Apple Tours vest waiting to meet us and to sign me out.

"Attention, soul mate travelers, we've reached our final destination."

"Actually, our 'final destination' might be light years away, Michael!"

"Good point, Jon. But the bus stops here." A few groans, to be expected. "Anyway, this has been a really awesome experience for me and I hope you've enjoyed it, too. Thank you so much for coming along!" Applause and Thank you's in response.

"So when is your book coming out, Michael?"

"Well, I need to finish it first, Dan. Couple more months probably. Then I need to find a publisher, so…"

"So we could all be dead from natural causes by then, right?"

"Thanks yet again, Todd. Yes, I'll probably publish it posthumously.

Look, when it's all done and ready, you'll be the first to get a copy, compliments of the author. Now if anyone would care to join me for a little lunch, there's a cafe in the park near Columbus Circle—my treat if you'd like to take a short walk. But if you're on your way from here, I bid you farewell and a very happy holiday. And watch your step getting off!"

I exit first and thank Flo for taking us around safely, pressing a twenty in her hand. She says it was a lot of fun, says I'm crazy and gives me a kiss. Roger that. On the sidewalk, Bob has a big smile as I assure him everything was fine with Tommy and suggest that a visit to the Guitar Center might be a winner. And as the others exit, there are handshakes and hugs. Most have plans for the afternoon, including Teresa, Dan, Sting, Angela and José, whose shift at the restaurant starts at one. We have a warm embrace and I wish him a joyful Christmas holiday with his family. Daryl is next off the bus. I offer my hand and a slightly guarded smile. "Thanks for joining us, Ms. Gordon. You were surprisingly quiet during the entire tour—I hope you didn't feel trapped on the bus."

"Not at all. In fact I got some great iPhone video, Michael. Why don't you tune in to CBS2 at 10…you might find it informative!"

"Oh, God. Well I guess I asked for it. Please don't make us look too foolish, okay?"

"Of course not. You were great. Everybody was and the whole thing was a totally different experience. Good luck with your book—I'll look forward to my signed copy." With that Daryl Gordon turns and walks toward a waiting black SUV. Must be nice. Amy and Liz, Todd and Jon are waiting around to join in for lunch. To my surprise, Corinne and Ginny ask if they could come as well, having never been to Central Park or seen anything like the pop-up holiday retail kiosks there. "Sure, that'd be great!"

Mabel and Teri are last to get off the bus and I'm a little uncertain what to say. Fortunately, Teri is not uncertain. "This was so much fun, Michael, thanks for letting me join you!"

"And thank you for jumping into the conversation so enthusiastically, Teri. You definitely brought the outside world onto the bus back there."

"My pleasure!" Mabel smiles at her friend then turns to me.

"Sorry we can't join you for lunch, Michael—Teri and I are seeing a movie in Union Square this afternoon. But this was really great, and now I'm convinced, you are a little bit crazy." I wondered then if I'd ever see Mabel again. I'm not sure what I felt. A little sad, I guess. "But we're having dinner later at Lucien, a little French bistro on the Lower East Side, do you know it?"

"I do."

"Would you like to join us?"

"Um, well, yes, that sounds nice. I'd love to."

"Great! Shall we say nine o'clock?"

What Vienna Saw

It's safe to say there was no residence in New York's far West Village in 1982 quite like Jordan Eklund's. In SoHo, of course, artists had been converting warehouse and factory lofts into studios and living spaces for years. Enormous, trashy-cool places to live and work and be a part of a still vibrant artistic community. But in 1982, the blocks close to the Hudson River, and the Meatpacking District were still Manhattan's 'wild west.' The idiosyncratic all-night bistro Florent didn't even exist then—the place was still a diner called the M&L, serving truck drivers and meatpacking workers in blood-stained butcher frocks in the daylight hours. The Belgian block streets were sticky with oil from the trucks and forklifts.

Jordan Eklund's residence occupied just over one-half of the 8th floor at 600 Washington Street. The one hundred ten-year-old factory building, which spanned the entire block between Horatio and Gansevoort streets, had been converted to warehouse lofts in the 70s, and he'd purchased the entire thing in 1979 for $985,000 cash, leaving the rental tenants where they were, till the leases expired. No rush. A cardboard warehouse, an office furniture warehouse, a restaurant supply place. The 8th floor, however, had been vacant for 7 years, since the previous tenant, Garnet Printing Company, had closed down and moved out, leaving two one-ton presses behind.

In the five years since Jordan Eklund had moved to the United States from Austria, he'd earned a small fortune in the art world serving, among other endeavors, as an associate curator at the Guggenheim, an advisor-buyer to several private client collectors, a forgery consultant to Sotheby's, as well as a collector of modern works himself. He even consulted for the NYPD and FBI in matters of art theft and forgery, identifying potential buyers of stolen works worldwide. Three years earlier Eklund had advised a discreet buyer from Tokyo, a friend of his father's, but the matter did not involve illegal property.

The Horatio St. entrance to the building looked blandly inhospitable, with its worn, faded marble floors, walls the color of coffee stains, battered metal elevator doors painted grey many times over, a heavy brass door leading to the stairwell. The elevator transported both people and freight. Only Jordan Eklund possessed the key to the 8th floor. A first-time visitor might gasp as the door slid open to the improbable sight of a vast open space of polished wooden floors, 14 ft. ceilings, white walls, giant double-hung windows facing the Hudson River to the west and partial views of the harbor and ferry boats to the south. In the center of this austere space a Bauhaus sofa and chairs surrounded a low, 8 ft. cast iron coffee table, overhung with an antique crystal chandelier. Ninety feet from the elevator an open kitchen and bar faced the room. To the right of that, an enormous workbench of thick, pitted wood served as a dining table. Behind the bench, a door leading to a large bath with floor and walls of ancient herringbone tile, a massive pedestal sink, and chipped claw foot tub. Next to the bath was the door to Jordan's bedroom, closed. And to the right hung a ten by ten-foot mirror framed in decorative cast iron.

Positioned here and there about the floor in a seemingly random yet precisely calculated display, sculptures by Inge King, Naum Gabo, Jacques Lipchitz, and Ben Nichelson silently demanded attention. A single Calder dangled above a lone wingback chair and cigar stand. Between the windows hung works by Robert Motherwell, Agnes Martin, Jean-Michel Basquiat, Bridget Riley, Warhol and others as yet unknown to the public.

At the age of 29, Jordan Eklund seemed an unlikely figure to command the respect and reputation he enjoyed. Physically, he appeared much younger, with his chiseled yet soft features, pale flesh, his thick, groomed dark blonde hair. Yet his tailored suits, Brioni or Huntsman, the bespoke shirts and ties, they made a certain statement. He wore them exclusively, whether in meetings or informal social gatherings in his gallery-loft. He never raised his voice but his facility with the language, in an unplaceable

English-Austrian accent, demanded the listener lean forward and not interrupt. His demeanor was warm and welcoming, but not gregarious. Women found Jordan beautiful. Men did as well. All were confused by him, and mesmerized. In the end, that was a large part of the authority he possessed.

Late on the evening of Thursday, October 28, Jordan was gently ushering his guests out the door of his loft. The social 'meeting,' which had included dinner (Chinese takeout) and drinks, had been attended by Jean-Michel Basquiat and his girlfriend Abrielle, gallerist Annina Nosei and representatives from her gallery, a publicist, and a somewhat detached John Perreault, art critic for the *Village Voice*. The purpose of the meeting involved the planning and publicizing of a brief showing of Basquiat's paintings at Annina Nosei Gallery, prior to their shipment to Fruitmarket Gallery in Edinburgh, Scotland for a major exhibition. Two of the works in that show were being loaned by Jordan—they would also travel the following week to Edinburgh.

As they waited for the elevator Annina turned to her host. "Thank you so much for putting up with us this evening, Jordan. I think it's going to be a fabulous show."

"I'm really quite excited about it, Annina. The exposure you've given Jean-Michel's work has been perfect—what a wonderful next step."

To which Basquiat replied, "Exposure? I've got a Krylon crew ready to spray a masterpiece on the side of your building, Jordan—say the word, my friend!" Which brought a chorus of laughter from the group.

"Perhaps when you return from Edinburgh we can discuss, Jean—you don't want to be distracted from the business at hand, now do you?"

The elevator arrived at the 8th floor with a chunking halt, the door opened, the guests exchanged handshakes, hugs, kisses and said their goodnights. When he heard the car reach the lobby floor, Jordan locked the door to 8. He brought plates and glasses to the kitchen sink and disposed of the takeout boxes and bags. Karina would clean up in the morning. He then walked over to the large mirror, staring at himself for a moment, removed his shoes then reached behind the raised iron frame for a recessed button, pressing it with his middle finger. With his right hand, he pushed the mirror easily three feet to the right, opened a heavy wooden door and walked forward into a dimly lit space. The door and mirror closed again behind him.

Jordan lifted a light switch on his left, illuminating three chandeliers hanging at 12-foot intervals through the center of a large room whose walls were covered in floral maroon velvet wallpaper bordered by gold-leafed crown and chair-rail moldings and hung with gold-framed mirrors and portraits of presumably 'royal' persons from a bygone era, as well as photographs of contemporary artists—Picasso, Warhol, Pollock, Haring—and of Josephine Baker. The room was furnished and arranged as a near replica of Tsaritsa Alexandra's sitting room in the Winter Palace in St. Petersburg.

Jordan heard the phone ring in the room he had left behind. He would let a message be left and perhaps return the call in the morning, continuing past a plush canopy bed draped with silk tapestries and into an intimate alcove. Jordan stood in front of a Victorian dressing table, divided in the middle by a full-length mirror, and removed all of his clothing, folding each item—jacket, shirt, pants—and placing them on a nearby settee. He watched himself in the mirror, his slender nearly hairless white body, his straight shoulders, narrow, childlike torso and hips. The long arms and fingers, and delicate neck.

He sat before the mirror on a velvet dressing stool and opened one of the table drawers, removing two small silicone breasts, which he sprayed lightly with an adhesive mist and placed carefully over his own pale breasts. At once they seemed a natural part of his body. From the same drawer, she removed a black silk lace brassiere, placing it over her breasts and fastening it in back and around her neck. On the dressing table top was a soapstone bust of Lillian Gish, and upon her head a raven black wig with short, feathered bangs, shoulder length on the sides and back and a small bun woven on top, made from the hair of a young Chinese girl. She removed the wig from Miss Gish's head and carefully fitted and pinned it onto her own. Already her beauty could gaze back at her and she paused to reflect. Then, from a palette of makeup choices, she began applying a light cake to her face, above and below her eyes, emphasizing her porcelain skin. Next, she brushed the slightest albinos pêche dust onto her cheeks, painted the thinnest possible black line along her eyelids, carefully brushed her lashes and eyebrows a midnight rouge. Finally, she delicately brushed her lips with a dark, scarlet gloss, taking care to stay within the lip line.

Opening a walnut jewelry box, she stirred the glittering contents, picking out a blue tanzanite necklace and earrings, a gold band bracelet and sculptured silver rings for each finger of her right hand.

She stood before the mirror and whispered something to herself, then removed from another drawer a sheer, black brief and stockings, pulling them over her legs, buttocks and genitalia effortlessly. Against the wall to her left stood a large, open armoire. Without hesitation she chose a vintage three-quarter length black satin sheath with a high neckline and long sleeves, a short-waisted, midnight blue jacket, blue Victorian ankle booties, and dressed. The open doors of the armoire were mirrored, and she approved of herself from all angles. Turning back to the dressing table again she pulled a black Coq plume from a pin cushion and pushed the quill into her hair. In the mirror, a faint smile glanced approval. She grabbed a black, beaded clutch, left the dressing alcove and walked across the great room to a large, framed mural-like painting of Furore, on the Amalfi Coast. To the left, from a row of iron Mission hooks, she chose a cerulean blue silk scarf, throwing it around her neck and shoulders, then pushed the painting to the right, revealing the open door of an enormous freight elevator on the Horatio Street side of the building. She walked in, moved the painting, whose backside was simply unfinished plywood with the word C L O S E D stenciled on it, to its former position obscuring the elevator. She pressed 1 for the ground floor freight entrance and loading dock.

It was after midnight when she left the building, the heavy steel door locking behind her. Clutching her scarf close to her neck against the late October chill, she walked down the concrete steps and across Gansevoort to a waiting car. The driver got out, wearing a grey tweed jacket and Scottish tam, and opened the rear door.

"Good evening, Miss Martel."

"Good evening, Thomas, nice to see you on this chilly night," she replied in a voice approximately one semitone higher in pitch than Jordan's, with a faint French inflection and timbre far softer, more sensual.

"Yes, ma'am, not too warm, but the heater's on." Vienna Martel stepped into the back seat. "Will you be going to Ruby's tonight?"

"Yes, Ruby's." Thomas closed the door, returned to the driver's seat and circled the one-way blocks back onto Washington Street then, eight blocks later, right on Charles Street, right again on West Street and finally right onto tiny Charles Lane. Halfway into the block a dozen people were milling about, smoking cigarettes and joints near a short velvet rope leading to an unmarked red door three steps below the sidewalk.

Ruby's was a very different experience from what were considered the 'rough' gay bars and clubs just a short distance away. Places like The Mine Shaft and The Anvil, where patrons from all over the city would gather, seeking hard-core adventure among a simpatico tribe. Ruby's offered something far less carnal—a sensual fantasy set to music in a sophisticated parlor lounge. Thomas pulled up slowly near the curb, got out and opened the door for his passenger. "Miss Martel."

"Thank you, Thomas—I shouldn't be more than 2 hours."

"Yes, ma'am. I'll be right here." With that, she turned toward the small crowd and the red door, as several familiar faces greeted her. "Hi, Vienna!" "Hello, beautiful!" To which she replied warmly, "Hello, Alex… Hi, Manny." Music could be heard coming from inside. Duran Duran, fomenting the mood. *"Mouth is alive with juices like wine…and I'm hungry like the wolf...*" A tall black doorman in suit and tie welcomed her and opened the door.

"Hello, Miss Vienna. Have a wonderful night."

"Thank you, Jerome—I'll be sure to." And into the dark space she walked, the music much louder, past a narrow vestibule and cloakroom, into an intimate lounge area with patrons, many in Venetian or Mardi Gras masks, crowded near a mahogany bar on the right and in plush banquettes and ottomans to the left. Beyond the bar, a low archway led to a packed dance floor surrounded by low candlelit tables and chairs against brick walls hung with sconces and black and white photographs of Downtown street people. A small stage at the back of the room sometimes hosted unannounced performances from early New Wave legends and a weekly drag fashion show. This night a DJ was playing dance hits and 70's funk for the pre-Halloween celebrants jumping wildly and singing along to Culture Club and Human League. "*DON'T YOU WANT ME BABY? DON'T YOU WANT ME OOOH?*"

Vienna didn't pass through the archway. Instead, she was greeted by Ruby himself, a short, round man wearing a blue satin jacket, black shirt and ascot who spoke in a high, theatrical voice.

"Welcome, Vienna!" he nearly shouted, touching her shoulder and kissing both cheeks. "So good to see you always! Your usual place?"

"That would be lovely, Ruby. Everyone looks so festive," she said as he led her to an elevated banquette facing the bar.

"Well it is Thursday night...oops, Friday morning! And Halloween is coming. Actually, it's already *here!* Can I bring you something with bubbles?"

"You know me well." Ruby bowed and turned back to the bar. Vienna was more than a 'regular' at Ruby's. Since shortly after its opening in '80 she'd come three, even four times a week. Jordan had heard about the place from one of Jean-Michel's friends, but Jordan Eklund seldom went out late at night. Vienna had thought it sounded interesting, and so it turned out to be. She knew and was friendly with many of the patrons, and of course the bartender and staff, but never intimate with any. Pleasantries and small talk. When asked about herself she pulled from a menu of responses. "Everything's wonderful, and you?" "Yes, it's unbearably cold!" "I'm meeting a friend from Rome for lunch." "No, I'm much too tired to dance." Her beauty and reserve conveyed a certain mystery in an otherwise uninhibited spot and with it, an unspoken deference.

She recognized many faces of course, but others were hidden behind their masks. Near the end of the bar, she noticed an older Japanese gentleman in a light grey suit, holding a soft leather bag. He had a thin, white mustache. He appeared to be alone, glancing toward the entrance frequently, sipping a short, brown drink. She knew him. Actually, Jordan knew him. Moments later Ruby returned with a glass of Champagne. "Voila!"

"Merci, Ruby." Vienna took the stem and raised it to her host, then her lips.

"De rien, Vienna—enjoy!" And with that Ruby pirouetted and returned to the front of the house.

Vienna took a sip from her glass, then noticed that the Japanese man was now speaking with two men wearing feathered mardi gras masks. One wore a long leather coat, the other a sport jacket over a red tee shirt. There seemed to be some disagreement among them. The old man shook his head and waved off whatever had been said with his finger. The man in the long coat held up both hands, palms facing out, as if insisting. The old man continued to shake his head. With his right hand obscured by the bar, the masked man removed a gun with a long barrel from his pocket and fired the gun at the old man's chest three times. He stood, frozen in shock for an instant, and reached for the mask facing him as his assailant pulled the bag from his hand. Vienna saw the gunman's face and their eyes met…she thought she recognized him, but from where? He dropped the bag, quickly put the mask back in place and the gun in his pocket. She saw the old man buckling. Nothing could be heard above the music and the crowd. She stood and stared as the accomplice held the old man up. The shooter picked up the bag, grabbed his partner by the shoulder, shouted something in his ear and he let the body fall to the floor and they left the club, bag in hand, as Vienna ran toward the bar, shouting Ruby's name.

The bartender, seeing Vienna, quickly moved toward her, assuming she'd wanted something, but now she was on the floor, loosening the old man's collar. She looked up, anguished, and spoke firmly, "A man's been shot, Tony, call the police!" Kneeling beside the body, Vienna opened his blood-soaked suit jacket, his white shirt glistening crimson. Ruby made his way to Vienna and gasped.

"Oh my god, Oh my god! Get back, get back everyone," as he pushed people away from where the body lay.

"We need water and towels…and an ambulance," Vienna demanded. "He's been shot—two men did it, and now they've gone."

"Yes, of course! Of course!" Ruby shouted instructions to the bartender who was already on the house phone.

"Police are on the way! An ambulance, too," Tony announced as he hung up the phone.

On the dance floor, the crowd was oblivious to what had happened. The DJ had his headphones on, "Tainted Love" filled the room. Ruby felt it best to contain the crisis to the bar area, till police came. Out on the sidewalk, no one knew what had happened. The two men had left the club, calmly if briskly, entered a waiting car and driven off. Within 5 minutes sirens screamed and two police cars pulled up abruptly, effectively blocking Charles Lane. Three cops rushed out and into the club. One stayed outside, instructing the now curious onlookers to stay where they were, and away from the door. Thomas got out of the limousine and rushed over to the cop.

"Officer, can you tell me what's going on?"

"Someone's been shot—stay clear of the entrance, an ambulance is on the way."

"My passenger is inside, sir, and she's alone—I have to see that she's all right." With that Thomas bolted toward the door but was grabbed at the elbow by Officer White, a large, muscular black man.

"Sir, no one's going inside at this point. You'll wait outside till the crime scene is cleared. Now back away."

Charging inside to the bar area the cops wedged into the crowd and quickly saw the body on the floor, Ruby and the bartender crouched, and Vienna kneeling, applying clean towels to the gushing wounds. Officer Molina spoke first. "Please stand back everyone. Stand back! What happened here?"

Ruby, gasping for breath, answered. "This man was shot. I don't know if he's alive." One of the cops, Officer Huang, knelt by the body and tried to find a pulse at his neck.

"He has no pulse," she informed routinely.

"Are you the owner here?" Officer Molina asked.

"Yes."

"No one is allowed to leave the premises—tell your people now." Ruby instructed Tony to inform the staff.

"Did anyone see the shooting?"

Ruby looked down at Vienna. "She may have seen it—Vienna was the first to alert us."

Vienna shot a frozen glance at her friend and stood.

"Ma'am, did you see what happened here?"

"Yes. I saw the shooter."

"Could you give me a little more detail please?" Molina drilled, a bit impatiently.

"He fired his gun three times. There were two men—first, they were all talking, then they grabbed a leather bag from him, shot him and left the club."

"Could you identify the two men?"

Vienna hesitated, considering her answer. There was much to consider. "Perhaps one of them. They were both wearing masks."

"Like ski masks?"

"No. Like mardi gras masks."

"If they were wearing masks, how could you identify them, or one?"

"When he fired his gun the old man reached for his mask and pulled it down before collapsing."

140

"Were you standing here, close by?"

"I was sitting there," she pointed to the banquette against the wall."

"Did anyone else see what happened?"

"I don't know. It was crowded and the music loud."

"And how did you…happen to notice what was happening?"

Vienna paused but held her gaze on the officer. "I thought it odd, seeing the older Japanese man here, wearing a suit, holding his bag—I was, I guess you could say, studying him."

"Do you know this man?" Officer Molina asked, indicating the body at his feet.

"No, I do not."

A siren could be heard outside as an ambulance step van from New York Presbyterian arrived. A nurse and EMT got out, pulled a gurney from the rear and headed into the club. Those standing near the bar were herded into the banquette area. The music stopped and the third cop, Officer Riley, shouted instructions that no one was to leave the club. There's been a shooting. The situation is under control. You will be free to go shortly… please stand or sit quietly.

The gurney was beside the body now as the nurse knelt to find a pulse. There was none. He quickly opened the man's shirt and applied defibrillator suctions to his chest, near the bullet holes, and started the device. The torso shook, but after a full 50 seconds there was no heartbeat, no breathing. The nurse looked up. "He's gone, I'm afraid. We'll take him to Presbyterian." The body was lifted onto the gurney, strapped in and rolled toward the door. Officer Molina interrupted before they could exit.

"Wait, please. Does he have a wallet?" He didn't wait for an answer, reaching inside the suit jacket and pulling out a leather billfold, rifling through it. Several hundred in cash, credit cards, driver's license. He read the name out loud. "Yusaku Saji, 985 Fifth Avenue. "Yusaku Saji," he repeated under his breath. Vienna recognized the name but remained silent.

"Officer, we need to take the wallet with us—you can claim it in an hour, once the body's been checked into the morgue. We copy all the documents." Officer Molina handed the wallet to the nurse, the gurney proceeded to the sidewalk.

"Officer, I need to let my customers go home and clean this up!" Ruby pleaded, but the cop was unmoved.

"Sir, this is a crime scene. The crime was murder. Everyone will leave but only when we see the ID and have the names and contact information of each person in the premises, including the staff and yourself. Officer Riley, Huang, please inform everyone here—names, addresses, ID. Then they can leave." Turning to Vienna, who stood beside Ruby, he spoke evenly, "Miss, it appears you may have been the only witness to this. I'll need you to come to the station with me and give a statement. Sorry for the inconvenience." A great sense of alarm flashed through Vienna's mind and body, though not betrayed on her face.

"I've told you everything that I saw," she protested, "everything I know, and I know nothing further."

"It's just procedure ma'am. You're not a suspect, but we'll need your statement. It'll be another half hour here at most."

"My driver is waiting outside."

"Then he can follow us, understood?" Vienna returned to the banquette where she'd been sitting just 22 minutes earlier. A million thoughts rushed through her head. Jordan had meetings, starting in mid-morning. He would need at least a few hours' sleep.

The cops processed the exiting partiers with surprising efficiency—they had no interest in hanging around Ruby's either. Masks off, check ID, make note of names, addresses, phone. A couple underage boys, who would simply be warned. Photos had been taken of the body where it lay, and the room, the bar. There was no way to dust for prints—a hundred hands had been on that bar. The assailants weren't drinking. The only thing they'd gripped was the bag and the gun, both of which left the club with them. Frustrating. By 1:40 a.m. the place was nearly empty, except for the staff, and Vienna. Ruby was instructed to do nothing at the spot of the shooting, the perimeter of which had been taped off on the floor and bar. No cleaning, no moving stools. Detectives would return in the morning to fill in any missing details. He should be available to let them in—they would call first. Officer Molina looked over to Vienna. "Miss, please come with me—this shouldn't take long."

Vienna and Molina left the club with Officer Huang. Officers Riley and White would follow once the place was empty and locked and the street cleared of lingering patrons wanting to talk, speculate, argue about what had happened. Thomas approached Vienna as she was being ushered to the police vehicle. "Miss Martel…"

"It's all right, Thomas. I have to go with the police. Can you follow us and wait please?"

"Yes, ma'am, of course."

"Thank you." Officer Huang opened the back door of the police car and Vienna stepped inside. The light bar flashed, the siren screamed as Thomas ran back to the Mercedes and followed the speeding car to the West 10th Street station.

Inside, it may have been the 'graveyard shift' but in the relentless wash of fluorescent lighting, time stood still. Dispatcher on two phones, booking desks occupied, men in cuffs waiting to be 'processed,' metal partitions taped with photos of wives, kids, parents, the smell of thirty-year-old upholstery and day-old coffee. Officer Molina led Vienna to his cubicle and a chair by his desk. Pen in hand and a stained yellow legal pad at the ready, he began the tedious line of questioning. "Please state your full name."

"Vienna Juliette Martel."

"Could I see your ID?" Vienna pulled a thin wallet from her clutch and produced a drivers license, betraying none of the anxiety she felt churning inside her. "It's French," observed Molina as he examined the car.

"Yes."

"Is that where you're from? France?"

"Yes, Paris. I'm living here temporarily."

"What is it you do, Miss Martel?"

"I'm a writer."

"What is it you write?"

"Fiction and non-fiction. It depends. Is this what you wanted to speak with me about, Officer?" Molina massaged his forehead and returned to mundane protocol.

"Your address in New York..."

"600 Washington Street. The entrance is on Gansevoort."

"Is there an apartment number?"

"The 8th floor. Number 801."

"Your phone number please."

"2-1-2...3-4-2-6-8-1-6"

"Tell me what you saw tonight at the club. Every detail, please, from the moment you entered." Vienna repeated everything she had already reported to the officer as they'd stood beside the body. There was no inconsistency though perhaps more detail: what the assailants wore, the long barrel of the gun, presumably a silencer, how long the encounter lasted, what she did when she saw the shooting... "And you said that you saw the shooter's face..."

"Briefly, when his mask was pulled down."

"Do you think you would recognize him if you saw him again?" She paused, trying to imagine the consequences of her answer.

"I believe so."

"And did he see you?" She reflected on this for a moment. "Did the killer see you, Miss Martel?" Officer Molina repeated.

"Yes. I think so." Molina paused, then looked up.

"How old do you think he was? His race? The basics please."

"Perhaps in his mid-thirties. White, maybe 185 centimeters. Angular features, thick, medium length hair..." Molina interrupted, while still writing.

"And you said you didn't recognize the victim, um, Yusaku Saji?"

"I did not."

"All right, this is good, Miss Martel. We'll need you to return later today and sit with a sketch artist and give this description again, in as much detail as possible."

"No. I have business during the day. I'm sorry but I can't come back here."

"Then he can meet you at your home if you prefer." Her thoughts raced from her mind to her stomach with sickening speed.

"No. I could come in the late afternoon."

"Could we say 4p.m.? I'll make the arrangements."

"Yes. May I leave here now?" It was just after 2:50 on Friday morning.

"Of course. I'll walk you to the door, make sure your ride is still waiting." Her car was parked directly in front and Thomas stepped out immediately upon seeing his client.

"Thank you for your time, Miss Martel. We'll see you tomorrow—I mean later today." Vienna nodded "Yes," not looking back as she hurried to the car. Thomas opened the door.

"Thank you, Thomas."

"Home now, Miss Martel?"

"Please." No words were spoken on the short ride to Gansevoort. Vienna manipulated the puzzle over and over again in her mind. How could she come to the police station…in daylight? Jordan had work to do, and meetings. Probably just a few calls to be made in the morning. The car pulled up to the dimly lit curbside and Thomas got out to open the door for Vienna.

"Can I walk you to your door, Miss Martel?"

"Thank you, Thomas, that won't be necessary."

"I'm sorry about this terrible thing tonight, I wish…"

"The police will sort it out, I'm sure. Would you be able to pick me up tomorrow, well this afternoon, at 3:50, Thomas? I have to go back there."

"Yes, ma'am, I can be here." She reached into her clutch and removed two one hundred dollar bills, pressing them into his hand.

"Thank you for staying tonight. Now get some rest and I'll see you this afternoon." Vienna turned and walked to the building, up the concrete steps and into the freight elevator.

It was Jordan who'd provided Thomas with an introduction to Vienna three years earlier. At the time, Thomas was driving a Checker Cab four nights a week. On one of those nights, he'd picked Jordan up on Washington Street and driven him to Brooklyn Heights, for a dinner party hosted by an East Side gallery owner. A twenty-minute ride across town and over the Brooklyn Bridge. Enough time to learn that the driver had left his "dead end" union job unloading shipping containers on the docks in Baltimore, that his younger brother had been shot and killed in the street after a bar fight, that he'd thought he should get his shit together and go back to school, was enrolled as a freshman, at the age of 31, at St. Francis College in Brooklyn, was studying psychology and criminal justice with the idea of maybe going to law school, was living with his sister in Queens, but just for now. Enough time for Jordan to sense that his driver was street-smart, and working to get something better than what he'd come from, enough time to tell him he knew of someone who was looking for a driver, usually at night, who could provide a car...and would he be interested in speaking with her? "Sure, I'd be willing to talk to her," he'd replied as the cab pulled in front of a brownstone on Clark Street. And the car that Vienna could provide was Jordan's 1960 Mercedes 300D, ownership of which he'd assigned to her after realizing it was simpler to walk or take cabs than bother with a car. But *she* shouldn't be walking *or* looking for a cab at 2 in the morning in the far West Village.

"Her name is Vienna Martel and she lives on Gansevoort Street. I'll let her know to expect your call. You can tell her Jordan gave you her number—if you have a piece of paper, I'll write it down for you." The driver handed Jordan his copy of *The Daily News* and a pen, indicating the white space above the masthead. Jordan filled in the space and handed the paper back along with a twenty dollar bill. "I'm sorry, I didn't get your name."

"Thomas. Thomas Finnegan."

"Nice talking with you, Mr. Finnegan. Good luck in school."

"Thanks. I'll definitely call your friend." With that, Jordan left the cab and Thomas drove back to Manhattan.

Inside her home, Vienna locked the elevator to the 8th floor and slid the mural over the door again. She walked directly to the dressing alcove and studied her troubled face in the mirror. She held the back of her hand to her lips, whispering, "I'm sorry. It will be fine. It will be all right...I promise." Still standing, Vienna removed the Coq plume from her hair, then the wig, placing it back upon the bust of Miss Gish. She undressed, carefully returning her dress, jacket and shoes to the armoire. Next, the jewelry. Then her brassiere, followed by her breasts, which he placed back into the dressing table drawer. Jordan wearily stared at himself. "Sleep," he whispered and finished. Undergarments would go in the bottom drawer of the armoire for now. Naked, he gathered up his clothing, closed the French doors to the alcove and left Vienna's home, returning to his own.

The '78 Plymouth pulled into the warehouse garage on Pacific Street in Jersey City just before 2 a.m. A one-story, cinder block building with a few filthy wire security windows and two steel garage doors that housed Teddy Misko's trucking business. Which consisted of a small fleet of step vans he rented out to mostly commercial plumbing and electrical suppliers. The driver was Teddy's nephew, Dimitri. His passengers were freelancers who'd worked for Teddy in the past. They watched as he thumbed through the stacks of bills emptied from the leather bag onto a steel desk. Ten stacks, a hundred thousand per. A million dollars. He handed one to the taller man in the long leather coat. "Why the fuck would you kill him in the club for Christ' sake? You were supposed to take him out to the street, to the car…now it's a murder. They have a body…fucking hell."

"He refused to go outside. He wanted the thing brought inside. We didn't have it, you know that. The place was loud and crowded. Made sense."

"So no one saw you?"

"No. Maybe one person, at a distance."

"But you were wearing masks."

The accomplice, Danny, broke in. "After he was shot, and he's falling, the guy pulled Mika's mask down. But he had it back on in a second."

"But someone *might* have seen you?"

"This one chick," Mika answered. Teddy stared at him, disgusted.

"That's called a witness."

"Look, you've got your 900 thousand *and* the property—we'll take care of this."

"How the fuck are you going to 'take care of this'?"

"We'll find out who she is."

"You think the police are just giving out her name? Jesus."

"Danny will go back to the club tonight, when they reopen the place."

Danny shook his head. "No, no way, I'm not going back in the fucking club!"

"No one fucking saw you…you're just another party boy. People will be talking about the shooting. You'll be shocked and buy a few drinks and wonder if anyone saw what happened. Then we'll have a name. Easy. Just change your fucking clothes—it's Friday night." Danny shook his head but kept quiet, resigned to what he had to do next. Teddy was unmoved by Mika's scheme.

"Hey! We have other business to do, but it can't get done till this is fixed. Dimitri, leave the Plymouth here—maybe somebody saw it. Take the blue Galaxy behind the shop and drive this one where he needs to go, then go straight home." Turning a hard look to Danny he ordered, "Don't take a car to the club. Probably be cops on the block. Taxi, subway, whatever. Call me by Sunday night and tell me this is handled."

It was 2:45 when they pulled away from Teddy Misko's garage in the Galaxy. Dimitri took the Holland Tunnel back to Manhattan and dropped Mika at his place on the Lower East Side, then over the Brooklyn Bridge taking 278 and Ocean Parkway to Sheepshead Bay and the walkup he and Danny shared in a nondescript row house. There was no traffic and little spoken along the way, the three running through the night's events in their heads. Danny mumbled, "This is fucked up" to himself. No answer required. Mika counted out 25 thousand from his stack and handed it to Danny, who stopped mumbling and recounted it. Dimitri would get his from Uncle Teddy—but only when everything was "handled."

Jordan Eklund was awakened from a fitful sleep by the phone beside his bed, just after 8:30 a.m. He rolled over, cleared his throat and picked up the receiver. "Hello, this is Jordan."

"Mr. Eklund, this is Detective Ronson from the Major Case Squad, NYPD downtown." This was not a social call.

"How can I help you, detective?" Now sitting on the bed, naked, Jordan quickly summoned his senses.

"Are you aware of the theft of a Kandinsky painting from a private residence yesterday morning?"

Jordan sat rigidly. "I was not aware. Who was the painting stolen from?"

"The Kellerman home, in Oyster Bay Cove."

"My god, I know the Kellerman's and I know the work...so..."

"We believe this theft may be related to a murder that took place last night at a club on Charles Lane in the Village. It's called Ruby's."

Jordan had not assembled the pieces in his brain at this point. "I don't understand."

"The victim was a Japanese businessman named Yusaku Saji. He was also a collector of fine art. And he was seen handing a leather bag to a man who then shot him three times and left the club with the bag. There was one witness, who will meet with a police sketch person today. Do you know Mr. Saji, Mr. Eklund?"

"Yes, I negotiated two sales on his behalf several years ago. Both recorded transactions—I'm shocked to hear this. You believe he was involved in the Kandinsky theft?" Jordan asked incredulously.

"We're not certain, but we'd like to get on top of this before the FBI gets involved, which will probably be Monday morning."

"Of what assistance could I be, detective?" Jordan Eklund found the thought of any involvement in this case extremely disturbing. Yet his calm belied his fears. "Of course, I want to help in any way I can. Do you know how the break-in occurred?"

"Well that's another reason we're seeking your expertise, sir. The theft was not a break-in."

"I'm sorry?" Jordan replied, confused.

"It was not a break-in," the detective repeated. "The painting was to be loaned to the Guggenheim as part of a Kandinsky exhibit. It was scheduled to be picked up by the museum's transport service yesterday afternoon. Two men in white jackets arrived in a step van at the Kellerman home late yesterday morning, claiming to be from Harrison Transport and were shown into the house by Mrs. Kellerman. She said they'd displayed

149

proper ID. They carefully wrapped and removed the painting and were gone within fifteen minutes, even leaving her a copy of the signed receipt. Approximately four hours later the real transport vehicle, and the actual Harrison art handlers, showed up. That's when we got the call."

"Good god. And you believe these two events are somehow connected, the theft and the murder?" Jordan had already made the connection. The man whose face had been exposed to Vienna eight hours earlier was a security guard at the Guggenheim whom he had seen, though never known, on several occasions. Detective Ronson's call had set in motion a hallucinogenic collision of places and images inside Jordan Eklund's mind. His left hand pressed against his chest, his eyes closed.

"Yes, we think the timing's too close to call it a coincidence. We'd like you to come downtown tomorrow morning, Mr. Eklund—I can show you the sketch of the suspect then and perhaps you can tell me more about the victim, Mr. Saji…who else he might be doing business with, that kind of thing. Can we say 9 a.m.?" Jordan was silent, thinking about the hours that lay before him, like narrow boards strung across a bottomless canyon. Vienna had to be protected. "Will 9 a.m. work for you, Mr. Eklund?" the detective repeated.

"Yes. Yes, I can be there at 9, detective."

"Oh, and one more thing, Mr. Eklund. It seems that the witness lives in your building, on Gansevoort Street."

"In *my* building?" Jordan asked, with a combination of real and amplified alarm. "What is his, or her, name?"

"Her name is Vienna Martel. She lives on the 8th floor. I presume you know her."

"Yes, of course I know her. She's rented the space from me since 1980, though I seldom encounter her as I live and work on the Horatio Street side. But that's very interesting indeed, detective." In truth, it was more than "interesting" to Jordan that the police had already placed Vienna in his building. It was unnerving.

"Well we can speak more about your tenant tomorrow, Mr. Eklund. It's 1 Police Plaza, Park Row."

"Yes, I know where you are. Till then." Jordan hung up the phone and stood. There wasn't time to review his 'options' at the moment, nor Vienna's for that matter. Karina would arrive at 10 to clean the loft. Annina's people would arrive at 11 to wrap and remove the two Basquiat's to her gallery before they departed for the Edinburgh show. Vienna needed time to prepare for her appointment at the 6th Precinct station. He would reschedule his luncheon meeting with one of Sotheby's 'client liaisons.' Jordan quickly made his bed, walked to the bath and stepped into a hot shower. A cleansing, a calming of the surface. If only the water could run over his brain, and his organs, comfort them like a fetus in the womb. After five minutes he shut off the hot water and rinsed with the cold. His senses jumped to attention, shutting down his reverie and focusing on the things to be done in the next six hours. Addressing the first of those, he stood in front of the old pedestal sink, leaned close to the mirror and shaved the barely visible fine hairs from his face. He dressed in a light grey wool and silk suit, white shirt, dark blue tie with muted maroon stripes. Business could begin.

Jordan pushed the enormous mirror to the side and entered Vienna's home. He seldom saw the place in daylight and it was a bit disarming— colder certainly in the indiscriminate light of day than beneath the soft highlights of the chandeliers. He felt almost as though he were invading her privacy. Entering the dressing alcove he considered himself for a moment in front of the mirror. He removed his clothing and once again sat on the dressing stool and placed the small breasts over his own. Then a blue silk brassiere and, again, the wig, which she positioned on her head. Today, no coq plume. Today, a 'practical' face, a matte pêche-rose lipstick. There weren't so many daytime options in Vienna's wardrobe. She chose a simple cerise silk blouse, pleated wool slacks, ankle boots, cerulean leather waist jacket. A plain silver ring for the forefinger of her right hand. Finally, a burnt umber and saffron silk scarf tied close to her neck. It was autumn, after all. She picked up the beaded clutch again and gave a faint smile to herself—quite stunning for a late midday appearance.

Vienna left the alcove and lingered near the bed briefly. The bed she had rarely lay upon. She lay across it now and, closing her eyes, began to conjure the events of last night, rather, early that morning, in Ruby's. The man's face. How she would describe him to the police sketch person. Definitely not his identity. That would be up to Jordan, once they showed him the sketch. She sat up, stood up and left the daylit room, locking the doors behind her. Outside, Thomas stood waiting beside the Mercedes on Horatio Street.

"Hello, Miss Martel," he offered, opening the rear door.

"Hello, Thomas—thank you for being here."

"Yes, ma'am, always a pleasure." She stepped inside and he returned to the driver's seat. "You said the 6th Precinct station? I hope everything is all right."

"Yes, they want me to describe the man I saw to a sketch person—I'm sure it will be fine. Can you wait for me there?"

"Of course."

It was exactly 4:00 p.m. when Vienna walked into the station house on West 10th. The place looked exactly as it had 13 hours earlier except there were more cops milling around inside, more clerks at desks and more people waiting to be processed or listened to. She approached a receiving desk and announced herself to a sturdy female police officer, Officer McGrath. "Can I help you?" she asked blankly.

"I have a 4 o'clock appointment, arranged by Officer Molina."

"Your name."

"Vienna Martel."

"Officer Molina is gone for the day. You'll be meeting with Mr. Kwan. Please take a seat, I'll let him know you're here."

"I'll stand, thank you." Officer McGrath dialed the sketch artist's extension, spoke, hung up.

"He's coming out."

Mr. Heng Kwan was not in uniform because he was not a cop. A wiry, middle-aged man with straight grey hair and inquisitive brown eyes, he wore khaki pants, a flannel shirt, corduroy jacket and wire-rimmed glasses. He was friendly and approachable. "Miss Martel?"

"Yes."

"I'm Heng Kwan. Can you come with me, please?" He led Vienna out of the common area and down a hall to a small, windowless office on the right. Three vinyl upholstered steel chairs, one steel desk, metal file cabinets, one wooden drawing table and rolling stool, and on the walls, an assortment of faces in pencil from crimes gone by. He positioned one of the chairs beside the table and the stool behind it, where he would work.

"Please sit here, Miss Martel," Kwan said, holding the chair for her.

He then sat behind the table and picked up a pencil. "Before we begin, do you have any questions?"

Vienna, annoyed, answered quickly. "How long do you expect this to take, Mr. Kwan?"

"Well, that will depend upon how quickly we can closely render on paper the face you recall seeing, miss. It could be a half hour…it could be over an hour. Shall we begin?"

"Yes, please."

"Let's start with the most basic features first—he is male, is that correct?"

"Yes."

"Okay, his ethnicity, age, the shape of his head, neck, hair—then we can begin to fill in the features."

Vienna placed his age at 36. Caucasian. His head fairly large, not bulbous. Slightly chiseled, somewhat prominent jaw, perhaps Eastern European. Kwan sketched quickly, like the caricature artists in Central Park. As Vienna watched she corrected his lines: *raise the cheekbones a bit…his chin has a slight cleft…a prominent ridge above the eyebrows…* Erase. Sketch. Erase. Sketch. Erase… Even as the portrait drew closer to a likeness, she grew impatient with the process. Vienna rose from her chair and stood near the artist, leaning over his shoulder.

"Mr. Kwan, would you mind please, just for a moment?" she asked but actually instructed as she reached for his pencil and bent over the drawing table. Kwan was nonplussed, but pushed his stool backwards to make room for the interloper. Vienna erased the hairline, then lowered and thickened it slightly. Erased the tip of the nose, squaring it somewhat and bringing the nostrils closer to center. Softened the cheekbones, thinned the lips, deepened the nasolabial folds. In moments Vienna's alterations brought the portrait closer to a photographic representation of the man she had seen at Ruby's and whom Jordan now recognized as a security guard at the Guggenheim. She studied the rendering, feathered the sideburns partially over the ears, then stood, satisfied, handing the pencil back to Kwan. "Thank you. That's the man I saw." She began to turn away from the drawing board.

"But miss, we haven't quite, um, finished…" He felt an instinctive need to regain control of the session's outcome. But the session was over.

"That's the man I saw," Vienna repeated, "thank you, Mr. Kwan." She turned and left the office and the 6th Precinct station. Waiting idly beside the car, Thomas quickly focused when Vienna emerged onto the sidewalk.

"Everything all right, Miss Martel?" he asked while opening the passenger door.

"Yes, thank you, Thomas. A bit tedious is all."

"Is there anywhere else?"

"Just home, please. And I won't be going out this evening, but I will call you again tomorrow."

"Yes, ma'am." Thomas drove back to Gansevoort Street. There were no further words between driver and passenger as Vienna stared out the window and deep into her thoughts. Jordan would have calls to return. Dinner at Raoul's had been planned with Jean-Michel, Abrielle and Annina—an early celebration of the gallery show. Sleep would be important. If difficult to imagine.

It was already after 5 as Vienna reentered her home. Still daylit, she illuminated the chandeliers—a shimmering, familiar comfort. Sitting on her bedside she constructed the future. Then reconstructed. She could not be a 'witness' in a court of law. She could not make herself a public figure. Jordan would be asked to testify, for god's sake. She shook her head and walked into the dressing alcove. Staring into the mirror, her eyes moistened. She saw her very existence fluttering like a rippled reflection on the surface of a pond. She and Jordan had been born of the same womb, on the same day in 1954, at the University Hospital of Zurich. Yet he hadn't recognized her presence inside of him until he was ten, or eleven. An age when he was too young to understand his feelings, or what she was trying to tell him. Too ashamed to acknowledge his longings. But it was the art world his parents inhabited that had helped him see and feel what was possible, through the erotic images of Balthus, Picasso, Édouard-Henri Avril, and others—and through the lives of those strange creatures themselves. By age thirteen, Jordan and Vienna had begun to exist as equals, their minds and souls inseparable since their shared cognizance. She would never have chosen to leave him, but now the question of choice, of so-called "free will," had been narrowed. Perhaps shut down entirely. When we are told we have three months to live, or three weeks, or three days, do we think about living that time to the fullest? Preparing our soul for what might or might not be next? Making amends for…whatever? Or anesthetizing ourselves from the terrifying clarity at hand? Would Vienna ever see herself again? Would she ever *be* herself again? She touched her face softly with her hand.

And undressed herself. But this time Jordan would leave Vienna's home with her silk blouse, her pleated slacks, cerulean jacket, scarf, the ankle boots, the clutch. He also took her silicone breasts, brassiere, and Vienna's wig, all that she was last seen wearing, being, in public, uncertain she would ever return.

In his loft, Jordan was careful to remove all traces of Vienna's makeup. He fingered the slightest bit of pomade into his hair and brushed it into place. There were messages from the Curator of Contemporary Art at the Guggenheim (undoubtedly calling about the Kandinsky theft); Annina confirming dinner; Chiaki Saji, daughter of Yusaku Saji; an insurance adjuster; the cardboard warehouse tenant (a water leak). He would call Annina and Chiaki, deal with the water leak and wait till tomorrow for the rest. It was too much for now.

Over dinner at Raoul's the conversation could hardly be described as a 'celebration' of Jean-Michel's brilliant successes. Instead, the topics turned quickly to theft and murder.

"So, the woman actually *let* the thieves into her home and *watched them* wrap and remove the painting?" Basquiat asked mockingly.

"It appears that's exactly what happened," Jordan replied. "The actual transport handlers from the museum arrived hours later, as originally scheduled."

"That's fucking crazy," Abrielle dropped, incredulously.

"And police are imagining there may be some connection between the theft and the murder at Ruby's, Jordan?"

"They believe it shouldn't be ruled out, Annina, given that the victim was a well-known art collector, and a client of mine—it's a bit unnerving, but we shall see. But why don't we offer a toast to our dear friend, who happens to be very much alive at this table right now!".

At 10:15 p.m. Danny took the Q, then the 3 train from Sheepshead Bay to 14th Street in Manhattan. Just under an hour. He would walk the rest of the way to Ruby's on Charles Lane. Maybe 20 minutes, or a little more. A chilly, clear night—a chance to gather his thoughts before reentering the scene of the crime. His crime. Danny hated the idea. Wished he was having a beer and a shot back at the Towne Cafe right now. Fuck it—this was the deal. In his blue sateen shirt, sensible gold chain, black leather sport jacket and tight black jeans Danny looked like he might 'fit in' at Ruby's, even if he didn't feel he fit in. Fuck it.

It was nearly midnight when he arrived in front of the club, wound tightly but looking forward to a first drink. He saw a police car parked maybe 50 feet away, two cops inside. A few young men loitered on the sidewalk with their smokes. Jerome was once again at the door as Danny approached the short velvet rope. "That's 25 dollars, sir," he said, interrupting his forward motion.

"Oh, right," he replied, fishing for cash from his back pocket and handing over two 10s and a 5.

"I'll just stamp your hand," which he did quickly, leaving "Ruby's" in ruby red ink on the back of Danny's right hand. Jerome held the door and he proceeded inside the club, where he'd been less than 24 hours earlier.

He hated being there. Ruby stood, soberly, by the near end of the bar. There were only six others at the bar and just a few seated on the ottomans and banquettes to the left. Fewer still in the other room, and no one on the dance floor. The music mix was strangely disconnected, from Stan Getz's Bossa Nova to Donna Summer, Sinatra, Culture Club… The patrons spoke quietly. There was no revelry inside Ruby's on this night. Danny stood with both hands on the bar rail and Tony acknowledged immediately.

"What can I get you?"

"Stoli and tonic. Slice of lime." Seconds later the bartender pushed a tall glass in front of Danny.

"Do you want to start a tab?"

"No, I'll settle."

"That'll be nine dollars." Danny pulled out his wallet and handed Tony a ten. He was searching for words. They weren't coming easily.

"My friend told me about this place—said it was a great spot. But it seems kinda quiet for a Friday night…" Tony was uncertain how much to engage with this guy. Whom he didn't know.

"Well, there was an incident here last night, so it'll probably be quiet for a couple days. But Halloween will be another story."

"An incident?" Danny probed. A young man standing close by seized his opportunity to tell the tale.

"There was a shooting—a man was killed!" he blurted out as if privileged information.

"Jesus Christ, you're kidding!" Danny replied, feigning surprise.

"Not kidding!" Tony, eyeing Ruby, was not happy with this conversation. But Danny had found his opening.

"Did they get whoever did it?" he asked, feigning concern. The young man's companion jumped in.

"He was wearing a mask and he walked out before anyone knew what happened. Gone!"

"Holy shit!" Danny exclaimed. "That's crazy!" Ruby moved closer to the three men, hoping to end the tiresome rehashing, which he found genuinely upsetting.

"My friends, it would be good if we didn't make last night's tragedy the topic of this evening's chit chat at Ruby's. You're welcome to do that outside, would that be all right?" he instructed.

"So nobody saw the guy who shot him?" Danny pursued.

"Vienna might have seen him, when his mask came off!" the young man's companion volunteered eagerly.

"Jason, respect Vienna's privacy for god's sake! This matter is in the hands of the police now."

"I'm sorry…this is just so…wild," Danny said apologetically. "Maybe I'll try to come back Halloween."

"It will be a proper party, I promise," Ruby said, walking back to his station at the front. Behind him, Danny continued out to the sidewalk again. He approached Jerome.

"Excuse me, have you seen Vienna tonight? I was supposed to meet her here."

"If you don't see Thomas, you don't see Miss Martel."

"Thomas?"

"Her driver."

"Sure, right, of course. I wonder where she could be?"

"Stay here—I'll see what I can find out." Danny thought he'd landed the prize as Jerome disappeared into the club.

"Everything all right, Jerome?" Ruby asked his gatekeeper.

"Maybe. There's a guy outside asking about Miss Martel. Says he was supposed to meet her here—but I think he's bullshit 'cause he didn't know about Thomas."

"Is he wearing a black leather jacket?"

"Yea, he was just inside."

"I'm going to call Vienna now—please wait a moment." Ruby picked up the house phone and called 342-6816. Vienna's phone sat on her dressing room table, but it was also tied into Jordan's bedroom line. He was startled from his sleep when the call came in and quickly gathered himself, assuming her voice.

"Hello, this is Vienna."

"I'm so sorry to bother you this late, darling, but there's someone at the club asking for you." Vienna felt a note of urgency in Ruby's voice.

"Who is it, Ruby?"

"I haven't seen him before—he told Jerome you were supposed to meet tonight, but he didn't know about Thomas. I thought it suspicious."

Vienna thought intently on this. Jordan did as well; this double-think, while not unprecedented, was particularly taxing given the physical exhaustion they both felt.

"Is he still there?" she asked quietly.

"Yes, Vienna—he's waiting for Jerome to give him some information, should you wish to give any whatsoever."

"Have Jerome give him my cross streets, Ruby, but not the address. And tell him I'm away this evening but perhaps will be at the club tomorrow night or Sunday. That will be fine."

"Are you sure, Vienna?" Something about this felt strange to Ruby. Especially after last night.

"Yes, I'm certain, and thank you. I have to go now." Jordan placed the receiver in its cradle and continued sitting on the side of the bed, navigating their thoughts. Perhaps someone would be waiting for Vienna in the daylight. She didn't relish the idea of going back to Ruby's so soon, fielding questions from the likes of Jason and the other gossipy boys. He lay back down, exhausted. Jordan had a 9 a.m. appointment with Detective Ronson, 1 Police Plaza. To view the sketch. To talk about Mr. Saji. He would need his sleep.

Jerome dutifully passed along the limited information that Miss Martel had approved and Danny left the club, believing he'd succeeded in getting what Mika had demanded. On his way to 14th Street, he stopped at the Corner Bistro to call him from a pay phone. Mika said, "Nice job," and hung up. Danny ordered a Stoli and tonic and drank it quickly. Then he ordered another and drank it quickly. *What a fucked up night*, he thought, left a 5 dollar tip and left the bar to catch the trains back to Sheepshead Bay.

Jordan dressed conservatively for his meeting downtown, in suit, tie and double-breasted trench coat. He arrived early—little traffic on a Saturday morning—but was not kept waiting. Detective Ronson himself met Jordan in the lobby and led him to his 4th-floor office. The Major Case Squad did not normally concern itself with homicides, but because of the potential link between Saji's murder and the Kandinsky theft the departments were "cooperating" with each other. The detective led with a few questions about Yusaku Saji. *How long have you known Mr. Saji? What was your relationship exactly? Under what circumstances did you meet? Do you know where his money came from? Have you ever known him to engage in theft, or any transaction that could be considered grand larceny?*

Jordan delivered his answers plainly, no subtext. He'd known Yusaku Saji for approximately 3 years. Had been contacted by him through a mutual acquaintance—Andreas Eklund, Jordan's father. He'd helped Saji negotiate the purchase of two signed Warhol prints, one of Einstein, the other Mao, and a sculpture by David Smith, all documented transactions. He believed he was involved in some sort of finance in Japan. Had never been aware of any illegal activity. Could not fathom a connection between the Kandinsky theft and murder in a night club.

Then Detective Ronson opened his desk drawer and pulled out the sketch. The sketch that Vienna had completed the previous afternoon at the 6th Precinct Station. "Mr. Eklund, please look at this rendering of the murderer as recalled by our one witness." He gave the sketch to Jordan. In spite of the fact that many of the lines and facial shadings had been drawn in her own hand, Jordan nonetheless felt a pang of alarm and discomfort seeing the image. He knew absolutely that this was the killer. But he could not know that—only Vienna could possess that knowledge. He also knew this face in another context. Not the name. The face.

Jordan looked up from the sketch.

"I'm quite certain this man is a security guard at the Guggenheim." Ronson made the connection immediately.

"And the Kandinsky was supposed to be on its way to the Guggenheim," the detective muttered, thinking aloud.

"I might suggest you consider doing two things, detective," Jordan offered. "Show your sketch to Mrs. Kellerman. And bring it to the museum. I believe the connection you're trying to draw between the murder and the theft might become clearer. Assuming this is the murderer." He handed the sketch back to Ronson. "Is there anything else you wanted to ask me?" The detective seemed lost in thought for a moment as if trying to assemble pieces of a puzzle that didn't quite belong together. "Detective? Anything else?" Jordan repeated.

"Um, just one thing, Mr. Eklund. Your connection to all of these individuals—Saji, the Kellerman's, the security guard, your tenant Miss Martel…that's a big coincidence in this line of work, wouldn't you think?"

"The art world is a very small universe, detective. Still, yes, I do find it all a bit disturbing—perhaps especially that my tenant has witnessed a murder…it can't be easy for her. But if these connections lead to the same conclusion, perhaps a fuller picture will be revealed." Ronson widened his eyes.

"A fuller picture?"

"Meaning, I might assume the thief is on someone else's payroll—other than the museum's, of course. And I believe it's possible the buyer for this painting is someone other than Saji. He may simply have been the courier, in behalf of a friend or business associate. There is a market for this sort of thing in Japan, and not all transactions are made through normal channels." Jordan rose from his chair, as did Detective Ronson, extending his hand.

"This has been very helpful, Mr. Eklund, thank you for your time."

"You're welcome, detective. If there's anything else I can be of assistance with, please…"

"That's very kind of you. If Mrs. Kellerman and the Guggenheim confirm what you're saying I'm certain we'll be bringing the suspect in for more than questioning. We'll alert you to any developments."

"Good luck, detective."

Jordan arrived at the Horatio Street entrance to his building just after 10:15. He decided to walk around the corner, to Vienna's side. A car was parked directly across the street from the freight entrance—a blue Ford Galaxy, with two men in the front seat. They were just sitting there, one reading a tabloid the other glancing left to the building. Jordan kept walking, toward the river. Jersey plates. He didn't recognize either man but believed he knew what—who—they were waiting for. But she would never appear. He turned left onto 10th Avenue, then to Horatio again, and up the elevator to his home. The reception for Jean-Michel at Annina's gallery would start at 6 p.m. and end when it ended. By mid-afternoon the men waiting on Gansevoort would be thinking about a Plan B—maybe waiting outside Ruby's. She'd said she would probably be there.

Jordan felt a hollowness inside, a longing for Vienna, as if she had gone far away and could not be reached. Standing in front of the mirror he could barely face himself, unable to summon the logic that might locate a missing person. But this rumination was an indulgence he could little afford at the moment. He was meeting Chiaki Saji for tea in a few hours, to offer his condolences and shock, and perhaps learn something he didn't know about her father. And she—Vienna—would call Thomas and ask him to pick her up at four. Then what? Jordan could think clearly enough to realize he was operating in a state of exhaustion, propelled only by the adrenaline events had sent rushing through his nervous system. Nervous system—he hated believing his actions could be controlled by such a mundane thing. He would need sleep before venturing out again. Was that even possible?

The murmurs, footsteps and shuffling papers seemed amplified in the cavernous courtroom on Centre Street. The gavel, the announcement that Court was "now in session" seemed barely to silence the noise inside Vienna's head. The chamber was stifling with the air of a thousand trials. She felt nauseous, yet determined to maintain her composure.

"The prosecution may call its first witness."

"Your Honor, the People call Vienna Martel to the witness stand."

"Stand here, please. Raise your right hand. Do you promise that the testimony you shall give in the case before this court shall be the truth, the whole truth, and nothing but the truth, so help you God?"

"I do."

"Please state your full name."

"*Vienna Juliette Martel.*"

"*You may be seated.*"

"*Miss Martel, please tell the Court where you were on the night of October 28th.*"

"*I believe you're referring to the morning of October 29th?*"

"*Yes, of course. Approximately 1 a.m. on the morning of October 29. Where were you at that time, Miss Martel?*"

"*I was seated in a night club in the West Village.*"

"*A place called Ruby's, on Charles Lane?*"

"*Yes.*"

"*You were called here today because you were a witness to a murder in that club. Is that correct?*"

"*Yes.*"

"*A man was shot three times in the chest, at point blank range. Is that correct.*"

"*Yes.*"

"*And the shooter took something from the victim…*"

"*Yes, a leather bag he'd been holding.*"

"*Is the killer in this courtroom, Miss Martel.*"

"*Yes. That man, sitting over there.*"

"*In your testimony, you stated there were two men involved in the murder.*"

"*Yes.*"

"*But you could only identify one?*"

"*Both men were wearing masks…but…*"

"*They were wearing masks? Wouldn't two men wearing masks stand out in a crowd?*"

"*Mardi Gras masks…party masks—other people were wearing masks too. You've heard of Halloween?*"

"*Yes, of course. Coming in a few days at that point.*"

"*Yes.*"

"*So the two men were wearing masks, but you were able to identify one of them.*"

"*As he was falling the victim pulled the gunman's mask down, so his face was briefly exposed.*"

"Miss Martel, we understand the shooting took place at the bar. Were you standing at the bar?"

"I was seated on the other side of the room, as I've said."

"If you were on the other side of the room, and the gunman was facing the victim, how could you see his face?"

"He looked around the room quickly, presumably to see if anyone had seen him."

"And he saw you looking at him…"

"Objection, Your Honor!"

"Overruled. You may answer the question."

"Our eyes met for an instant."

"And what happened next?"

"He put the gun in his coat pocket, placed the mask back over his face, said something to his partner and both men left with the leather bag."

"Thank you, Miss Martel. I have no further questions at this time."

"Does the Defense have any questions for this witness."

"We do, Your Honor. Miss Martel, you've stated that you were not standing at the bar but you were seated across the room."

"Yes."

"How far away from the bar do you think you were seated?"

"I don't know—perhaps fifteen feet."

"And was the bar area crowded?"

"It was fairly crowded, yes."

"And yet nothing impaired your view of these three men?"

"People were walking to and from the bar but none preventing me from seeing these men."

"Had you been drinking, Miss Martel."

"Objection!"

"Your Honor, Defense would like to establish whether the witness might have been impaired in any other way."

"Continue."

"Miss Martel, had you been drinking that evening?"

"I'd had one sip of my Champagne."

"And that's it, one sip."

"Yes. I'd only just arrived at Ruby's ten minutes earlier."

"Had you been drinking, or used any substances such as cocaine or marijuana, prior to going to the club?"

"Objection!"

"I'll answer the question. The answer is No, I had not."

"So mere moments after entering the club your attention was focused on three men at the bar, which you've said was crowded. Why would that be, Miss Martel?"

"The man with the leather bag—he was an older, Japanese gentleman, wearing a business suit. I found it odd seeing such a person in this club. So, yes, you could say my attention was fixed on him, and then the two others."

"How long did you say the face of the gunman was exposed?"

"I didn't say."

"Do you think one second? Two seconds?"

"Perhaps two."

"And sitting across the room, in a crowded bar, you believe you could identify a man whose face might have been exposed for two seconds? Miss Martel?

"Yes."

"Beyond a doubt?"

"I believe so."

"Defense has no further questions at this time, Your Honor."

"You may step down, Miss Martel. Do the People wish to call its next witness in this case?"

"We do, Your Honor. The People call Jordan Eklund to the witness stand."

"Jordan Eklund. Is Jordan Eklund in this courtroom?"

Jordan bolted upright from a theta state of half-sleep, exhausted and perspiring. He would need to shower. He would need to change his suit...

By noon Detective Ronson was showing Vienna's sketch to Mrs. Kellerman in her home, though she'd already sat with a sketch person at the Oyster Bay Cove Police Department the day before, describing the two men who'd removed her Kandinsky. But the image presented to her by Ronson was far more detailed and realistic a portrait than the ones she'd helped create. Still, there was uncertainty in her reaction. "I–I do see a resemblance to one of the men. But he had horn-rimmed glasses and wore a grey woolen flat cap. Weren't you shown the sketch done by the Oyster Bay Cove police, detective?" Detective Ronson admitted he had not seen the other rendering, but said he would make a point of comparing the two. Somewhat embarrassed, he thanked Mrs. Kellerman for her time and left.

An hour later the detective was in the office of Daniel Russo, head of security at the Guggenheim, a tall, thick-boned man who fit the profile of a retired cop. He looked at the sketch, then looked up. "He worked here for about two years, up until last Tuesday—didn't show up for his shift, hasn't shown up since. Mika Pavlou. Is he in trouble?"

"Yes, I'd say so. He's a suspect in the theft of the Kandinsky painting on Thursday, and a murder that took place at a club late Thursday night-Friday morning."

"Jesus Christ. What can I do for you, detective?"

"If you could provide his address, any details on his background, a photo—those things would help a great deal."

"We've got all of that, detective—the museum has a pretty extensive clearance procedure, especially for security hires. Though maybe we missed somethin' with this guy." Russo stood and walked to a white file cabinet, pulling one of the drawers, then fingering through the folders. "Pavlou…here we go," he said as he plucked out one of the files, handing it to Detective Ronson. "I can make you a copy of any of this." And there it was: a resume covering nearly a lifetime leading to this moment—from grade school near Omonoia Square in Athens to brief service with the Hellenic Police, jumping to porter at the Roosevelt Hotel in Manhattan, waiter, then security guard at Pace Gallery 1977–1980. He'd started at the Guggenheim in late 1980. A phone number and address: 156 Essex Street on the Lower East Side, apartment 3C. Several short letters of recommendation from his former employers. Who wouldn't trust Mr. Pavlou? And a photocopy of his Guggenheim security photo—a near perfect match of the sketch brought by Detective Ronson.

"A copy of these things would be very helpful, Mr. Russo."

"Sure. I'll make them right here, detective." Which he did at the Xerox machine on the shelf behind his desk.

By mid-afternoon the detective had obtained a search warrant for Mika Pavlou's apartment and an arrest warrant for his suspected role in the theft of the Kandinsky, and for the murder of Yusaku Saji. As a courtesy, he would contact Officer Molina from the 6th Precinct and invite him to meet at the apartment. "Yes, of course I'll be there." Molina was a little pissed that these next steps were initiated downtown. *Arrogant pricks.* But that's what "cooperation" was supposed to be about, right? And at least the FBI had been preempted. So, fine.

At 3:45 p.m. Jordan put on his overcoat. He took Vienna's beaded clutch from the lower dresser drawer. It still contained her wallet and a few makeup items. He removed the cash but left her French driver's license and a photo of herself taken during her year at École des Beaux-Arts in Paris. The clutch fit snugly in his coat pocket. He left his home and locked the 8th floor behind him. Outside, the descending sun behind his building cast a shadow over Washington Street. The temperature had already fallen into the low 50's. Tomorrow was Halloween. Then came November. Jordan walked to the corner of Gansevoort. The Galaxy was gone and the block was empty. He walked into the street and stopped directly opposite the service entrance, where he knew Thomas would park in a matter of minutes. He pulled the clutch from his pocket and dropped it close to the center of the road, then walked quickly to the sidewalk and west, looking back to see if anyone had watched. No pedestrians, no commercial traffic. Hopefully, Thomas would recognize the clutch and find Vienna's wallet inside. He would wait a few minutes for her to come out of the building. She was never late. He'd become anxious, cross the street, enter the building and ring her floor. No answer. There was a pay phone in the White Horse Tavern on Hudson and 11th. He would call Ruby's first. *No, we haven't seen Vienna.* His concern merging with fear for

her life, he would call the 6th Precinct and report that he had found her purse and wallet in the street in front of her building and that Miss Martel had not kept her appointment to meet him at four and that she did not answer the bell to her floor.

If someone else found the clutch before Thomas, hopefully they would report it to the police—there was nothing of value inside. Well, except for the thing itself, and the Saint Laurent wallet. Hopefully, a good citizen. Then Thomas would wait a bit longer for Vienna, perhaps 15 minutes, before going to the building to ring her floor. He would go back and sit in the car and think about calling Ruby's…maybe even the police…

By 4:15 Jordan had circled the block and was back to the corner of Washington and Horatio. Anxiety and longing filled his body. He felt ill. No one would ever describe him as sentimental, a romantic. But his heart was bursting. Vienna was gone now. Could he actually have taken her life? Soon she would be yet another police report, a 'missing person.' There would be a bulletin and a search. A search of her home. Jordan would be called. Details collided with feelings in his mind. He decided to walk to Chiaki's apartment building on East 17th Street. Breathing would steady with the tempo of his steps. Blood would flow more rapidly from his heart and arteries into his brain. The tide of emotions would ebb, some perspective regained, at least for a while.

But once seated beside Chiaki another wave of emotion flooded Jordan's heart. Her sorrow and shock, more powerful than his fear and emptiness, forced him to absorb someone else's pain. Chiaki's father, Jordan's friend, was dead.

Yusaku Saji had been his first client in New York City, a meeting arranged by Jordan's father in 1979. In part through the successful acquisitions they had consummated together, the art world wunderkind and the Japanese businessman had developed a mutual trust and friendship. If there was an exhibit of particular interest, or a special piece coming on the market, Jordan would make a point of informing Saji. And when his daughter moved to New York City to finish her degree in International Studies Jordan helped her find an apartment in the Gramercy area, not far from the university, and introduced her to many of his young colleagues.

"I'm so sorry, Chiaki—there are no words." No words, and no way to console someone in the face of a fatal loss.

"Thank you for coming, Jordan," she said, trying to steady her voice. "It's impossible to understand. My father had no enemies, only people who respected him. Who would do this?"

"There had to have been people involved whom he didn't know, a scheme he was unaware of. I don't know if you could have heard, but the police are linking your father's killers with the theft of a valuable painting the morning before."

"He would never steal from anyone!"

"Of course not, Chiaki, but perhaps someone in whose behalf he was acting made Mr. Saji an unknowing participant. They've identified the man with the gun—when he is found more will be known. But nothing that could incriminate your father, I'm certain of that."

"I am in mourning, yet I am angry and frustrated to be powerless and without answers. And there's nothing I can do for my father now." Tears welled up in Chiaki's unblinking eyes. Jordan searched the place where there were no words.

"Even when the answers come and the murderers are caught, it won't be nearly enough. But I will do what I can, to assist the police, and to help you, Chiaki. Are arrangements being made now for your father?"

"I will take father to Tokyo on Monday—the earliest they would allow. My uncle is taking care of the arrangements. He will meet me at the airport...the funeral will be Thursday...and father will be buried with my mother in Yanaka Cemetery."

"I could accompany you, Chiaki. This is a terrible burden for a daughter to bear alone."

"That's very kind of you, Jordan—but I'm just going through the motions now. The details are taken care of; I'll be there for the documentation, his and mine. I'll sleep on the flight, visit and mourn with my relatives, struggle with their questions. Then return the following week to resume school. But thank you."

Jordan shared what he knew of the Kandinsky theft, and of the suspect who had worked at the Guggenheim. Then he left the topic and asked Chiaki about her school year, but there were difficult silences as they sipped their cups of sencha tea. No words. Finally he rose.

"I am here if you need anything, Chiaki—please know that."

"I do, and I'm grateful, Jordan." They held each other for a long moment before Jordan left the apartment and resumed walking.

It was after 7 and dark when he arrived at Annina's gallery on Prince Street. Inside, animated chatter filled the room, along with clinking glasses and smoke from cigarettes and weed. Jean-Michel's paintings took up all of two walls, his drawings covered a third. Gitanes in one hand, Chablis in the other, the artist held court for friends and hangers-on. Abrielle, never the clinging girlfriend, flitted about the room, making "connections." Warhol, out of deference to his friend, stood in a far corner, surrounded by a few of his ersatz "superstars." Annina herself mingled from friend to patron, never letting the party distract from business. Then she sighted Jordan and quickly excused herself to meet him at the door. "So happy you made it, Jordan—I was starting to worry! The gallery's been packed practically since I opened the door!"

Jordan summoned all of himself to the moment. "I would *never* have missed a chance to celebrate Jean-Michel, Annina."

"Of course you wouldn't! Now let me take your coat and let's get you a glass of something—I think it's going to be a long night." Annina pulled Jordan's coat from his shoulders, took his hand and ushered him through the crowd toward a counter where the bar had been set up. She turned to her bartender with instructions, "Adrian, please pour our friend a drink while I hang up his coat." But Jordan's emotions had not waited outside the gallery.

"Annina, I need to use your phone for a moment, then we'll celebrate, I promise."

"Oh for Christ' sake. Follow me." She led him to her office and pointed to the desk. "You have five minutes before I come back for you!"

Annina closed the door behind her and Jordan picked up the phone. First directory assistance, then 1 Police Plaza. The number rang 12 times before a disinterested female voice came on the line.

"NYPD can I help you."

"Detective Ronson, please."

"Detective Ronson is tied up—who's calling?"

"Please tell him Jordan Eklund is on the line."

"Hold please." Instead of being put on "hold" she'd just laid the phone on her desk. Jordan listened to the sounds of a busy police station on a Saturday night. Voices, phones, intercom. Several minutes passed before the detective picked up.

"This is Ronson."

"This is Jordan Eklund, detective. I hope it's not inappropriate to have called."

"Not at all, Mr. Eklund. In fact, I tried to reach you earlier...but go ahead."

"I'm at a gallery event on Prince Street and all anyone can speak of is the Kandinsky theft. It's not my intention to comment on this matter publicly, detective, but I do wonder if there were any developments since we met."

"Yes, a few. The man you'd identified from the sketch did in fact work at the Guggenheim, though he hasn't shown up there since last week. His name is Mika Pavlou. Unfortunately, Mrs. Kellerman was unable to make a positive ID from our sketch—it seems he was wearing a cap and glasses at the time of the robbery."

"That is unfortunate."

"Well the sketch she helped render with the Oyster Bay Cove police showed enough resemblance that we were able to get search and arrest warrants for both crimes."

"So that sounds like good news, detective."

"*Not quite* good news, I'm afraid. The apartment was empty—no

Pavlou, no weapons, cash, anything we could call evidence. It's unclear whether he knows he's being sought, but he's definitely not taking chances. Of course we have his building under surveillance. But the reason for my earlier call, Mr. Eklund, is that a half hour ago I heard from Officer Molina at the 6th Precinct. It seems Vienna Martel is missing." Jordan paused, as the action he had plotted played out in real time, with the ending unknown.

"Miss Martel is *missing?* How could that be, detective?"

"Her driver found her purse and wallet in the street, in front of her building. She was supposed to meet him there three hours ago, but she never showed up."

"This is very disturbing…do you think she's in danger? Have you begun a search?" At that moment Annina opened the door and was about to lunge for the phone when Jordan raised his hand, waving her off impatiently.

"Of course we have. But little is known about her. She hangs out sometimes at a place called Ruby's. The driver takes her on errands, shopping, visiting friends at night…"

"And she's the murder witness."

"Indeed, Mr. Eklund. And if she doesn't appear by morning we'll need to search her residence. You have the key I presume."

"Yes, of course."

"Please be available in the morning. And thank you again for your assistance in identifying the suspect. Very helpful."

"You're welcome, detective. Hopefully Miss Martel is safe and will return to her home."

"We hope so, too. Have a good night, Mr. Eklund." Jordan placed the phone on its receiver then was motionless. All these hidden pieces, now in plain sight. Except that Vienna was missing. The emptiness was returning. He shook his head sharply, turned away from the desk then stopped, searching for another piece. He could feel her inside. She was watching him, wondering, *What will you do now?* What made him believe she would simply die in the street, inside a beaded clutch? How presumptuous. Cowardly. Vienna could not be dead, because the man who killed Yusaku Saji was still alive. Jordan left Annina's office. The gallery was loud and festive. Annina, now beside Jean-Michel, had been watching her door and spotted Jordan immediately, waving him to come. And he did, smiling broadly.

"It's about time, darling—no more phone calls tonight!"

"Where have you been for fuck's sake?!" the artist chided as he took his friend's hand and pulled him closer for a hug.

"I'm fully present, my friend, you have my word. It's been a long day, with this Kandinsky thing, and the murder—I was just on the phone with the detective downtown, but that's enough for tonight. This seems to be a brilliant opening…you both must be thrilled."

"Yea, it's really cool—look at all these crazies!" Jean-Michel smiled sarcastically. "But truth is, man, I'm really looking forward to Edinburgh—I've never been." Annina pretended to take offense.

"Oh, and this is *nothing*," she sneered.

"Of course it's not *nothing*, Annina—you're half the reason for the show in Scotland, darling!"

"You two souls are perfect for each other," Jordan mediated. "I may actually come see you for the Fruitmarket show, Jean-Michel."

"You'd fly to Edinburgh just for the show, Jordan?" the artist asked incredulously.

"I thought of going to Paris first, and trying to connect with a friend there…so perhaps after."

"New York, Paris, Edinburgh—you're too much, Jordan. I'll go fetch you that drink you never got…what will it be?"

"Something with bubbles, Annina. Then we'll have a toast."

Guests—invited and not—were still arriving at Annina's gallery when Jordan excused himself just before 9:30, in spite of protests from gallerist and artist alike. "I have a 10:00 p.m. call to Tokyo—where it will be 11 a.m. tomorrow—which I'm *definitely* not making from your office, Annina. But I will see you both sooner than later."

The 10:00 p.m. call would actually be to Thomas. Mika Pavlou had not been arrested. Therefore he needed to believe that the witness to the murder was still alive, still needing to be "handled." And Jordan needed to know that Yusaku Saji was not an accomplice in the events that led to his murder. And to acknowledge a raw pulse beating inside him—Vienna's plea for her freedom.

"Hello, Thomas."

"Miss Martel?"

"I'm sorry I couldn't keep our appointment this afternoon…"

"I–I was worried. When I found your purse and wallet in the street I thought something terrible might have happened—so I called the police."

"You did the right thing, Thomas. I was frightened, too. I saw two men waiting in a car outside my building this morning—I believe they're somehow involved with the murder. I believe they were waiting for me."

"Jesus Christ! I mean, how did your purse get there? Did they attack you?"

"I put it there, after they'd left, and just before you were to arrive. I wanted to disappear, not be involved in this ugly business any further… to be 'missing.' And that's what happened. But these men—whoever they are—are free. Which means I cannot be."

"So what will you do, Miss Martel? What can *I* do?"

"There's nothing to do at this moment, Thomas. But I'd like you to take me back to Ruby's tomorrow night."

"But the police think you're missing!"

"I'll call them in the morning and tell them what I've just told you. Do you have my purse and wallet?"

"Yes, ma'am."

"Then perhaps you could bring it tomorrow night. Can you pick me up at 10:45, Thomas?"

"Sure, of course. But…"

"Yes?"

"Tomorrow is…"

"Halloween."

"It will be crowded—it could be dangerous…"

"I suppose. But I'll protect you, Thomas." Vienna couldn't resist the tease. "Now have a good night, and thank you."

"No, I'll protect you, Miss Martel. And *you* have a good night."

When Jordan first provided Thomas with an introduction to Vienna, he didn't fully imagine the importance this driver might have in her life. Of course he'd considered her safety and comfort during downtown late night excursions—that was the idea. But he hadn't anticipated their unforced closeness, nor what a relationship with her sole heterosexual companion might mean. Had Thomas become as much the older, protective brother as the responsible employee? Right now the employee was focused on the unfolding events, trying to understand what was happening, but he could not. He knew nothing of the Kandinsky theft, nor of Mr. Saji's relationship to Jordan. Only that there was a murder and Miss Martel was the witness and now her life was in danger. At least she was alive.

Jordan hung up Vienna's phone and stared in the direction of her home, on the other side of his bedroom wall. His anxiety had ebbed, a calm come over him. He felt her there, which was reassuring. Still, it was too early to sleep, no matter how much his body required it. He brushed his hair, straightened his tie and took the elevator to the lobby. It was less than a fifteen-minute walk to Ruby's, where it was unlikely anyone would know him. He would simply walk by on the other side of Charles Lane as if to another destination. Just look to see if the club was busy on a Saturday night. See if the Galaxy was nearby. Forty people or so waited along a velvet rope to enter Ruby's, many in masks. Busy night. A blue Galaxy parked a hundred feet away, close to Washington Street. No one inside.

Having resolved what their course of action would be over the next 24 hours, Jordan collapsed into a deep sleep. Yet it would be Vienna's dreams he would awaken from. A dream of Paris. Her beloved Hotel Caron de Beaumarchais, with its ancient furnishings and artwork, where she'd lived for nearly a month at the start of a school year. Lost in reverie at the Jeu de Paume. Ending the day at Les Deux Magots. The short walk to Quai Voltaire…being followed, by an admirer? She never found out. They must return to Paris, he thought, as soon as things were finished here. Hopefully, very soon.

Jordan made a light breakfast for himself. Coffee, toast with blackberry jam, slices of orange. Then Vienna called the 6th Precinct station and asked for Officer Molina. "He's not on duty today, can someone else help you?"

"This is Vienna Martel—yesterday someone called your station and reported that I was missing. I'm calling to report that I'm not."

"Please hold, ma'am." She waited a full minute, listening to the babel and din in the station. Then an Asian woman's voice came on the line.

"Miss Martel, this is Officer Huang. I accompanied you to the station with Officer Molina the night of the murder."

"Yes, I remember you."

"And we did hear, from your driver I believe, that you were missing—that he'd found your purse and wallet in the street." Vienna shared the details of her scheme with Officer Huang. Her fear of being hunted by the murderers, the men waiting outside her building. Her plan to be "missing," to arrange for her own disappearance.

"It seemed you'd succeeded, but you're calling us now..."

"This morning I realized that until these men are caught I will remain in danger."

"If they are in fact looking for you, that is correct, Miss Martel."

"I did not leave my home Friday night, officer, but I was told that a man was asking for me at Ruby's. I'm planning to go back there tonight, which is the reason I've called you."

"I would caution you against doing that, ma'am. Halloween is a crazy night downtown, especially in the Village. If someone is looking for you there will be enough noise and confusion to cover their actions—as there was three nights ago."

"I'm well aware of that, officer. But the club's owner and staff know me well and will look after me. If the police decide to come I would suggest after eleven, and not in uniform, nor in official cars. If you see a blue Galaxy on the street, you will know they are there."

"Miss Martel, we can't guarantee your safety if you do this. I strongly urge you..."

"Thank you for your concern, Officer Huang. I will be careful." Vienna hung up the phone leaving Huang without another rebuttal. Frustrated, she thought for a moment, then reluctantly decided to call Officer Molina at his home on Staten Island—after all, this was pretty much his case. Molina was not happy. The family was getting ready for church. Not that he was a believer, but his wife liked the ritual for the kids. No point in arguing with that. It was Sunday. Halloween. Later he would take the kids trick or treating—the streets in New Brighton were safe enough. But that would be early. *Shit, it's fucking Sunday.* He decided to call Detective Ronson. After all, the departments were "cooperating." Ronson was actually excited by this development—he had no other plans for Halloween.

Next Vienna called Ruby's and left a message on the machine—she would be coming to the club tonight, looked forward to seeing everyone. This way if anyone asked for her, the answer might be 'She's expected.' Then a call to Thomas, asking that he bring a mask for himself when he came to pick her up so that he might accompany her into Ruby's. He understood that to mean *Be my bodyguard for the night.* He was honored to be asked, but what kind of mask? Vienna would wear her silver Venetian Swan mask.

Twelve hours until Thomas would come for Vienna. Normally so organized, so in control of details and outcomes, Jordan was restive, with no plan for filling the time. He realized he hadn't spoken with his father since before the murder of his friend. Is it possible he hadn't heard? Neither crime would have been in the papers yet and Andreas Eklund never watched— did not possess—a television. Only listened to classical music on the radio. It would be late afternoon in Salzburg. The call would be nearly as difficult as his meeting with Chiaki. They spoke in Austro-Bavarian, Mr. Eklund's native dialect. Devastated by the news of his friend Yusaku, Jordan waited as his father stammered for words and his breathing settled. "I'm sorry, father, I'm so sorry to bring you this news." Jordan asked if he had spoken with Mr. Saji recently. His father hesitated.

"Yes. I spoke with Yusaku in September. I asked if I might put another Japanese business man in contact with him…"

The other Japanese businessman, Tomiichi Nakano, had been seeking a trusted individual who could assist in expediting a large financial transaction in the United States. The purchase of a painting. Mr. Saji had been happy to accommodate his friend. Father and son did not speak of the obvious connection. Jordan urged Mr. Eklund not to attempt to contact Mr. Nakano. There was no purpose until more was known of both crimes and those who had plotted them. He told his father of his meeting with Chiaki and the plans for Mr. Saji's funeral in Tokyo. Mr. Eklund wondered aloud, as Jordan had, whether he should attend. His son told him it would not be the right time, but he would keep him informed of developments. "Much more will be known very soon, I'm certain of that, father."

Jordan walked to one of the south-facing windows in his loft. Hands clasped behind his back, he stared at the distant harbor, and the boats. He couldn't possibly spend the rest of the day and half the night pacing the floor, so he decided to walk around the Village. Kids would already be trick-or-treating. The bridge and tunnel revelers would be arriving early to the Irish pubs. Barricades and police would have taken their positions on 10th Street in preparation for the parade. Plenty of distractions before indulging in a long brunch at La Ripaille.

It was nearly 5 when he left the bistro, the taste of jambon et fromage crepe and three café noisettes still in his mouth. The cool air was bracing, the sidewalks alive with costumed partiers and the merely curious. Jordan kept moving, east from Hudson Street, then south on Bleecker. Bars, clubs, second-hand clothing shops, head shops, the now fading markers of the folkie and new wave eras. A mix of fallen leaves and trash blown to the curb. Then something caught his eye in a parlor floor shop window. Along with the hookahs and beads, costumed mannequins. Standing next to Richard Nixon and Darth Vader was David Bowie, as "Aladdin Sane," one of his many alter egos. Jordan had met Bowie a few years earlier, at a gallery in London. In their eyes, he'd sensed recognition of a kindred identity, their androgynous beauty. Though formally courteous and deferential, inside Jordan had suppressed a profound attraction. Or was he simply star stricken by the beautiful rock idol?

What if he—she—Vienna—were to arrive at Ruby's *as Bowie*…as Aladdin Sane? Physically, they could easily have been brothers, or sisters. And how difficult could it be to mimic Bowie's South London accent? To most Americans, his Volksschule-learned English sounded perfectly British. Jordan walked up the stoop and into the store. She wouldn't need the Aladdin mask. Just some glitter and face paint. The two-tone lightning bolt across her forehead and right cheek would take time. But there was time. Vienna had extravagant leotards a friend had brought from Milan she'd sworn she'd never wear. And maroon knee boots. Jordan could color his hair orange-blonde and tease it to a fluffy crown, like Bowie's. He could shave his eyebrows—well, they'd have to think about that.

By eight-thirty Jordan had dyed, blown and sprayed his hair. He thought it looked quite silly, so very *not* Jordan—*or* Vienna—yet he felt a mix of excitement and trepidation. Was this really a disguise? Would her face not be fully visible? Well of course it would, yet completely unexpected, and that was the point, wasn't it? They would finish dressing in Vienna's suite, where the facial lighting and mirrors were more practical. Now, wearing only his briefs, Jordan walked from his bath to the bedroom. From the lowest drawer of his desk, he removed a Baretta M1935, a gift from his father, who'd served in the Austrian Resistance during Nazi occupation. He checked the magazine. It contained eight rounds. He then went to his dresser and removed Vienna's breasts and brassiere. With this incongruous collection in both hands, he left his loft and entered Vienna's home. She was no longer a missing person.

It took over an hour and a half to complete her 'mask.' White eyeliner applied to the brows (no shaving—they couldn't imagine how Jordan might explain that to…whomever); a pale magenta gloss on the eyelids and lips; a thin, black tracing along the hairline, to suggest the possibility of a wig? It seemed plausible. And, most time consuming, creating the two-toned bolt across the face. Fortunately, Vienna was quite proficient at figure rendering. When finally finished she considered herself in the mirror, and in fact found him quite attractive. It even seemed somehow wrong to apply her breasts, as if she would be violating him. *It's a costume, Vienna…please remember that.* She had to search another dresser for the boldly striped, Italian leotards. Skin-tight and shiny, she began to feel aroused. A fitted yellow-metallic off-shoulder top (which she would *never* wear) and vintage flamenco vest nearly completed the look and distracted from her small breasts as well. Now the knee boots. *Awful.* And, eyes closed, a pinch of glitter on the face. *Jesus Christ, who am I?*

Hanging from the armoire door, a gold, beaded clutch—it seemed a fitting accessory for Bowie—inside she placed the Baretta, and on top of the gun, a carefully folded silk scarf. She stood for a final appraisal of her new persona, singing softly with a faint smile, *Turn and face the strange… Ch-ch-changes.*

It was almost eleven when Vienna stepped out of her building and onto Gansevoort. Thomas, waiting outside the Mercedes, ignored her as she approached. It couldn't be her.

"Hello, Thomas. Thank you for waiting," she greeted, channeling the voice of the famous Londoner.

"Miss Martel? Is that…you?" Thomas slapped his forehead in disbelief.

"It *was* me, Thomas. But now it's David Bowie. What do you think?"

"Um. I…can hardly believe what I'm seeing!"

"Well it's Halloween, after all. And nothing is quite what it seems, is it?"

"No, ma'am, it certainly isn't." Thomas moved to open the passenger door but Vienna interrupted.

"You go ahead, Thomas, I'm going to walk to Ruby's."

"But it's cold outside, ma'am."

"It's a short walk. If someone sees the car they'll assume I'm inside. But when Mr. Bowie arrives no one will have a clue. Do you understand, Thomas?"

"I think so, Miss Martel."

"So wait before you come in. I'll let Jerome know. Did you bring a mask?"

"Yes, ma'am." He reached into the front window and pulled out a Ronald Reagan mask.

"Good Lord," she mocked, shaking her head. "Okay, I'll see you at Ruby's. And don't park too close. Oh, and my purse, Thomas?"

"Yes, right here."

"Leave it for now." With that, Vienna turned and walked south on Washington and Thomas got in the car. By now the streets and sidewalks were crowded and noisy with costumed life. The parade was over and thousands of freakish marchers and onlookers had dispersed to bars, parties, stoops and empty lots with open bottles and joints. The cops couldn't be bothered unless there was a real problem. A stabbing, whatever. Vienna was recipient of a few catcalls and sideways glances as she walked. The gay boys *loved* Aladdin Sane. She smiled and waved and kept walking.

On Charles Lane, she could see the big Mercedes parked down the block from the club, close to West Street. She approached the car and nodded to Thomas, holding up a hand to say "Not just yet." In front of Ruby's there were dozens of people milling about, half of them in line to get in, the others smoking, plotting, hooking up. Some in costumes, some with painted faces, all with temporary identities. Sunday night in the Village. Vienna paused and surveyed the scene. Then another vehicle appeared, pulling up directly behind Thomas. A blue Galaxy. There were three men inside. Her heart began to race. *Will the police come?* she wondered. But no one could possibly know who she was. She walked decisively along the velvet rope to the head of the line.

"Sir, there is a line and you'll have to wait, like everyone else," Jerome instructed with impassive authority.

"Jerome, it's Vienna."

"Miss Martel?" he responded, genuinely confused.

"Yes…I've come in disguise you might say."

"We heard you might come, but I never never would have…"

"Well it's good to be here again. I've missed everyone!"

"Go right inside, and tell Ruby it's you."

As Jerome held the door for Vienna she breezily instructed, "Oh, and I've asked Thomas to join me as well, and if any of my friends ask for me please tell them to look for David Bowie."

"Of course, Mr. Bowie. Happy Halloween!"

Inside, the house was already filled—the lounge seating, the bar, the standing room in between. The music and raised voices were a cacophonous mix as "Sympathy For The Devil" howled from the dance floor. This was one night the Fire Marshals would pass on. Vienna snaked her way forward and found Ruby at his usual station, helplessly 'chaperoning' his party. She moved in close, inches from his ear. "Ruby, it's Vienna." Startled, he turned and believed he was staring at David Bowie. "It's me, Vienna," she repeated.

"My God! I would *never* have known that, Vienna!" He kissed her on both cheeks and pulled her close. "It is so good to know that you're all right, that you're here tonight!"

"I couldn't be anywhere else, my friend—it's Halloween, after all."

"Let's get you Champagne…then we'll make room on your banquette…" But Vienna waved a finger in protest.

"Not just yet, Ruby. Believe it or not, I'm going to the dance floor—I'm quite certain it's what my alter ego would do. If any one asks for me, please tell them to look for Mr. Bowie…and I'll see you in a bit."

"Absolutely, darling." With that, she touched Ruby's cheek and inched toward the dance floor, where the crowd bent to the will of the DJ.

Billy Idol, "Dancing With Myself." Perfect. And that's what Vienna did, in the center of the floor, her beaded clutch in hand, with the modestly seductive moves of an androgynous rock star. Boys and girls alike moved in to share a dance with this alluring beauty, and she accommodated them all, in their turn, with a faint smile.

Inside the blue Galaxy, the man in the back seat spoke. "If that's her car and driver, then she's inside, and I'll recognize her."

"Want me to come too?" Danny asked, hoping the answer was No.

"No, wait here for me. This can't get fucking messed up." Pavlou put on a mask—this time a generic clown face—and left the car. Thomas had noticed. He quickly removed his jacket and shirt, revealing a black tank top and the tattoo of a snake running from his left wrist to his bicep, roughly parallel with a three-inch scar on his forearm—vestiges of an earlier time in the Seton Hill neighborhood of Baltimore. He put on the Reagan mask and left the car quickly. Dimitri and Danny had been looking ahead, at Mika. Hadn't seen Thomas leave the car behind them, didn't think twice about a man in a wife beater wearing a mask. The street was filled with gay men. Jockeying to the front of the line, Pavlou was face-to-face with Jerome, who wasn't having it.

"You'll have to wait in line, buddy, like everyone else."

"Vienna asked me to meet her here…do you know if she's arrived?"

Jerome stamped the back of the clown's hand. "Look for David Bowie," he replied impatiently, waving him past. Moments later, Thomas was standing at the front of the line, but before Jerome could send him to the rear, he lifted his mask.

"Jerome, it's Thomas, Miss Martel's driver. She asked me to come inside tonight," he spoke with urgency in his voice.

"Yes, she said to expect you. Look for David Bowie." Thomas put his Reagan face back on and entered the fray.

Vienna moved fluidly to the rhythm of each song, from "Tainted Love" to "Sexual Healing," which the DJ had brought back from Belgium months before its release in the States. Her eyes were half shut, as if in an induced trance. At the art auctions, at the negotiating table, you never revealed your emotions. Remained impassive. But always alert. She noticed someone standing on the perimeter of the dance floor, not moving. Wearing a clown mask, a long coat, not moving. She ignored his gaze and kept turning slowly to the sensuous beat, the dancers pulsating around her. Then she spotted the Reagan mask near the back of the room. She nodded, acknowledging Thomas' presence. When the song transitioned to the opening bassline of "Under Pressure," she stopped dancing, bowing appreciatively to her admirers. And, walking past Thomas, she said without looking at him, "If a clown follows me, wait one minute before coming down." She continued, unhurriedly, to the basement steps, illuminated by candle sconces, which led to the two WC's. Vienna entered the one whose door was cracked open. There was a toilet with no stall, a urinal, a sink, more candle lighting. She left the door unlocked and faced the mirror above the sink. How beautiful she was in the low lighting. She rested her open clutch in the sink well and with her right hand gripped the Baretta firmly. The door opened and was quickly shut and locked by a man in a clown mask, whom she now saw in the mirror.

"I know who you are," he said. She turned to face him as he was pulling something from his coat pocket.

"I don't believe you do, sir," Vienna replied and fired into his forearm. He recoiled in pain, pulling his empty hand from the pocket, gripping his arm with the other. "But I'm quite sure I know who you are."

"Fucking bitch!" Pavlou shouted, angrily rushing Vienna before she could fire again. He pinned her against the brick wall by the sink, his upper body pushing the wounded forearm against her throat, his left hand gripping her wrist. "You saw something you shouldn't have the other night, lady." He couldn't have anticipated the sinewy strength of Vienna and Jordan's limbs. Her right knee jerked sharply into his groin, sending a bolt of pain up his spine. "Aggh…fucking…you are dead!" he screamed, pushing harder against her throat and effectively neutralizing the Baretta. Vienna was unable to speak or cry out as she gasped for breath.

On the other side of the door, Thomas knocked loudly, calling her name, shaking the handle. He backed up two feet and threw his entire weight, shoulder first, into the door. It flew open. Seeing Vienna pinned against the wall, he gripped his hands together over his head and brought them down decisively into the back of Pavlou's neck causing him to buckle to his knees. Thomas bent down, placed his neck in a stranglehold, pulled the injured arm behind his back and stood him upright. Vienna pulled the gun from Pavlou's coat pocket and lifted the mask from his head.

"This is the one I saw murder the Japanese man. And this is the gun." Thomas saw that Vienna had a gun in each hand.

"But you could have killed him!"

"He'd have very little to say if he were dead, wouldn't you agree, Thomas?" She put the mask back over Pavlou's head. "We'll walk him to the front of the house—there's no reason to make a scene, he'll just be another drunken clown at a Halloween party." She then addressed the murderer. "If you try anything, Thomas will break your arm and your neck simultaneously—and I *will* shoot you. I hope that's understood." Under the circumstances, he could neither speak nor nod, but offered no resistance. Vienna put both weapons in her clutch and they left the john, which two men in matching costumes immediately entered. Another bathroom break.

It was a challenge getting through the crowded dance floor and more so the narrow bar, but Bowie blithely led the way. At the front of the bar, she could see Ruby talking with a man in a grey suit. It was Detective Ronson, whom Vienna had never met and whom she now ignored.

"Ruby, may I speak with you?" she interrupted, with Thomas and their captive standing behind her.

"Vienna! This man is looking for you. He says he's with the police downtown. I hope there's no trouble tonight!" Ronson stared at the strange creature speaking with Ruby. She seemed familiar…because she so closely resembled the figure she had costumed to be? Perhaps.

"Miss Martel?" he probed.

"Yes, and you are?"

"Detective Ronson, from the Major Crime Unit downtown. You were the witness to a murder here last Thursday, is that correct?"

"Friday morning, to be precise. And this is the murderer." Vienna turned and pulled the mask over Mika's head. "Does he look familiar to you, detective?"

"Yes, but how…" Vienna cut him off, opening her clutch and pulling out the long-barreled weapon.

"And this is the gun he used to kill that man, and intended to use to kill me tonight." She handed over the weapon but kept her own concealed. "I'm sorry, I should have introduced my dear friend Thomas, who helped me greatly this evening." Ronson, attempting to take control, pulled handcuffs from his suit pocket.

"We'll take it from here, Miss Martel," he assured her, fastening the steel ring to the prisoner's free hand as Thomas released the other. Mika winced in pain. The detective noticed the wound. "What happened to his arm?"

"I had to defend myself, detective." Vienna quickly changed the subject. "And there may be others waiting for him outside."

"There are four officers on the street, holding two men who were sitting in a blue Ford Galaxy. They'll all be going to the 6th Precinct tonight. I'm sure we'll be in touch with you, ma'am."

"I've given my statement, sat with your sketch person and now delivered your murderer, detective," Vienna replied dismissively. "I'm sure these men will have stories to tell but, as you suggested, perhaps you can 'take it from here.'" Ronson left Ruby's, leading Mika Pavlou by his elbow. Vienna followed to see what she had hoped—two unmarked sedans down the street from the blue Galaxy, a man sitting in the back seat of each, a plain-clothed cop at the wheel, two plain-clothed cops waiting, backs against the cars. Officer Molina and Officer Huang. As she walked back into the club she saw the puzzled look on the gatekeeper's face. "Everything's fine, Jerome—there's always a bit of craziness on Halloween, isn't there?"

"Yes, indeed, Miss Vienna."

Vienna knew Detective Ronson would call Jordan in the morning. Mrs. Kellerman would positively identify the men who'd taken the Kandinsky painting from her home. There would be negotiations for further information. Time served for names and places.

"Is everything all right, Vienna?"

"Yes, Ruby, it's fine. And it's Halloween, perhaps we should celebrate."

"Something with bubbles?"

"You know me well. And you, Thomas?"

On Wednesday, November 3rd, Jordan flew to Paris, where he and Vienna would spend eight nights—it would be a much-needed respite from the tragedy and uncertainties of the previous days. And a chance for each to reconnect with their respective friends and colleagues in La Ville Lumière. Then, on the 12th, he would fly to Edinburgh for the opening of Jean-Michel's show at Fruitmarket Gallery. He'd said he might, but it would still be a great surprise for the artist-provocateur. On his answering machine Jordan left word of his travel dates, that he would be staying in Paris in the apartment of a friend, would be checking daily for messages, looked forward to returning to New York City on the 16th. But left no overseas contact information.

On Tuesday, November 2nd, Vienna recorded a message on her answering machine informing any who might call that she would be traveling Upstate for the next few weeks, would unfortunately not be able to check her messages but looked forward to returning after Thanksgiving. "…Please enjoy your holiday and I'll see you after." She then phoned Thomas to tell him she was going away for a few weeks, to stay with a friend on Lake George and take a much-needed break from the city. No, she wouldn't need a ride—she'd take the bus or train and just do some reading. And he would have time to focus on his studies. "But I expect to be back on the 28th. And what will you do for Thanksgiving, Thomas?"

Thomas felt a pang of sadness at the thought that Miss Martel would be away for so long, a feeling he hadn't experienced before. "Um, I won't have any classes that week…I guess my sister and I will drive to Baltimore early and spend it with my mom and some of the other relatives. I hadn't thought about it, though." There was an awkward pause as Vienna lingered over an emotion she hadn't felt, or acknowledged before. The way that a part of Thomas might somehow be inside of her now. The possibility that she could miss him, even for a brief few weeks.

"Well, hmm. Why don't we have an early Thanksgiving together, Thomas, just you and I? Do you have plans this evening?"

"I…no, I don't." Stumbling for words, stumbling for thoughts.

"Pick me up at seven then—I'd love to show you a wonderful little bistro in the Village, my treat. Would that be all right?"

"Yes, um, that would be fine, Miss Martel—but please, uh, we have to go Dutch."

"As you wish. And tonight you'll have to call me 'Vienna,' Thomas."

"Yes, Miss Vienna."

"Just 'Vienna.'"

Letters to the Editor
of *The East Hampton Star*

As noted in the Foreward, it is the policy of *The East Hampton Star* to publish *every* signed letter submitted. This idiosyncratic editorial position, in effect since the 1950s, quickly became a psychogenic discharge valve to me, and I took unfair advantage I fear, writing letters of 1,000 to 2,000 words in length, on any viewpoint, fantasy or personal humiliation I cared to share.

The Star has been under the ownership of the Rattray family since 1935 and its editors a succession of dedicated family members. My first letters, starting in 1998, were addressed to Mrs. Helen S. Rattray (who remains the paper's publisher). In 2001 her son, David E. Rattray, assumed the role of editor and it was he who would be forced to endure my lengthy air castles, digressions and yes, soul-searching, all the while attending to other more pressing news of the day, I am certain.

The letters that follow were selected because they still made me smile or laugh out loud, or weep. Some have been edited for length (you're welcome) or grammar. That said, all were published in *The East Hampton Star,* and for that, I thank the editor.

February 18, 1999

To The Editor
The East Hampton Star

Dear Mrs. Rattray:

News of the scarcity of burial sites in the East Hampton Township, as recently reported on the front page of the New York Times, and subsequently examined in your newspaper, will certainly strike a poignant chord for a generation coming-of-a-certain-age, of long-time and part-time residents alike—those who have presumed that they, and their children, and their children's children would one day be interred near the resting places of their parents and grandparents, as well as those "outsiders" who have traveled far from their own birthplaces to call this beautiful community home. And the three-decades-long trend toward the increasing popularity of cremation has apparently had little effect on the pressure impacting real estate for the deceased.

The problem, of course, is the historically low turnover rate in cemeteries. Most people remain where they are buried for what seems like an eternity; you seldom hear of opportunities for plot acquisition arising from relocation or subletting. ("Deceased cubist sculptor moving to Normandy Coast indefinitely; will sell lovely Main Street Amagansett grave site 'as is' for $29,500 or best offer. Steps to beach, train, Farmers Market. Will consider suitable swap. No brokers.")

Whether for religious or personal reasons, the matter of one's post mortem is a highly emotional topic for many people. And the absence of attractive options will only serve to make it more so in the years ahead. My own father died unexpectedly in the first year of his retirement, on the Gulf Coast of Florida. My mother didn't know what to do— she, like her three children, was ill-prepared for the unholy moment. We buried Dad in Clearwater. Less than a year later Mom moved back to Rochester, "so I could go to the weddings and the funerals ... and see the leaves turn again." Two years after that, she married one of her childhood sweethearts—a good story for some other time. That was almost twenty-five years ago. Now, Mom talks about someday bringing Dad back to Rochester, to rest beside she and my stepfather. Pretty sweet. These things stay in people's hearts, and they're of greater import in that region of the being than the mind can properly capture.

I myself have strolled by the charming cemetery at the corner of Main Street and Atlantic Avenue on my way home from the Jitney drop and cast an admiring glance at the peaceful site. It appears fully occupied. I don't see any "For Sale" signs. No "Open House Sunday" signs. But I sometimes imagine that there's certainly room for one more, somewhere between the ancient markers. That's where I want to be buried—posthumously, of course. Easy access for my friends, who might want to throw a little Chardonnay on the grass in my memory. (I promise, it won't be wasted!) For the convenience of my loved ones and executors, I've even planned the headstone. (No marble, please—local limestone only.) "Lyle John Greenfield. 1947–2068. I'm not here—did you try the beach?" Simple. And no 'Thanks' necessary—it was fun!

In truth, at a certain time in your life it is hard not to think of death from time to time. I, for one, love it here. This planet. And I'm certain that I'll miss me terribly when I'm gone. But these reports that there may be no place to go when we're gone are exasperating! Has anyone thought about the site where they're not going to allow a new supermarket to be built? Traffic patterns wouldn't be impacted, and there'd be plenty of room for generations to come. The fact that the area is commercially zoned may seem like a bummer to persons of deep religious faith, but with discreet signage and tasteful landscaping, the property could present the appearance of blissful tranquility for ages to come. In keeping with traditions of nomenclature well-established in our community, I would name

this acreage Finhampton. But at the time when fundraising must be initiated for its development, it might be a good idea for The East Hampton Star to sponsor a contest to come up with a name. Raise awareness. Make folks feel like part of the process. People with historic generational ties to the community, and celebrities, should be offered an incentive to secure plots in the new cemetery, just to get things moving. A 'groundbreaking' prize awarded to the family of the very first body in. And something at the Talkhouse afterward! There are tons of ideas that can help make the new site work, and make it fun at the same time.

Another possible site—and a meaningful one to weekend residents of the Hamptons—is the lovely grassy strip that divides the east and westbound lanes of Rt. 27 between Manorville and Southampton. Strategically placed overpasses, approved, of course, by the Department of Highways, would make access a breeze—a huge plus for weekend guests of the deceased who might want to pay their respects before gassing up, grocery shopping, visiting Pumpkin Town, etc. And I feel comfortable in saying that this site would provide virtually limitless availability of plots—at least until 2006. Dare I suggest that this resting place be called "Sunset Byway?" Or "The R.I.P Lane." (It might be a good idea to get Dan's

191

Papers involved. Maybe they'd like to sponsor a "Run For The Graves."

You think that some of these ideas have been frivolous, don't you? And yet everything you've been reading over the past two weeks has forced you to contemplate the matter on some level, hasn't it? Maybe you've only said to yourself, 'Thank God I've made arrangements to be cremated, and my ashes thrown into the surf. No one need be burdened with my lifeless remains.' But not everybody wants to be fodder for a Dustbuster. I will tell you a story that illustrates this human fact in an achingly human way.

In early November of 1996 a dear friend and business associate of mine passed away. I will call him Robert. He died of heart failure, in his mid-seventies. Robert was a long-time, part-time resident of Amagansett, and no place on the surface of this planet meant more to him than the shores of our hamlet, where he strolled and fished and swam and pondered life's unfathomable questions for the greater part of his adult life. Following his demise, Robert's Last Will and Testament was read by his executor, another dear friend who is a well-established surgeon at a well known Manhattan hospital. It was Robert's wish, as written in his Will, that he be buried on the beach, in the Walking Dunes between Indian Wells and Two Mile Hollow. A very

beautiful place that is reasonably safe from rising storm tides. And very, very expensive real estate, I might add.

Dr. Tom (as I'll call him) and Robert had actually worked out a plan that would make it possible for Robert's oceanfront dream to become reality following his death. So simple, yet I tremble still just thinking about it. Tremble with exhilaration, I suppose. Here's what the plan was, and how it came to pass: The relevant portion of Robert's Will, the portion in question, was actually an addendum to the actual Will, which specified that Robert would be cremated in Dr. Tom's hospital, his ashes released into the sea, etc. With this document, and the authority vested in the good doctor by virtue of his stature at the hospital, and of his executorial position, Dr. Tom was able to arrange the completion of the documentation attesting to the cremation of our friend Robert, prior to said actual cremation. (I confess now that this required a cash payment of several thousand dollars to two individuals employed in the crematorium, who were moved by the doctor's verbal explanation, and his assurance of personal indemnification. These fine individuals also assisted Dr. Tom in removing Robert's body, in his body bag, to the back of an idle ambulance where it was placed upon a gurney and covered with a white sheet. Dr. Tom, behind the wheel of the vehicle, exited the building. According to signed documents, Robert had been cremated. God rest his ashes.)

It was, of course, very late at night. "Night shift" at the hospital, so to speak. Dr. Tom and Robert now drove directly to a gas station on Tenth Avenue—one that had a tire pump on the side of the building, just out of the flow of customer traffic. That's where three of us were waiting, in another close friend's Jeep Cherokee, rear end facing the pump, "filling" the tires. The doctor backed in close to us so that the two vehicles were tail-to-tail.

A station attendant asked if he needed any help, but Dr. Tom said, "No, it's no trouble, thank you." It took less than thirty seconds to get Robert in the back of the Cherokee. We pulled out of the station moments later, followed moments after that by the ambulance. And twenty minutes later the hospital vehicle was back in the hospital garage and Dr. Tom was sitting in the back seat of the Cherokee, heading toward the Midtown Tunnel with his best friends, probably wishing he hadn't come of age in the Sixties.

On a weeknight in November, at 1:30 in the morning, it doesn't take that long to drive to Amagansett. Even keeping close to the speed limit—and there was no question

that we would—we were heading south on Indian Wells Highway toward the beach by 3:15. I must say, it was a lovely evening. Chilly, but no breeze, and every star in the Heavens shimmering right above us. The driver—I'll call him Jeff—threw the Jeep into 4-wheel mode and we hit the sand without a slip. Jeff drove slowly to the west, toward Two Mile Hollow, staying close to the dune. Do you want me to try to describe how nervous we felt inside? Impossible. Even with surf rods laying on the roof rack, we knew we must appear guilty of something. Maybe of burying a friend on the beach. You're not even supposed to bury your dog in your own back yard, you know. It's in the Health Codes. A quarter mile or so later I shouted out, "Up there, let's do it there."

"Why there?" Dr. Tom asked, puzzled by my sudden revelation.

"There's a big log there—look. It'll be our personal grave marker!"

It made sense to everyone immediately. There, at the edge of the dune grass, lay a giant silver-white log whose girth must have been six feet. Half buried in the sand, it wasn't going anywhere for a good long time. Jeff turned left toward the ocean and backed up beside the log, toward the beach grass. Felix—or so I shall name him—began removing the rods from the roof. It was his assignment to stake them in the sand near the surf. We were there to fish, that had to be apparent. But we needn't have worried—no one was around. No lights were shining from the gracious homes, no head-lights coming or going on the beach. It was just us, the five of us.

Jeff opened the back end of the Jeep, and there was Robert, zipped up in his bag. It sounds gruesome, doesn't it? But if I possessed a greater gift, I could convey to you the solemnity and joy of this moment. We've all buried a loved one, all been to the ceremonies and the services. We just all haven't buried someone in the dunes late at night. I removed four shovels from the back of the Jeep and handed them to the guys. Dr. Tom removed a lovely wool blanket—one of Robert's. I then grabbed a bottle of Champagne and four stems from a side compartment. Leaving Robert behind for the moment, we walked into the dune grass to locate just the right spot to lay our friend to rest. It turned out to be about a hundred fifty feet from the Jeep.

Stabbing the shovels upright in the sand, and leaving the blanket and Champagne where we stood, we went back for Robert. Lifting him carefully from the vehicle, the four of us walked slowly back to his final resting place. In our chosen pocket of the dune, we dug a hole for Robert. It took no more than fifteen minutes.

The Champagne was opened and poured, and very fine words were spoken of our friend by each of us. Then we lowered him into his bed, which was not so easy. Dr. Tom unzipped the bag partially, revealing Robert's pale head and shoulders. He then picked up the blanket, which we helped him outstretch and place over Robert's body. Another toast to our dearly departed friend. And the grave was covered, and the sand above it brushed over gently. We walked backward toward the Jeep, crouched over, covering our tracks carefully.

It was very strange, driving in the early commuter traffic, back to Manhattan, following the night that we were leaving behind. No one slept a wink on the road. We ate ravenously at a diner not far from the Midtown Tunnel and made plans to have brunch in East Hampton the following Saturday. And to take a walk on the beach afterward.

Resolving the issue of burial sites, and how to provide them to an expanding small community, and how to regulate their availability— the "real estate" part of it—will inevitably end up being about politics and money. Too bad, because none of it will address the other stuff. You know, the "resting in peace" thing.

To a long, happy life,
Lyle Greenfield

———— ⋯ ————

January 20, 2003

To The Editor
The East Hampton Star

Dear Mr. Rattray:

I'm sorry I didn't finish this letter in time to make a recent deadline. Unfortunately, I became quite sick to my stomach and decided it would be a good idea to just stay in the bathroom (I have cable and a flatscreen there, so I took in the Godfather Trilogy).

That was a lie. Actually, I'd flown to Miami that weekend to visit my daughter and grandson. She'd asked me if I wanted to see Joseph sing on Sunday with the other second and third graders in a church service performance at his new school—a private Lutheran grade school. (He had just transferred there from a terribly over-crowded public school where his teacher spent the entire day yelling at the restless kids.) I said "Absolutely!" We arrived a little late and were thus led to seats in the very front of the hall, which turned out to be a large chapel attached to the school itself. And the kids' performances turned out to be part of a total-involvement mass. I was raised Catholic, so the only parts of this that were familiar to me were the readings and the sermons…and the announcements.

As you know, I can be a bit cynical at times, but I'm a fatal sucker for innocence and romance.

The kids broke my heart. Seventy or so of them. Racially mixed? Indeed. Mostly African-American, plenty of Hispanic, a handful of Caucasians—beautiful faces performing for their proud parents. My eyes scanned back and forth across the chorus, and I fought the tears. My grandson saw me looking at him and he smiled awkwardly, hiding for a moment behind the head of the kid in front of him— then peeking out again. Praise the Lord!

Then there was a "special treat." We would all bear witness to a baptism! A young couple with three children and a newborn stepped up to the altar and approached one of the senior ministers, who happened to be the grandfather of the children. And this minister took the little baby in his hands and showed him to all of us. The proud parents stood by. And the minister said unto us, "This wonderful couple has brought little Zachary here today to be joined with Jesus Christ our Lord. As you know, this little baby arrived in the world with sin. The original sin we are all of us born with. And that is why Jesus gave His life for us—to lose our original sin and be given the opportunity to join Him by the side of the Heavenly Father…" (and so forth).

And then the minister spoke with the other children, telling them that they must pledge to see to the spiritual well-being of Zachary—in the event that their parents died, or drifted from the Church. And I thought, 'Holy shit, this is crazy! This baby wasn't born with any sin—he's a totally sin-free boy and God loves him unconditionally.' Then the minister brought the baby over to the baptismal font, dipped a cup into the water and, pouring it onto Zachary's head said, "I baptize you, Zachary, in the name of the Father, the Son and the Holy Spirit..." etc., etc. He held the baby up for us to see, then handed him to the proud parents. Done. Zachary was in. And sound asleep. The baby was with Christ and thus, with good prospects.

I basically let go of my own Catholicism shortly after reaching adulthood (whenever, if ever, that was), having pondered the notion that un-baptized persons would never see the face of God. It didn't make sense, and couldn't be justified with the notion of a "just" god. Thus, my sense of enchantment with, and detachment from this baptism was palpable. Someday, I imagined, Zachary might have to think about these things for himself. Good luck, Zach. And God be with you.

A recent issue of Newsweek blared the headline "Bush & God... How Faith Changed His Life and Shapes His Presidency." The photograph of our President on the cover, hands folded earnestly in prayer, was actually frightening to me. Oh yes, I pray...to whomever or whatever's out there—when the plane is flying through turbulence, when my daughter is traveling, when a loved one has fallen ill...I pray.

Our President has told us that he prays, too. He prays for strength, he prays for wisdom...he prays for peace. That's what he said during his prime time press conference in the East Room of the White House just over a week ago. Why does that scare the shit out of me? Because I don't trust faith-based calls to arms. I have a picture in my head: Jesus is handcuffed, with his arms across the front of his torso. The sleeves of his robe are long, so we can't see that his wrists are locked together. He is being pushed along, behind an entourage of the righteous, who are marching up a hill. He is told to look straight ahead, not to speak. It is not in his nature to speak out...to admonish those who push and prod him forward.

In this same issue of Newsweek, the columnist Anna Quindlen has "The Last Word" (thank God). And in her "last words" she worries that "Our history books say we fight for freedom. They don't say anything about going to battle to save face... What is required of a nation that is...the greatest democracy on earth at this moment...? That it must live up to its principles, not down to its enemies." Millions of people in this country, and tens of millions more around the world agree deeply with this. And still, we do not hear a vibrant debate concerning this issue among our elected officials in this great democracy. What the hell is going on?

The most recent issue of Time trumpets the words "Bound For Baghdad" on its cover, over a picture of Army General Tommy Franks. And this banner sidebar: "Foldout Map—A Guide To The Battlefield." War? This is Spring Break 2003! And here's a must-read guide to the hot places we'll be hitting before they get too hot to hit—so don't miss 'em! And inside this same issue is a photograph of a chaplain baptizing a Marine in a pool of water somewhere in the Middle East during a "service" at Life Support Area 7. The headline reads, "Our soldiers have already asked for forgiveness for what we're going to do to the Iraqi army."

How did my country get to this place? What are we doing here? What happened to what we stand for, and the "last resort" we require before unleashing our terrible swift sword in the name of justice? Has it been traded down, to a baser instinct, by elected "officials" who don't fully understand what America is defined by? If I were Bin Laden, hiding out in my little TV videotaping cave studio, I'd be pretty self-satisfied right now. Watching America's relationships

around the world imploding. Like a big building. It makes me ache inside.

The other night I was up pretty late, channel-surfing through my sleeplessness. I stopped at CNN— the "Showdown Iraq" channel. And here was the story I landed on: It has been discovered that the "documents" proving Iraq's purchase of plutonium from an African nation for the purpose of developing nuclear weapons were forged. They were not real documents—a discovery made shortly after our President referred to them as further proof of the need to disarm Iraq. I would have assumed this would be a front-page story. So where was it?

Just a few days ago the father of our president, the senior President Bush, gave a speech at Tufts University in Massachusetts. In his address, he sounded words of caution against unilateral action on the part of the United States. He inferred that the case against Saddam was "less clear" than in 1991. Objectives were "a little fuzzier today," he said. You might have missed this—after all, it wasn't reported in the Times, The Wall Street Journal, National Public Radio. It was reported in The Times UK.

It's difficult to argue about what might or might not happen "down the road," isn't it? Incredibly well-briefed people are standing around a table right now. On the table is a great relief map—with the Middle East in the middle, and Africa, and Europe (we're not on this map). These well-briefed people are talking about "the big picture," how people and oil and power will flow differently after the change is made. These people know things that we don't know. Maybe they are right, and all the "peaceniks," as we're being called again, will be proven wrong. I'm no sore loser—I'll be happy to be proven wrong! Still, I'm troubled greatly by the way we've unfolded this map.

When a U.S. diplomat in the United States Embassy in Athens quit recently, protesting "Our fervent pursuit of war," it was buried news. When the A.F.L.-C.I.O Executive Council unanimously approved a resolution urging the president to embrace a "broad multilateral approach to Iraq," the administration accused it of Democratic Party politics. When millions gathered around the country recently to say "Let the inspections work," the president's response was that he didn't base his decisions on "focus groups." I'm very interested in knowing what exactly he bases his decisions on,

this being a democracy and all, so to speak.

If this all ended tomorrow, in some unexpectedly peaceful disarmament, then the party in power could take credit for "applying the necessary pressure" that made it impossible for Saddam to continue with his "deceptions" a moment longer. A great majority of people in this country would applaud that "victory" over one-third of the "axis of evil." And the Democrats would struggle, again, to find their footing on the political landscape. Yet I fully believe that a majority of the world's citizens would hold us in contempt—and in fear—for wielding our might without their support, even against their will. When Vice President Cheney said that "9/11 changed everything," and suggested that the rest of the world may not fully understand that right now, my greatest fear was that what changed was what the United States now stands for. The "freedom" that our president so frequently refers to is something that must be won on the merits—not just at the point of a missile, or at the close of a payout.

Sincerely,
Lyle Greenfield

—— ··· ——

February 10, 2003

To The Editor
The East Hampton Star

Dear Mr. Rattray:

This letter could have been prevented, you're well aware of that. The ink could have been used to print other words or images— words or images that might have been more useful to your readership, and to the community. But now the letter is begun and there is no way that it can be stopped, except by my untimely death. Yet very few people know where I am right now, and those who do would not harm me. And my breathing is relatively steady— so the letter cannot be stopped.

Why am I writing this letter? What's the difference? The main thing is, the letter is being written, four or five people will read it (a couple of my readers have returned from their vacations) and, based upon reasonable assumptions concerning circulation of The East Hampton Star (local and out-of-town), it will consume several pounds of paper or the equivalent of a large log. So, apologies to the tree from which the log was extracted.

In truth, the letter is being written for several reasons. First, to voice my disapproval with the tone of the letter itself. Given the gravity of some of the subject matter which the letter will touch upon, it seems inappropriate that I would stoop to sarcasm and name-calling for the purpose of fortifying a political or philosophical position. Hopefully, this "preemptive" attack on the letter will yield a better letter.

Also, the letter is being written, of course, to express my continuing dismay at the posture my government has taken with regard to the "resolution" of certain international crisis. In spite of my initial belief, just two weeks ago, that the president was considering a more measured, diplomacy-driven approach to Iraq, as I had urged in my letter of January 20, all present evidence suggests that he is hell-bent on the precipitation of war. This despite a growing outcry of opposition from the citizens of his own country, from important allies in Europe and Asia, and in spite of cautionary pleas for patience by Kofi Annan, Secretary General of the United Nations. The president's position is now being "pitched" so aggressively by Secretary of State Colin Powell, Defense Secretary Donald Rumsfeld and National Security Advisor Condoleezza Rice it's beginning to sound like an infomercial. (Maybe they'll bring in Tony Robbins to help close the deal.)

I'm beginning to calm down a bit. It would probably be a good idea to end the previous two digressions with an anecdote. (It would probably be a better idea to get to the main point of this letter, but who cares?) A few weeks ago I was heading downtown in a cab to join friends who were having a celebration at some little club on Orchard Street (in honor of a dear friend who'd just been hired in a very high-level position at a large soft drink company).

My cab driver turned to me and said, "Ees da music too loud?" And I said it was fine. He proceeded to tell me that it was Duke Ellington and Ella Fitzgerald, and he loved this music more than the modern stuff. Then—I swear to God—a black guy (How would I know if he's 'African-American'?) pulled up beside us in a very big SUV. The two drivers talked to each other like they were friends. So I assumed they were. My guy turns up his jazz...and the other guy turns up his truck-thumping hip-hop track. They're both smiling, and then the light turns and the SUV speeds away. And I say, "Was that your buddy?"

And he says, "I don't know the guy—but I hate that hip-hop shit! That's all my daughter listens to, and the lyrics are, you know, disgusting!"

I couldn't tell from his hack license where he was from, so I asked. "Madagascar," he said. Where's that? "In the Indian Ocean, Southeast of Africa." Jesus. There are 400,000 Madagascans in the U. S. His wife is one. They have two daughters. They all speak Madagascan...but the oldest daughter, "She doesn't like to."

Why would I tell a little story like that? Because I just liked the interaction between these two men in their cars, sharing their music... like offering a stick of gum, here in America, here in New York City, where over one hundred languages are spoken. We are the great melting pot. We defend and protect the oppressed. We defend our borders. If our friends are attacked, we will fight for them. We don't start wars because we are "sick and tired" of somebody's lies. We better watch our ass...we better be careful about what we think we're doing "in the name of God." We need our friends as much as they need us.

(If you are presently employed, or have laundry to do, or need to sharpen the blades of your lawnmower just in case Spring comes this year, you should probably skip the next several paragraphs. Hey, don't mention it!)

On Saturday afternoon I stopped into the Pottery Barn on Broadway near Lincoln Center. I like to watch young, attractive couples pick out bedding and accessories for the bathroom. It just makes me feel good inside. So, I was wandering around the street-level showroom, checking out the furniture, lamps, serving trays, etc., when over the in-store sound system the song "True" by Spandau Ballet started playing. Within seconds, I began to cry…cry uncontrollably. I didn't know what was happening to me—it's a beautiful song and all, but something just snapped, and suddenly I was lying face down on a queen-size sleigh bed, sobbing like a baby. One of the sales "consultants" rushed over, stroked me on the back of the head and asked me if everything was all right. Turning towards her, I tried to collect myself, and slowly stopped heaving. Her name tag said Debra. I said, "Debra, have you seen the Saturday Times?"

"Not yet," she replied, "I've been working here all day. Why do you ask?" I told Debra that, practically buried inside the first section, was a story under the headline "Britain Admits That Much of Its Report on Iraq Came From Magazines." And I elaborated that the article referred to a 19-page report published by the British government, praised by Colin Powell in his speech to the United Nations, and heralded as an "up-to-date and unsettling assessment by British intelligence …of Iraq's security apparatus" was, in fact, largely plagiarized from several non-secret articles—some published over six years ago! And we are using this "intelligence" to bolster our case for attacking Iraq! "Debra, don't you find that unsettling?" I cried.

"Yes, I do, Sir," she said, "but I need to assist some customers in 'shower curtains' downstairs…and you need to get off this bed and seek a different kind of assistance elsewhere." Quite a few people had gathered around the bed at this point—some running their hands over the sheets and squeezing the duvet. I respected Debra's suggestion, and left the store (not before picking up six Bordeaux glasses, however, which were on sale for $20).

You know I love your newspaper, don't you? All of this would never fit on a sandwich board, or I'd walk around town with it. And, in spite of my frustrations with their apparent ambivalence over the White House's posture, I need The Times, too (No, I do not wish to receive home delivery, so don't bother calling.). So, let us turn to the last page of the Sunday Magazine. It's called "Lives." There are four photographs of a woman and her family from Coppell, Texas. After she was diagnosed with breast cancer, she required a lumpectomy, then a mastectomy. Her 51-year old husband lost his $100,000-a-year job, and months later found something—for $11-an-hour. The family had to give up their health insurance after the premium jumped to $832 a month. The woman has been doing some clerical work…and she begs in the street. Her six-year-old daughter doesn't understand what's happening. Her mom had to stop chemotherapy because the money ran out, and the family might lose their home.

So, Mr. President, in conclusion…let's see, where was I?

Sincerely,
Lyle Greenfield

——— ··· ———

May 21, 2006

To The Editor
The East Hampton Star

Dear Mr. Rattray:

I'm writing to you because I'm disturbed, and at the same time, unable to pinpoint the source of the disturbance. I believe you could help me by allowing me to examine several of the disturbing possibilities in the pages of your newspaper. I will then be able to read about myself, as written by myself, and perhaps glean an insight into the unrest and pain I feel every day. And maybe the nine (eight?) readers who have in the past read my letters will read this one…will reach out to me, and share their insights into my disturbance. So thank you in advance. And thank you in retrospect.

I hope you had a wonderful Mothers' Day. I don't know if you watch Channel 2 News, or read The Daily News, but the story about the small, shirtless man who was found lodged in the chimney of a building on the West Side of Manhattan the morning of Mother's Day—that was my sister's building. She and her partner were awakened at 7 a.m. by

the faint cry of a human voice. They thought it was a cry for help, but could not identify the source of the sound. Disturbing! They thought it might be coming from the adjoining building—possibly an elderly person who had fallen down (we all know the story) and couldn't get up.

Finally, they called 911 and explained the quandary. Within moments, two New York City police detectives arrived on the scene and went through the house with the ladies. They too heard the voice, but could not identify its source. Dominique then went into the basement, to check for a possible break-in there. And the voice was even louder, though there was no evidence of wrongdoing. The cops came downstairs, too, and determined that the voice was coming from the chimney in their boiler room. They then called in "back-up"—the fire department and EMS. Within ten minutes, according to my sister, there were "sixteen burly men" in their basement, and six vehicles— police cars, fire truck, EMS vehicles—outside on the street.

The fire chief asked the ladies to turn off the boiler, which they did.

They detached the aluminum flue pipe that vented the boiler into the brick chimney. Then the firemen proceeded to bash the bricks of the chimney with their pickaxes until there was a large enough opening to get a head inside and look up with a flashlight. And there, within arms' reach, were the dangling legs of a little man. They pulled him out of the chimney and onto the floor. He was covered in soot. Spoke very little English. Apparently had burglarized the building next door and, running along the 4-story rooftop, attempted to make his escape by crawling into my sister's chimney. He then slid down the chimney only to discover that there was no way out. Based upon the time of the burglary the night before, the detectives believe he spent about eight hours stuck at the bottom of the chimney. Disturbing.

As Dominique said, "Imagine if it was winter, and the furnace had been on to heat the building! Imagine if we'd gone away for the weekend!" Disturbing! One of the police detectives told them that they should be proud because they had "saved a life." He also urged them to contact their attorney, in case the guy in the chimney decided to sue…maybe because of the chimney opening. Even as I write that, I'm smashing a glass goblet into my forehead in disbelief! Maybe it's not helping me to write this, Mr. Rattray. Why can't you

respond to this letter in real time? Next time, can I come to your house to write my letter? I want milk and peanut butter cookies!

Channel 2 arrived on the scene before 10 a.m. and the reporter went up to the roof with the video crew, then into the basement, made the obvious reference to Santa Claus in describing the burglar's escape plan. Fox news wanted to come at 2 p.m., but my sister told them that we were having Mother's Day brunch then, and they would have to come after 3:30. I love Joan—she's so practical. She even told the Times they would have to wait till later because she and Dominique were going out to a movie! The reporter said, "The story will be 10 hours old by then!" And she said, "Hey, this happened 4 hours ago—where were you?!"

So now, at 12:30, it's Mothers' Day brunch time with the ladies—with my eighty-six-year-old mother from Rochester (still smoking Marlboro Reds), my daughter and grandson from Miami, me, Joan and Dominique. Fantastic. And, of course, we all went into the basement to examine the extrication scene—the hole in the busted chimney, the brick and rubble on the floor. Joan had made a beautiful avocado dip and a salad from their rooftop garden…and I made scrambled eggs. Yummy! Then Joan said, "Oh, yeah, and about an hour after they took the little soot-covered man away, the fire truck came back, and the fire chief came in and issued us a citation for a chimney and boiler violation—caused when they disconnected the flue and broke open the chimney with their pick axe!" What?! "But he said it was 'standard procedure;' we would have to take personal responsibility for curing the violation within fifteen days, at our expense, and then sue the City of New York to get our money back."

I involuntarily spit out my eggs after hearing that. Still, part of what is disturbing about that footnote to the chimney man saga is that it is so breathtakingly incongruous that it makes you—or me at least—love New York even more! Maybe this is a bad sign about certain fixations or impulses that we want to regard as "love-based" but which, in fact, are based in our own self-delusion, or even dementia. This possibility is upsetting to me.

Now, I don't have an opportunity to read The Star every week, because obviously I don't have the time to write a letter to The Star every week. But a very good friend of mine, someone who does read The Star every week, told me about a story that appeared in the paper recently, concerning a cat that was found hanged from a train trestle in East Hampton. I found that to be disturbing. And yet, for someone who reads The New York Times with some frequency, with its daily reports of car bombings in Iraq, genocide in Africa, random sidewalk shootings…the hanging cat story seemed almost like—please forgive me—lite news! Like 'Lite on the Bays.' "Here's an interesting item, people!" I don't feel good about myself, thinking this way. I guess that's why we're going through this process, Mr. Rattray—unless you have destroyed the letter before printing, in which case I'm just undressing for my laptop. Now I am sad, and lonely.

But allow me to continue, I beg you, on a somewhat still-more-morbid thread. I am told, on absolutely solid authority, that a man in our community was found dead in his home. To be more specific, on my street in Amagansett. And I am told that, based upon the condition in which the body was discovered, he had probably been dead for at least two months. Yet no one to my knowledge has ever seen an item about this in the news—local or otherwise. Am I missing something? The whole business is, of course, disturbing. And don't get me wrong, the hanging cat thing is very disturbing. But what is news, anyway? Gardening tips for May tubers? Flounder movement in the harbor? The hanging cat? Maybe there is a local news protocol. I'm searching myself for answers—but all I'm coming up with is a Metrocard and a post-it with my cell phone number on it. Maybe I'll call me later.

This very morning I was watching CNN (I know, why wasn't I watching "Barney?"). A report began under the heading, "Is Your Town Prepared For Disaster?" Meaning, what if a hurricane or tornado hit your town? Ready, or not ready? For a Category 5, or a Super Twister. Who knows? This subject had actually come up during dinner at my friend's house on Bluff Road not two weeks ago. My little house is down in the dunes. I'm building a small guest room there, in case I get a new friend. I expressed my concern that maybe our area is due to be hit with the Big One. I mean, it's been decades, right? What if a Cat 5 hurricane hits us on a full moon, at high tide? The sea surges over the dune, the oceanfront houses are ruined, standing precariously on their pressure-treated stilts, and houses like mine are flooded and destroyed. Where would my guest sleep then? And what would I do? Can I stay at your place, Mr. Rattray? I'll bring wine.

And then it hit me, like a perfect storm! After many years of anecdotal observation, we would have to agree that most tornados, and most hurricanes, will target a trailer park before any other part of a region. You almost believe that they love trailer parks—maybe

because it's just so easy to wreck them—even for a Category 2. What I suggested to the other guests at the dinner table was this: We should build a decoy trailer park, ideally somewhere west of East Hampton. Possibly on the western side of Southampton. (They have more flexible zoning rules in Southampton.) I further suggested that the park would contain between 50 and 70 empty trailers, so when things really got bad, it wouldn't matter that the roofs blew off, or there was massive flooding and looting—no lives lost, nothing to steal. When the hurricane was still approaching our coastline, what would the "eye" of the storm see? The trailer park! And that is exactly what the heading would be. And, BAM! By the time the storm realized that there was nobody in the trailer park, it would already be heading toward Southold! Too late to turn around and hit us in East Hampton!

Strangely, Mr. Rattray—as disturbing as it is to imagine new trailer homes being destroyed by a vengeful storm, the idea of saving lives and property values in our community actually makes me feel a little better. Thank you.

And you're welcome,
Lyle Greenfield

———— ⋯ ————

August, 2007

To The Editor
The East Hampton Star

Dear Mr. Rattray,

You knew that I turned sixty (60) at the end of July, but you did not send me a birthday card, or call to say "Guess who's getting old now, sucker!" (I didn't expect or want any gifts. I don't need anything, with the possible exception of better use of my faculties and a drip-bag filled with steel-fermented Chardonnay.)

You also knew my mother passed away in May, but, again, you did not send a card expressing your condolences, or call to say "Gosh… uh…sorry." Maybe you figured, 'Well, there goes another one of his readers…there should be seven left now.' Very funny, Mr. Rattray. My mother did not even read my letters. She thought they were stupid. She read the Rochester Democrat & Chronicle, and romance novels. And, to her credit, The New Yorker. She was a powerful and funny woman who outlived two great husbands (the first of whom helped conceive me, without an instruction manual), both of whom she said she was ready to join in Heaven. One in the smoking section, the other in non-smoking. She smoked a pack of Marlboro Reds a day till she was about eighty-five. We are wimps by comparison. I dedicate this letter to my mother—which probably places

the future of my soul at considerable risk. Forgive me, Mom!

I'm sure you read the article in The New York Times on Friday reporting on recent scientific experiments in which out-of-body experiences had been induced in "ordinary, healthy people." The article was largely based upon studies published just a few days ago in the journal Science. If you did not read this article, I encourage you to leave your body and read it now, because it is fascinating. (I am actually writing this letter from outside my body—partly from the deck, where the beach plum leaves are rustling in a light breeze, and partly from the ceiling of my dining room, from which position I can view my chiseled torso and the balding spot on top of my head.)

The author reminds us that, historically, the "near-death experience" has been characterized by the "sensation of floating over (ones) body, looking down, hearing what is said…" But in the experiments, virtual-reality goggles and projected images of, for example, an "illusory body," coupled with physical manipulation and stimulation of the subject with a stick, produced something very similar to the out-of-body experience. The subject would see the rubber mannequin rubbed with the stick, and feel it as well.

Now I fully realize that I'm not the go-to guy when it comes to comprehension of matters of scientific, neurological, psychic, or spiritual inquiry. But after reading this article twice I had to ask myself, How are these experiments different from the common dream state? Or masturbation? (Sorry, Mom.) Or the effect on one's mind/body of watching a sword fight scene in "Gladiator"? Isn't that experience "out-of-body" in nature? The sword is going through the neck of an actor on the screen... so why am I clutching my neck in response?

As many of us know, I was diagnosed several years ago with a small, benign tumor inside my skull—an acoustic neuroma. Not a big deal, so shut up and sit down. Or go back to sleep. Anyway, the brilliant neurosurgeon who examined my MRI, Dr. Chandranath Sen, Chairman of the Department of Neurosurgery at St. Luke's-Roosevelt Hospital, counseled that no surgery was required or called for at the present time, but we would monitor the situation periodically—to make sure that the tumor didn't begin to grow to beach plum size. Or fingerling potato size. Or begin manifesting symptoms such as those on exhibit in this letter.

Things have been encouragingly stable inside my skull (with the exception of a dream I had a year ago in which I became Michelle Pfeiffer, and she developed a huge crush on me, who then had to find a way to convince her that it was safe to express her/my feelings about me/Lyle. Fantastic—making out with me as Michelle Pfeiffer! Sorry again, Mom.

So. In late 2006, Dr. Chandranath Sen called me in my office and asked if I would visit him for a consultation. Nothing to be alarmed about, he assured me. But he had something to discuss he hoped would be of interest to me. Of course I agreed, and we met in his office the very next afternoon. I'll spare you, and any remaining readers, the lengthy preamble that Dr. Sen had prepared for me in this "consultation." Cutting to the chase, he wanted to pick my brain, literally. He explained that he'd been approached several months earlier by a team of computer and micro-engineers from M.I.T. who were developing a new micro-technology that would have the ability to intercept and "read" images and thoughts created in the mind, and then send these images and thoughts in digital form for projection/dissemination onto a receptor medium. A computer screen. (In addition to its academic and scholarly work, this team had done work-for-hire in research and systems development for the likes of Microsoft, Nokia and Apple.)

Dr. Sen reminded me that the most fragile nerve in the human body is the optic nerve. The optic nerve conveys signals/information (my phrasing) to the brain—the brain accepts this information, and stores and sorts the images. But until now, we have only been able to send pictures to the brain—not get them from the brain (except through narration, creation, interpretation, coercion). The idea here: We will view your dream on a computer screen, virtually in real time—exactly as you see it. If you have an idea for a film or a plot for a book, you don't have to write it out (yet)—the signal will be sent from your brain, as data, and will be projected to the computer. (Imagine the possible applications in criminal investigation, judicial testimony, psychology...)

Nearly two years earlier, Dr. Sen had told me that no surgery would be required for my condition. On this day, he was asking me if I would participate in an experiment. One which would require implantation of a minuscule chip into my brain for the purpose of this experimentation. He assured me that the procedure itself, which he would perform himself, would be minimally invasive. The chip would be far smaller than my tumor, and even more benign. It would not even need to be removed at the conclusion of the testing. It could simply be "shut down." I said, "Yes, let's do it."

The operation was simple and elegant. Even under magnification,

the chip is harmless looking, like a smooth grain of sand, or a little tapioca pudding ball. Not at all like those ridiculous tracking nodes they attach to giant sea turtles for their instinct-propelled oceanic journeys around the globe. Following a mild local anesthetic and partial sedation, the incision was made; positioning and placement by the fibrous "arm" of the surgeon was guided by live neuroimaging juxtaposed onto the MRI images already on the computer screen. I felt nothing, with the exception of a profound disturbance in my psyche—a condition you might regard as understandable, given the mission.

Because much of the "sorting" and in-brain imaging is performed in a fully integrated network involving several cranial regions, a decision had been made—at the suggestion of Dr. Sen—to place the chip deep inside the right hemisphere, nearest, he believed, to the "visual signals" the M.I.T. team felt they could record and digitize. And if they were off a bit? Hey, your cell phone gets stock updates from a satellite—so a millimeter, or an inch, in the brain... not a big deal.

My own concerns were more mundane: If everything worked just fine, what would start showing up on the computer screen? Would we really be seeing my dreams? And what of my innermost fears? Or my most loathsome thoughts and reveries? I began to wonder if I would attempt to "censure" my own thinking patterns, which in turn created even more bazaar ruminations and fantasies. Very difficult days for me, in the immediate aftermath of the procedure.

My non-disclosure agreement prevents me from revealing specifics of what has been documented to date during the experiment (which continues even now). Look for the November issues of The New England Journal of Medicine, and WIRED, if you're still reading this, for graphic details.

Respectfully submitted,
Lyle Greenfield

———— ··· ————

May 11, 2008

To The Editor
The East Hampton Star

Dear Mr. Rattray,

As you may not recall, I wrote a fascinating letter to this newspaper in August of 2007 chronicling a bold experiment being conducted by Dr. Chandranath Sen, Chairman of the Department of Neurosurgery at St. Luke's-Roosevelt Hospital, in cooperation with a team of computer engineer researchers from MIT—an experiment that I had agreed to participate in. To put it plainly, the idea was to literally see what the brain is seeing. To accomplish this, Dr. Sen inserted a newly-developed microchip into my brain for the purpose of transmitting not simply signals displaying levels of relative calm, excitement, arousal, etc., but visual motion images depicting exactly what I was "seeing," dreaming, imagining, to be viewed in real time on a computer monitor.

Six days ago I was riding the #1 Train from work to the Upper West Side when I heard my name called. "Lyle? It's Jan! Your neighbor from 30 years ago!"

This was pretty startling, because normally, even when the train is crowded, I "ride alone," deep in my special thoughts. And now, here was Jan, leaning over me excitedly. After the expected exchange of "How've you been's" and "You haven't changed a bit's!" Jan said, "I saw that amazing piece you wrote in the East Hampton newspaper last year, and I thought of you and wondered how the experiment came out! I even checked several issues of the New England Journal of Medicine, but never saw anything."

I was a bit embarrassed to have to explain to Jan that the experiment had been aborted due to an unforeseen technical glitch: While the early results and images were promising—and quite disturbing, I must add—after a few weeks the signal from the microchip began to fade and become intermittent, and finally, to cease. A subsequent MRI of my skull confirmed that there had been some calcification around the chip, blocking its ability to transmit wave patterns from my brain. Dr. Sen concluded that what had happened was similar to what happens when an oyster forms a pearl. There is a grain of sand—an irritant—inside the oyster, and this bivalve mollusk secretes a nacre substance similar to that of which its shell is made to protect itself. And this becomes a pearl. My brain was doing the same thing—creating a "pearl" of the same sort of enamel found in my teeth.

I apologized to Jan, saying that there would be no report in the medical journals until further tests could be undertaken, which would not happen until they had dealt with this problem. And I myself was not at liberty to reveal more information, or any of the images, as a condition of the non-disclosure agreements I'd signed. Jan stared at me and shook her head, and we said goodbye. I pray that she doesn't read this—but felt that all of my readers (now 14) deserved an update. A full disclosure. By the way, Dr. Sen assured me that the pearl forming in my brain was benign, and would probably grow no larger than a Le Sueur pea. But we would monitor it over the next few years. He said, "Think of it as a cultured pearl!" And I said, "Thanks." Still,

it is my intention to donate the pearl, upon my untimely demise in the latter part of this century, to the Ladies Village Improvement Society. Who can predict the value, many decades from now, of this little protected chip containing my dreams and reveries from the summer of '07?

But that's not why I'm writing this letter, Mr. Rattray. I'm writing because of my concern that your food and dining writer, Ms. Laura Donnelly, has become so desperate for establishments to review that she is being airlifted to destinations none of us in The Star reading area would ever travel to. Southold, for example.

So to help the newspaper, and Ms. Donnelly, find their way home again, I will review herewith one of our Township's most venerable and beloved bistros. One that has, inconceivably, never been reviewed in these pages. I am referring to Brent's in Amagansett— the East End's first tri-lingual dining experiment (Spanish, Irish, Bonackerian) and a place of extraordinary cultural diversity.

While there is no "table service" per se at Brent's, the restaurant does offer outdoor dining in an intimate garden setting for breakfast, lunch or dinner—and all meals in between. It is also true that there is no wine list, a fact that did not deter my dinner guests and I recently, as we had brought several bottles of a lovely steel-fermented North Fork Chardonnay to crack open for a modest corking fee. (Setting aside the wine shortfall, Brent's can boast a far greater selection of beers, juice and soda beverages than any other tavern or bistro in The Hamptons. They also offer Yoo-hoo, which you will not find at, for example, The Palm.)

The staff at Brent's is friendly, courteous and knowledgeable about the cuisine and preparations. They are also quite short, which made my guests feel at ease. For starters, we ordered a medium container of egg salad, a medium container of potato salad, a medium container of corn salad with some other produce in it, a small container of coleslaw and a large order of fries. As we sampled the different appetizers on our all-wooden table outside, we nodded and moaned in approval. (Only the cole slaw disappointed on this night, as it was a little bit dry and nondescript.) The excellent potato salad seemed to have a great deal of mayonnaise. The fries were both crisp and soggy, an effect that even The American Hotel has been unable to duplicate.

When it was time for main courses, we placed our bags and other used paper products in the convenient garbage receptacles on the perimeter of the garden and proceeded back inside. If you peer over the serving counter, you can see inside Brent's working kitchen, where the magic happens. This creates a sensation of the freshness of everything, much as one would experience at Nick & Toni's, where Joe waves his wand over the proceedings. At Brent's, if you order two scrambled eggs, bacon and American—a little soft—on a toasted roll, you can actually watch it being made if you look carefully as your little paper order is being pulled from the kitchen window shelf. Yum.

But we had bigger fish to fry than egg sandwiches—well, bigger chickens, actually. Our party had decided on sharing a 20-pc. bucket of Brent's renowned Southern Fried Chicken ($25.95) and a tub of shrimp (serves 5-6 for just $31.95).

We don't need to discuss the price of a single serving of free range-chicken at other East Hampton restaurants, do we, Mr. Rattray? No, we do not, because this is about Brent's. I cannot speculate on what range these chickens came from—free or otherwise—but I do know they came to please. Of all the parts we sampled, I would say the thighs and drumsticks were most savory—though one of the ladies did prefer the meat of the breast. Hey, you need at least one of those in every crowd.

As for our tub of shrimp, we successfully achieved collective crustacio, and I'm convinced we'd have gone back for more if we weren't slumped over our table like enormous pigs-in-blankets!

But 15 minutes later, when we finally came to, it was time for dessert. After carefully wrapping the chicken parts and shrimp tails in paper, stuffing them into the tubs and disposing in the convenient garbage receptacles (trash barrels, if you prefer), we went back inside. We let Jolie pick out something for the table—and she chose a wonderful box of Entenmann's assorted donuts while the rest of us prepared our caffès-of-choice from Brent's large communal coffee station. Here, you can choose from the regular coffee, or decaf if you prefer. From whole milk or 1% milk (for runners and triathletes), from real sugar to a selection of I-can't-believe-it's-not-sugar products. The "coffee bar" at Brent's is the place where anybody who is anybody goes. Or just anybody with a pulse. It's the real Who's Who and Who Cares of The Hamptons. On this night, Uma Thurman and Gwyneth Paltrow were refilling their paper cups and joking and shoving a couple of big landscaping guys. But fortunately it never got ugly.

Now everybody knows that I've dined at Nick & Toni's hundreds of times. Because I know that everybody has been counting. But Nick & Toni's cannot touch Brent's when it comes to even the most basic "ingredients" of the complete dining experience. Nor, in fairness, can any other restaurant in East Hampton or Southampton, or Southold for that matter. Name another restaurant that offers batteries and calling cards? Or crayons, coloring books and condoms! Name a restaurant where can you buy a pack of True Greens, an El Diario and a lottery ticket. You can't. Unless you said Brent's.

So whilst Laura Donnelly is wandering far afield exploring menu options at the Princess Diner in Southampton, or in the snack shop at Islip MacArthur Airport, I think it's important to make clear that there are plenty of choices right here, in our own home town. (Next week, I'll be visiting the IGA in Amagansett.)

I should mention, finally, that Brent's is open year-round, including Christmas Day, which I view as a sign of respect. Note also that Brent's does not close for weddings or special functions during the "high season"—May 15th through Labor Day. I'm told that several weddings are booked in the garden in late September and early October, so planning early is recommended.

To pearls of wisdom,
Lyle Greenfield

———— ··· ————

June 30, 2008

To The Editor
The East Hampton Star

Dear Mr. Rattray,

My feet are dangling far above the turbulent waters of the Sound. I'm held by my waist in the powerful grip of a large, well-dressed woman standing on the deck of the Susan B, bound for New London. Her face is red, the veins bulging on her neck, as she laughs and shakes me wildly over the side of the heaving boat. It is difficult to type.

"You should be ashamed! You should be ashamed!" she screams over and over.

I am already ashamed, Mr. Rattray, but can't think of the particular thing that she is referring to, so I'm fearful my silence may anger her further. I fear also that she will grip me by my ankles and slap my body violently against the side of the ferry, like King Kong did to the pterosaur that was trying to fly off with Naomi Watts. The winged dinosaur was smashed on the side of the mountain like a rag doll.

Please don't let that happen to me. If I cry for help, how will it look? A grown man being manhandled by a possessed woman. I don't know how to explain that. Let's hope she is just having a little fun, or expressing some inner conflict, and releases me on the deck. I would like to go below to the restroom and clean myself up.

Then have some pills and be alone with my thoughts.

I've taken far too much of our precious time in recent weeks talking about aging and how to "win the battle." Pretty strange preoccupation for someone who is built like a brick comfort station.

But we all have our purpose—for a few moments longer—and this apparently is mine: help others understand. I mean sometimes people will make assumptions about your level of awareness or sensitivity to certain topics, and they just open up to you. You don't turn your back on that confidence, and I won't now. Recently, two of my male friends revealed to me that they had had serious medical events related to their prostates. There were surgical procedures in both cases, and in both cases the results were successful.

Still, this sort of conversation in a casual social situation is alarming. It's not like hearing that your friend had traded in the Dodge Ram for a Smart car or his kid was out of prison and doing really well in trade school. Prostate stuff is a big deal. So now I'm thinking, 'I haven't even had a physical in three years. What if I've got a freaking melon in my lung? Or somewhere else!'

In this very real state of personal alarm, I phoned the walk-in clinics in East Hampton and Bridgehampton, and in both cases, of course, they were closed. It was Sunday. So I drove to CVS and purchased a home colonoscopy kit. I figured knowledge is power. Like the First Alert thing. Better to know.

This is pretty embarrassing, Mr. Rattray. I'm not even sure what I was looking for during my self-examination. The little fiber optic tube is not nearly as wide as the nylon string in a grass whip, so it was no problem getting about 28 feet of it into the mysterious tunnel. Yet, no matter how far the little cable went, nothing appeared on the monitor. Remembering the images from Katie Couric's televised special, this gave me even more concerns, and I believe that I have enough concerns, thank you.

And then I noticed on the side table beside my bed: the lens. I had failed to attach the tiny lens to the tip of the cable. Was my face red! But more than that, the discomfort I felt coming from the hose-like organ inside my lower torso began to be overwhelming. There was no one to help me. And you don't just yank out 28 feet of whatever no matter how nauseated you feel—you have to go very slowly—it's right there in the directions on the side of the box. I so wished I had read those directions prior to commencing the procedure. I would also have known that you do not attempt an at-home colonoscopy within 24 hours of eating dinner at La Fondita.

I'm happy to report that this story has no tragic ending. I feel much better, have scheduled a physical for next week, and for the next few days am just having juice and soups, though no seafood bisques. Looking forward to a Rowdy Burger by mid-July.

But that's not why I'm writing, Mr. Rattray. The purpose of this letter is to undo the extraordinary damage that has been done to our society through the propagation of a fear of aging, and promotion of the mythology of "anti-aging." We've created discomfort and insecurity for an entire generation: 60 million people frowning in front of the mirror every day. It makes me sick, and I was just beginning to feel better.

In an effort to address this thing (and my own vanity) head-on, I visited the regional Social Security offices in Jamaica, Queens, last week, the only physical location in our immediate area. Most people go in person for clarification of their retirement benefits, to make sure they're properly registered, to deal with identity theft, etc. I had another question. The place had the feel of a Motor Vehicle office— take a seat until your number is called. After nearly an hour, I was summoned to one of the windows and an extremely uninterested man said, "Can I help you?" I said, "I'd like to speak with someone about changing my age."

"Excuse me?" I had to repeat this slowly before the gentleman informed me that I would have to speak with one of the supervisors. Returning to my wooden bench, I waited another 30 minutes before someone named Phyllis Rodriguez emerged from behind the fortified counter and asked me to follow her.

I'm so grateful that I do not work in a windowless office with steel furniture and photographs of strange looking young people taped to my big tan computer. "How can I help you?" Ms. Rodriguez asked. And I explained to her very deliberately that I would like to change my age legally and would that be possible? She stared at me for a few moments, biting her lip slightly, then said, "How old would you like to be?"

"Just 14 years younger," I said, "So, I'd like to be 46."

"You're 60 now?" she asked.

"Yes, I'm 60. But most of my professional colleagues are much younger, and many of my friends as well. I just think it would be less awkward for all of us if I was closer to their age. Not fielding questions all the time about when I'm going to slow down, when I'm going to retire. I'm sick of that."

Ms. Rodriquez informed me that I was not the first person to inquire about changing their age, and that, in fact, several hundred people actually do it every year. She said that the Social Security Administration is more than happy to accommodate people who are more concerned about their social status than their Social Security benefits since, in effect, they would be removing their names from the list of those nearing entitlement to government pensions.

"We have no problem not sending you monthly checks for another 14 years, Mr. Greenfield. But you better be sure that's what you want to do." For 15 minutes she walked me through the procedure that would make my age change possible. There is a psychiatric evaluation (list of authorized clinics provided), a Request for Change of Age Form, an indemnification agreement, which must be witnessed by two persons, and notarized, and a fee of $175. Allow two weeks for processing, with notification via certified mail.

I've thought about this a great deal, Mr. Rattray. Every aspect of it. Giving up as much as $340,000 in benefits, explaining to my daughter that I'm only 10 years older than she, blaming my first wife for marrying me when I was 7. It's complicated. And, yes, it's tantalizing at the same time.

Ms. Rodriquez, staring at me again, asked, "Can I help you with anything else, Mr. Greenfield?"

I took the forms, stood up and said, "No, thank you, I'd just like to think about it all a little bit more."

"By all means, take your time. You're not getting any younger."

Indeed,
Lyle Greenfield

November 30, 2008

To The Editor
The East Hampton Star

Dear Mr. Rattray,

Please consider the environment before printing this letter. On the other hand, thank you for printing this letter without regard for the environment.

I'm writing because at least nineteen (19) of my now twenty-seven (27) readers have asked me, "Why haven't you written a letter lately?" My recollection was that I had, in fact, written a letter recently, but when I went back to re-read the letter, it wasn't there. Nor was the letter in my files, so it's not like I can suggest that you rejected the letter out of hand. I apologize to you for even thinking that, and to my readers for my failure to write. I know I have a responsibility. I also know that I may have a problem, and I'm just praying it's not related to the implant. Please pray with me, Mr. Rattray. I will contact Dr. Sen's office post-Thanksgiving weekend and get a prescription for an MRI.

And speaking of that blessed day, I hope you had a bountiful and Happy Thanksgiving, sir. I have so much to be thankful for that I sometimes feel my inappropriateness could put my well-being at risk. The karma smack-down. I don't think God finds me amusing. And why

should He or She? I've called Him or Her out more than once, demanding better performance, a show of greater interest and greater responsibility for what He or She has created here. Still, I tell myself I'm doing God's work by being clear: We have expectations, and You might try to do better. Is God listening to me? Hey, nobody else is, so what the hell. But Happy Thanksgiving to You, God—I know You have pardoned many turkeys. I hope you've included me. Thank you. Now do better!

Did you say 'Grace' before your Thanksgiving feast with family and friends, Mr. Rattray? It's a humbling moment, isn't it? Whether you speak the words or simply think about what you are about to receive, and what you might have to be thankful for. Does God think I'm faking it in those moments because they're so few and far between? I don't know. God should think good thoughts at Thanksgiving time. Join us at the table! Have some turkey and stuffing!

Obviously, I'm thankful that we will have Barack Obama as our new President. And Michelle and the kids as our new "First Family." I still feel a sense of buoyancy just thinking about it. A lightness of being. That's crazy, right? I don't care. It's nice. Remember when I canceled my subscription to The New Yorker because of that inflammatory cover depicting the Obamas as Muslim terrorists? They've continued sending me the magazine, along with notices asking if I've forgotten to renew my subscription! Maybe I will next year. I'm still pissed about it and continue to await an apology from David Remnick. Hmm, not the spirit of Thanksgiving. Sorry.

On election night I stayed late at my office. I lay on the floor with the lights out, just wishing for the hours to pass. Didn't want to go to my friend's place where a bunch of colleagues were watching the returns like it was the Super Bowl. But by 9 p.m. I finally got up & joined them till the networks called it. Then I went home and watched the acceptance speech by myself. That was satisfying, crying in my apartment, alone. I spoke with a few friends, and my daughter—the sense of relief and joy seemed to be everywhere. Though to my few dear ones who voted the other way it may have been a different "sense."

Just weeks prior to the election several of my most liberal friends had said to me, "The country will never elect a black man, Lyle. It won't happen." It shocked me—even frightened me. I wondered if there was a subtext to their words. I'd voted before breakfast on the Upper West Side. It's all liberal Democrats, so everyone pretty much knows where their "secret ballot" went. The looks of

satisfaction amongst the electorate were a little annoying. But maybe understandable. I forgive myself.

Something quite magical happened to me on election day. Would you like to hear about it, everyone? Then please move a little bit closer in and watch my eyes as I retell the story. Forgive me if my voice breaks—and do not get up to use the facility. Okay, let's begin:

A short while after voting I was in my office on 18th Street. There was a phone call, and it was for me. From a very long time ago. "Hello Lyle, this is Gene Zappitelli ...do you remember me?"

"Umm...I'm not certain, Gene..."

"We were at Bowling Green (University) together..."

"Well thanks to short, mid and long-term memory loss, I don't remember much from the Bowling Green days...um..."

"Lyle, there's been something on my mind all these years, and I was afraid I would never have a chance to tell you ... that I would carry it to my grave." Well I had chills at the thought of this, wondering what could have happened, what could I have done over 40 years ago.

"Jesus, Gene....is it something I did?"

"No, no ... it's something I did. Do you remember Gary Severs?"

"Uhhh...well I'm, I'm not sure...." (the year would be 1966)

"He was a black kid—you

217

brought him to DU (Delta Upsilon, the fraternity I was in for one semester). You brought him to us as your friend, and I'm one of the ones who made it impossible for him to get in, to join. And I have felt terrible about that ever since… and I just wanted to apologize. We were young and stupid then, but I wanted to tell you how sorry I am." At this point in our conversation, I was beside myself with emotion—I couldn't remember a moment like it.

"Gene, you don't have to apologize—but I'm overwhelmed that you would find me, and call. And on this particular day. Maybe a historic one, too—It's very powerful…"

And that's the story. I asked Gene what he'd been doing—he told me he still lives in Bowling Green; had married a "Townie,"

has taught at the high school and the University of Toledo. And I told him a little bit about myself, that I'd married a girl from college, had a daughter, was divorced. I asked if he would stay in touch, and he said that he would. I said I hoped he would put that distant moment away now, and he said he thought he could.

I often joke about how bad my memory is, and how I regard it as a blessing. Files always being deleted. No backup! Bear a grudge? I can't remember what the hell you did! But Gene had reminded me of why I'd quit the fraternity after one semester. God bless Gene, and Gary, too.

The day following Martin Luther King Day, Barack Obama will be inaugurated as President. God bless him.

With Thanks,
Lyle Greenfield

——— … ———

March 29, 2009

To The Editor
The East Hampton Star

Dear Mr. Rattray:

Several days ago I was having lunch in our New York recording studio with partner Brian, and our co-worker Chris. Brian and Chris were having salads, and I was having a delicious meatball hero from the Pizza Emporium downstairs. Ridiculously good.

Our conversation was animated, and I continued speaking excitedly even after taking a substantial bite of the meatball hero. Suddenly, for the first time in my life, I began gagging desperately. I'd attempted to swallow the contents of my mouth without completely masticating, and "it" became lodged in my throat—would not go down, would not come up. I stood up, choking and holding my neck.

Chris yelled, "Breathe through

your nose!" And Brian, who's six foot five and about 230, a bigass bear from Wyoming, came up behind me, wrapped his arms around me just below the rib cage and said, "Relax." I was so relaxed, Mr. Rattray, gasping in humiliation in the grasp of my young business colleague.

Next Brian gave three power hugs in succession—and on the third, an unpleasant looking projectile came flying out of my mouth. Brian said, "How do you feel now?" And I said, "Fantastic." Still coughing, I went to the sink and continued spitting the residuals of that fateful bite—some bread, tomato sauce, mozzarella cheese. Not unlike the disturbing follow-up to a vomiting incident. Then I drank some water and cleaned up the meatball from the rug. Almost 62 years old and look at me—a gagging wretch. So ashamed.

I thanked Brian and said, "Ya know, if you'd just let me choke the whole company would be yours right now." And he said, "I didn't think of that in time."

So we resumed our animated conversation, they finished their sissy salads and I finished my meatball hero, chewing like a professional. And what can we learn from Lyle's terrifying experience? The Heimlich Maneuver, stupid!

A short while later, Sara (7 months pregnant) and Brad returned to the office from their lunches outside. I decided to disclose the entire incident to them, rather than have them hear it around the "water cooler" (we don't actually have a water cooler at Bang). Sara gasped, "Oh, my God!!" with that strange little pause after "Oh" that young ladies do when saying "Oh—my God!" Then added, "Then what did you do?!"

And I said, "I picked up the meatball chunk, shoved it back in the sandwich and ate it of course."

"Oh Gross!!"

Then I said, "Just kidding." I did place it in a jar, though, as a special memory of a very special lunch.

Which brings me to the real "meat" (fish, actually) of this letter, Mr. Rattray—a wonderful dinner party we attended this past Friday at the home of The Star's esteemed food and restaurant journalist, Ms. Laura Donnelly. Nine fascinating guests, each more interesting than the next, though none quite as interesting as one of the guests whose name was hand-written on a little standing card that I ended up sitting behind.

I thought a wonderful way to thank Laura for her hospitality would be to review the meal she lovingly prepared and served in these pages! We began with great, homemade crackers that had some kind of cheddar cheese component, a nice soft crunchiness blah, blah. Perfect with tap water, or steel-fermented Chardonnay. After the crackers and some random pieces of cheese, we sat down in a chilly enclosed porch for the main course. Laura had prepared a stunning, tender baked flounder with a green curry sauce. Yum. We were all making provocative sexual sounds as we savored our first bites of the delicate fish. Accompanying the flounder, a brilliant rendition of Wasabi infused mashed potatoes. "Oh, my God!" everyone exclaimed in unison! Mary said, "I LOVE these, and I don't even like mashed potatoes!" And I thought, she just lied and it's Lent! Awesome.

Then, the salad. What can I say? Mixed greens, with some carrots and maybe red pepper—whatever. But the dressing! A subtle mingling of flavors including lemon, lime, white wine, baby fescue…I could only think of the name I saw on a Benjamin Moore paint chip a few weeks ago: Lime Sorbet. Paint my tongue, Laura!

Well, what an amazing repast. And when it was finished, we all remembered how cold we were in the unheated porch—except for Laura, who was sitting on the one space heater in the room. I don't mean 'space' as in the kind astronauts use to heat their space suits—I mean the kind that sits on a floor, plugs into a socket and looks like burning logs. Hmm, I'm just realizing there were no hot buns at the dinner table. Did not matter!

Laura noticed that the conversation had turned to the topic of global warming, and how everyone wished it would come to East Hampton soon, so she decided to heat things up a bit. "Okay, how many of you read about Matt Lauer hitting a deer while riding his bicycle?!" Within moments the guests were slumped on the table, fast asleep, heads resting in their dinner plates—which, thanks to our irresistible meal, were clean. As Laura continued speaking about Matt Lauer and the deer incident, I was able to remain awake by holding an ice cube against my right eyeball. I kept nodding and slapping my knee, repeating, "That's incredible. That's amazing."

Then I offered, "I think it's wrong for cyclists to intimidate the deer under any circumstances. Lauer was riding a metal framed device with spinning wheels and protruding bars—and wearing a helmet! The deer was unarmed. In fact, the deer had no arms, and no helmet—just a need to cross the road. Ergo, who was the victim here?"

With that pithy remark, the guests began to stir and wipe the sauce from their foreheads. "Good point, Lyle," they sang in unison. Then I lowered my voice, Mr. Rattray, and told my own East Hampton cycling story. Everyone leaned in to hear.

Each week I ride my bicycle on our beautiful roads—Old Stone

Hwy, Further Lane, Highway Behind the Pond...And I don't ride with a helmet, or those tight, shiny cycling outfits. I feel if you want to break the wind, have a meatball hero. Comfortable clothes, oxygen rushing along your skull, sounds filling your one good ear. Do I ride a 6 oz. titanium Italian engineering masterpiece? Never. Instead, a fat, nondescript bike I stole from the sidewalk in front of a Cuban restaurant on Amsterdam Avenue. No, I didn't.

Normally, I ride just before daylight, so there's very little traffic and few, if any, television personalities. But here's what makes my morning ride special: Before each outing, I will take an old stocking (usually obtained from the Home Exchange at the Recycling Center) and stuff the toe with a mixture of Smuckers Chunky Peanut Butter and Orange Blossom Honey. About 8 oz., the whole wad. I tie off the stocking and pin it to the back of my sweatshirt—then put on the sweatshirt and commence my ride.

Deer love peanut butter and honey—perhaps even more than you do, Mr. Rattray. Without fail, by the time I've gone no more than a half mile, at least several deer have come out of the woods to lick the sock hanging from my back. I ride slowly so they don't have to lick and run. In the coldest weeks of winter, when tender shoots are most scarce for the deer to eat, as many as 18 deer have followed me along Further Lane, taking turns, getting their licks in. Let me simply proclaim: It's a beautiful experience, to feel the closeness of these animals, their innocent curiosity, their apparent joy at having a taste of something they don't find in the woods of Hither Hills.

If it's early enough, sometimes I'll dismount near the duck pond off of David's Lane, and we'll rest by the stream. No, I'm not a "deer whisperer" or anything special like that. I assure you, deer are dumber than night crawlers. When it's time to go, I take off the stocking, rip it open and leave the remains for the herd, give them each a noogie, pick off a few ticks and ride away.

Whew. Well the porch was getting hot as we rose to leave, thanking Laura for a simply amazing dinner. I apologized for pretending to pick up the thread of our conversation and telling a long, pointless story. Then everyone apologized for listening to the story. Finally, Laura apologized for making me feel it was necessary to tell the story in the first place. "Accepted", I said. Kiss kiss, good night, let's do it again soon!

No helmet,
Lyle Greenfield

——— ... ———

May 25, 2009

To The Editor
The East Hampton Star

Dear Mr. Rattray:

As you know by now, I am a special person with special needs. That is why I ask you to use a rubber spoon when you feed me my tapioca pudding in the morning. And I thank you for that.

There are people in our community who believe that I am preoccupied with the organs of the lower digestive tract. To these people (you know who you are so I will not reveal your names in this letter) I would say this: maybe the small intestine, but that's the extent of it.

I reported recently a seldom discussed fact—that the small intestine of the adult human is approximately 23 feet in length. Among its important functions is the breaking down of large supramolecular aggregates into small molecules that can be transported across the epithelium. You could spend a week in Home Depot and not find something with that capability. It's hard to believe there isn't a song about the small intestine, or a national holiday honoring its service to our bodies.

Which brings me to a fact that I reveal publicly here for the first time: I love chicken. There is no doubt that I consume a half-roast chicken three times a week. If you do the math, Mr. Rattray, that comes to about 75 chickens per year. Let's say that the course of my "adult" lifetime has been 40 years (I'm including the "lost years" of my questionable adulthood for the purpose of this analysis, and subtracting two "chicken vacation" weeks per year). That's approximately three thousand (3,000) chickens eaten by me since 1969. And I clean the bones, people. I leave nothing for chicken stock or angry kitty.

Let's imagine that each chicken is approximately 12 inches long, from beak to tail. Standing single file, barely touching, there would be a contiguous line of chickens stretching from Stephen Talkhouse past Brent's. If the 3,000 chickens formed a precision marching unit, they would take up more space on a regulation football field than the Florida A&M band. If they all checked into the newly renovated, tastefully appointed Maidstone Hotel there would be wall-to-wall chickens in every room.

Now picture those chickens filing through my small intestine, and tell me that there is no God. You cannot, Mr. Rattray, because only a Supreme Being could get 3,000 chickens through a 3-centimeter diameter tube.

God bless,
Lyle Greenfield

——— ··· ———

222

January 10, 2010

To The Editor
The East Hampton Star

Dear Mr. Rattray,

Would you like to feel power, vitality, endurance and pure elation you haven't felt since you were sixteen? Then I urge you to read this letter.

If you have a history of heart disease, high blood pressure or are currently taking prescription medication for anxiety, depression, sleeplessness or restless face syndrome, you should not read this letter. Under rare circumstances, this letter, in combination with any of the above mitigating factors, could cause dizziness, loss of balance, despondency or thoughts of suicide.

Women who are pregnant or trying to become pregnant should not read this letter. If you have been on the pill for longer than six months, do not read the letter. This letter will not prevent socially transmitted diseases, therefore its contents should not be considered an alternative to widely recognized methods of transmission prevention.

Do not read this letter while driving or operating heaving machinery. If you should experience a feeling of euphoria, combined with sustained swelling or expulsion events for a period exceeding four hours call your doctor immediately.

Isn't it time you started living your life again? Wouldn't you like to hear these words each and every day? "You look amazing, Tim!" Well you can. Read this letter and say Hello to a new you.

A few days ago we ran into Larry, the legendary bartender from Stephen Talkhouse. He'd popped into Rowdy Hall for a visit, and noticed that neither of the TV screens had the hockey game on. "What's up with that?" he asked Joe. Joe replied, "Football. Basketball. I got no hockey."

Hearing this, my wife yelled, "I'm from Potsdam—we're all about hockey!"

Larry became reflective for a moment. "The other night this lady came into the Talkhouse just as we were about to close. She said, 'I drove all the way from Canada straight to this place'. So I handed her a beer."

We were riveted by Larry's enchanting story so, encouraging him to continue I said, "Then what?"

"So she says to me, 'Ya know why everybody in Canada does it doggie-style?' And I say, No, why?"

"So we can both watch the game!"

Awesome. Are you starting to feel the swelling, Mr. Rattray? Me too!

To your health,
Lyle Greenfield

— ... —

July 25, 2010

To The Editor
The East Hampton Star

Dear Mr. Rattray:

I recently discovered that I am engaged to be married. How did I find out? It was at Montauk Printing in East Hampton, of all places. I was there to pick up copies of my newly-proposed sign stating Beach Fire Rules for the Town of East Hampton. The sign looked great—clear, readable, plain English. Perfect for posting at the entrance to all the public beaches. And with the enthusiastic support of the Amagansett Citizens Advisory Council, the East Hampton Town Board, the heads of the East Hampton Marine Patrol and Parks Departments, FEMA and the Department of Homeland Security, the sign would surely be a winner.

But I digress. This isn't about our burning, smoldering, litter-strewn beaches with bad dog baggies every 75 ft. It's about what's happening that could shake the very foundation of my existence. Mary was with me at the printing store that day and remarked, innocently enough, "The sign looks great, Lyle! I can't imagine why they wouldn't love it! Hey, while we're here, we should see if the invitations are ready!"

Shut up, Mr. Rattray. For all I know you already knew what I was about to find out. Mary asked the young woman behind the counter if the "invitations" had arrived from Montauk. "I think this is for you," she said, producing a large cardboard box. Mary tore open the box with her bare hands and pulled out packages of cards in two sizes, and packages of envelopes, also in two sizes. "They look fantastic!" she exclaimed. "What do you think?"

I examined the larger card. It had words printed on it. These words were even clearer than the Beach Fire Rules words (though they were not signed by the East Hampton Fire Marshall). They made specific reference to "The Wedding of Mary and Lyle," giving an exact time, date and location this would take place, and inviting the card recipient to attend.

One of my lungs collapsed, so I began breathing rapidly through the other one. "So what do you think?" Mary repeated.

And I replied, "We're getting married?"

"Yes, we're getting married!"

"That's incredible news!" I said. And I thought to myself, 'Really incredible.'

We often focus on the negative aspects of memory loss—whether it be short, mid or long-term in nature. "Oh how sad," people will say, "David's memory is starting to slip," blah blah. But if one were to take a truly balanced view one would discover many positives, including extraordinary health benefits. Think of the surprise and exuberance that I experienced, for example, in learning that I was going to be married—four weeks after (apparently) co-writing the invitation! It was a great feeling I was able to enjoy for the rest of the day and into the beyond.

Mary gave me a big hug and my collapsed lung filled back up. "When did we get engaged?" I asked, still marveling at these impending nuptials.

"In February, stupid! You proposed to me on the beach in St. Barth and I fell to my knees in the sand! That's what this ring is about!" she said, thrusting her ring-bearing hand in my face.

"Wow, yea, that was an amazing moment!" Get it, Mr. Rattray? I call it the Theory of the Double Positive. Events, impressions, epiphanies, recurring in the brain as if for the first time (this is not a subtle reference to the regrettably unforgettable Foreigner song).

I've always believed that memory loss can be cleansing. Like deleting old emails. Most of the readers of The Star have significant memory loss, and that is a good thing (for The Star). They will not recall that this week's report on the movement of bluefish offshore in Napeague is a reprint of the same report from three weeks ago. So this news will be fresh as today's catch to them, and cost The Star nothing! Other readers will wake up and see The Star on their coffee tables, or under their pet's bowl, and believe it is a daily paper, and start reading it through, all over again.

My own readers can't remember the first sentence in this paragraph, and that is why I love them. Readers, remember to check the expiration date on your cottage cheese containers! Lyle, remember to bring your new suit to the tailor!

Now, where was I?
Lyle Greenfield

———— ··· ————

July 11, 2011

To The Editor
The East Hampton Star

Dear Mr. Rattray:

As I write this letter there is a video camera mounted on the opposite side of the dining table focused directly on my bare torso, recording the mystery and magic of my creative process for all to see, for all time. As you will observe once the clip is posted on YouTube, I'm wearing nothing but bright blue boxers with colorful starfish and seahorses printed on them. You will also notice a small sheep sitting on my lap. I have duck-taped a razor to the sheep's little front hoof, and I am making it shave my chest. It is not easy to type under the circumstances, of course, but I will persist. (Remember when these letters were hand-written? What did we do without 'delete'?!)

The sheep is not unhappy, let's be clear. It is well-fed and purring while we shave. So no hate mail from the animal wellness people, please. Oops, some shaving cream just squirted on my MacBook! Mr. Rattray, I am not writing simply to cause embarrassment to a fellow mammal. Like you, I love and revere my fellow mammals. I am writing to establish beyond reasonable doubt the certainty that I will never be able to seek nor attain elected office anywhere in the United States. The first paragraph of this letter should pretty much take care of it. The online edition of The Star will make the letter available to most of the people of Earth, and I will be judged unfit for a leadership role in this or any other community. My hope is that this will spare my family future public scrutiny and humiliation and my friends and supporters disappointment from my betrayal of their trust. I wish I was in a position to return their money, but luckily I have neither solicited nor received any, so it's all good.

I was speaking with my business partner Brian in New York City last week and found myself reflecting on the impressive number of things I have failed to accomplish over the course of my 40-plus year career. It was breathtaking, actually. The books, screenplays and treatments I could have written if I'd been more focused, worked harder, put in the time. The clever clothing line idea I had but never followed through on. The songs I never finished writing. Brian agreed that the list of great things I'd failed to achieve was long indeed, and probably unlike anything anyone else had failed to achieve. Realizing that, I think we both felt better about me. I know I did.

It's so easy for us to get down on ourselves for being just "average," or below average people, Mr. Rattray. But I feel absolutely certain that every one of us has a list of abandoned dreams and ideas that is completely unique to our selves. Think, for example, of the surfboard you never designed—so light yet stable, and able to be converted to a wind-powered snowboard. I say Bravo! That's part of what makes you you—what you failed to do. We should celebrate together. Just name the place!

A few days ago Mary and Anne went to see Ina Garten speak at Guild Hall. Mary asked me if I'd be interested in attending and I said, "Absolutely not!" Afterward, the ladies reported that Ms. Garten was amazing—funny and personable and the packed crowd simply adored her. "Here's this wonderful woman who taught herself to cook," Mary gushed, "and her recipes are all so simple with no fancy ingredients. She said 'If the meal is a disaster, just turn up the music and drink more!'"

And I thought That is exactly the point! Ina Garten is demonstrating that a cooking failure can be a totally unique and unforgettable experience. There are no recipes for disaster if we look at life with a lemon-fresh shine! Like the words printed on the back of my Kellogg's Raisin Bran box: "Bursting with wholesome and hearty goodness!" Damn right!

You're welcome. Cheers!
Lyle Greenfield

———— ⋯ ————

October 31, 2011

To The Editor
The East Hampton Star

Dear Mr. Rattray,

This is the dramatic conclusion of the meandering yet though-provoking letter which I submitted to your paper on October 17th and which you mutilated in an editorial hatchet job that makes Freddy Kruger seem like a physical therapist.

Before I begin, however, I would like to acknowledge the passing of one of my readers and a dear friend of the family, Nancy Mulligan of Amagansett. She fought a rare illness with courage and dignity for many years before finally slipping from her physical anguish last week. Nancy was a loving wife and the adoring mother of four handsome boys. As a pediatric nurse, she was herself a caregiver, thoughtful and gentle, a person who could be counted on by all who knew her. At the reception following her funeral mass at Most Holy Trinity Church last Friday, one of her sons said to me, "My mother loved your letters. Whenever she saw one in the paper she would call me up and read it to me." Hearing those words touched me, and at the same time made me question her judgment. Oh well, Nancy is in heaven and I'm sitting here typing this thing, so who's to question? Amen.

Summer seemed to end with a door slam, didn't it? It was barely mid-August when we drove my daughter and grandson to JFK for their return to Miami. He was starting junior year of high school one week later. Six feet tall, broad-shouldered, on the basketball team. And here's grandpa, 5 ft. 7-something, and shrinking. What the hell!

From the airport, Mary and I drove directly to Saratoga, to visit her mother in the assisted living facility known as Home of the Good Shepherd. HOGS, as the family is fond of calling it. This is a lovely, well-run place, with an amazing staff of people who are all far nicer and more patient than me. Jean resides in a "memory care" home

THE SOUL MATE EXPEDITIONS

on the HOGS campus with 16 or so other elderly women in various stages of Alzheimer's disease. When we arrived in mid-afternoon we could see through the front doors a number of ladies enthusiastically engaged in a game of balloon volleyball in the dining room.

Inside, we said our big Hellos, hugging and kissing Jean and greeting the other ladies. She seemed happy to see us and even remembered my name. Then, moments later, she resumed play with the other golden girls, knocking the balloon over the net strung across a couple of dining tables. "Come on! You should play!" she yelled to us, her shoulders heaving with laughter. Jean was safe and healthy, well cared for. Memories of her life in Amagansett receding to a distant place.

Mary and I took her mom out for an early dinner off campus—a place called The Ripe Tomato. An old fashioned family joint with wood paneling, checkered table cloths, paintings and photographs of tomatoes on the walls... and a certain musty smell. It was perfect. Jean finished her burger and most of her fries, I killed the tuna melt, Mary the Ceasar salad. "Isn't this a great place?" my mother-in-law said. The next day we decided to keep things familiar and went back to The Ripe Tomato for lunch. "Have you ever been to this place before?" Jean asked me.

"Just once, Jean, and I loved it!" Jean isn't thinking about Occupy Wall Street, Mr. Rattray. And she's not thinking about Arab Spring.

On the drive back to sweet home Amagansett, we decided to first spend the night in our small apartment in Manhattan. In order to determine the best route into the City, we phoned a trusted friend who strongly recommended avoiding the Tappan Zee and the George Washington Bridge, staying on Rt. 17 through New Jersey, right into the Lincoln Tunnel. Wonderful. I knew that I knew better than to follow this advice, but alas, I am a sheep. As we approached the chaos of major construction and intentionally deceptive signs to the Lincoln Tunnel a sense of remorse came over me. The Manhattan skyline was now in the rearview and signs for Newark began to appear. I suggested to Mary that we seek instruction at the nearest gas station and she numbly agreed. Moments later I pulled the yellow Focus into a small refueling outpost that I prayed was operated by Americans. (For obvious reasons, my prayers are seldom answered.) A friendly man wearing a turban informed us, "You must go back four lights and then make a left and then look for a sign and then bear right." I bowed and thanked him, filled the tank and away we went. Clear. Relieved.

Wake up, Mr. Rattray, it's almost over. Within 45 minutes (it was now rush hour) we had reached the "approach" to the Lincoln. This enormous loop leading to some minuscule orifice beneath the Hudson River was packed with vehicles in all lanes, like a terrible digestive event. I began to be aware that I needed to urinate and that a potentially unsolvable problem could arise prior to the expiration of the hour it would now take to reach the other side of the river. A river filled with a tremendous amount of water, flowing constantly. I looked out the windows of my not moving car and quickly realized that there would be no "rest area ahead," no wooded patch to pull over and run to. I saw no door marked "Rest Room" inside the car.

I decided to summon my strength and will, to force my bladder to read "half full." But twenty minutes later, still outside the Tunnel, I began perspiring, which is not the same as peeing. Mary said, "I have a Poland Spring bottle."

I replied, "I don't think that will work for me, but thanks." Ten minutes later I began giving myself

Last Rites and finally said, "Mary, I'm going to stop here, get out of the car and sit on your side. You are going to drive while I try to figure something out."

"Okay," she said. (This will be a great story for her to tell at my wake—remind her, okay, Mr. Rattray?)

Once on the passenger side, I gazed out the windows again. My car was shorter than the other vehicles, allowing the occupants to look down and see me. Especially the Hasidic gentlemen packed into an old bus to my immediate right. Am I profiling? It's just that they were all wearing black hats and had long curly sideburns. Did they know what was happening? A certain clarity washed over my being. I will never see these people again, I knew. I reached for the empty water bottle.

I've moved on, Mr. Rattray, to other digressions. But this one I dedicate to Nancy. Hopefully, she'll take it the right way (otherwise I'm screwed).

May your cup never runneth over,
Lyle Greenfield

———— ··· ————

January 13, 2013

To The Editor
The East Hampton Star

Dear Mr. Rattray:
Greetings of the season to you.

I've been scolded recently by a few avid readers for my lack of productivity in these pages, so I'm writing to assure them that I remain devoted to their amusement—and to mine—and to the greater mission of improving the quality of this newspaper. It is a daunting challenge. The East Hampton Star has been in my family for over 35 years now (remember when I taught you to ride a tricycle?) and for all this time, consistent quality and relevance have been an elusive goal. So let's reset this new year and make it our best ever, deal? Here's my rusty boy scout knife—cut your forefinger and press it against my forehead. Deal!

To digress for a moment from our mission, it pains me to report that I ended 2012 and began 2013 with a toothache (lower left molar, if you're still awake). Try reaching a dentist on Christmas Eve, or New Year's day—I hope you never need to. But I was able to secure an appointment with a highly recommended doctor of dentistry in Southampton just days ago and he had special news for me following a thorough examination of my mouth and a complete boxed set of fresh X-Rays. To paraphrase: "The tooth must go. There is no point in trying to save it. The roots are dying. You won't miss it."

But wait, that's not all! "I won't sugar coat it, Mr. Greenfield...you have serious periodontal issues. You should see a specialist. You probably need to have your gums pulled back so the bone can be scraped. The good news is I believe you'll be able to keep most of your teeth." What?

Later that very afternoon I

was sitting in the comfortable recliner of an oral surgeon, also in Southampton. My yellow Focus was parked outside next to a very large BMW SUV. Sub-digression: Cool young person, if you're thinking of forming a rock band, forget it. Become a dentist and play air guitar while listening to AC/DC records.

The oral surgeon was warm and understanding. He gave me several shots of Novocaine and asked me each time if I was comfortable. I squirmed and told him that I was needle-averse. He laughed and said he'd be back in a few minutes and we'd get me on my way.

There are a lot of excruciating problems in this troubled world of ours, Mr. Rattray. They require our thoughtful consideration, they cry out for solutions and assistance. This is nothing more than a tooth. And now it's gone. Now I massage the gummy hole where it once was with my tongue. Fortunately, Chardonnay does not require chewing, so don't cry for me. Just yet.

Three days later I was sitting in the comfortable recliner of a periodontist, also from Southampton. They all know each other, these oral people. They attend dentist conventions together, bring their significant others, check out the latest in hi-tech dental gear, play a few rounds of golf. Whatever. So this warm and experienced periodontist looked at all my teeth, probed under the gums, examined the boxed set of X-Rays (and took a few more for his own collection) and said, to paraphrase, "I'll be honest with you—there's a lot of biofilm in your teeth. Plaque buildup. It goes deep, deep into the roots. Filling the pockets. But the good news is, we can save your teeth—certainly most of them. I do want to take this upper left molar out. You don't need it. You won't even know I took it." What?

So I asked, "How long do you think this process will take, doctor?"

"Well, 18 visits or so. Maybe 19. Probably 10 or 11 months. But then you'll be clean, disease free, and you should be fine for the rest of your life with proper in-home care and checkups every 3 months."

"I look forward to it," I said. "Guess I won't be buying a new Focus this year."

And the cheerful periodontist said, "You know, my wife and daughter both have a Prius. Fantastic! 50 miles per gallon, I'm not kidding. For a hot minute, I thought about getting one—but I always wanted a Mercedes SL convertible. So I went for it. I figured I don't play golf, I've been doing this for 30 years…why not?"

And I said, "Doctor, you've been taking s**t from people like me, with their rotten teeth and stinking breath, for 30 years. You definitely deserve a Mercedes convertible."

He laughed. "You're funny!" And I thought, 'My teeth will be paying off the lease on his car, one visit at a time. Maybe that's where the phrase "sweet tooth" comes from.'

Remember to brush –
Lyle Greenfield

——— … ———

April 10, 2013

To The Editor
The East Hampton Star

Dear Mr. Rattray,

Please sit down. Over there is fine, near the aquarium. I didn't want you to fall down when you read a compliment, from me, on your editorial, "A Plea for Civility," in the recent Star. But here it is. Your tone is pitch-perfect and perfectly captures the exhaustion that so many of us feel with the absence of even tempers, basic

manners and a willingness to collaborate for the benefit of the common good among our elected officials. Oh how East Hampton's Board games seem like a microcosm of our Great Union.

Your observation of several exchanges from the recent Town Board meeting reminds me of why I've stayed away from these public hearings for so many moons. Almost unimaginable given my fondness for the sound of my own voice. Well, though I'm sorry for my loss, I'm sure for many the silence is golden.

Fine. Let all speak in civil tongues or forever … never mind.

On an equally painful topic, a number of readers have asked me how things are panning out with my ongoing periodontal journey. (Thank you, Paula Diamond, for admitting you read the letter. That took courage. And no one has ever referred to me as 'estimable'—not even my accountant!). There have been two more appointments with the periodontist since that first treatment. They both sucked. Far more than the device the hygienist sticks in your mouth to evacuate the water she's squirting on the drill while he's deep-scraping. He keeps asking, "Am I hurting you?" Read my lips! Oh wait, they can't move because there are two hands and three devices in my mouth. Anyway, it's going great and I get free dental floss and a toothbrush after each visit. Only 15 more to go. Bite me.

On an even more painful note, our cat Sami died three weeks ago. As you well know, Mr. Rattray, I don't much care for cats. Their passive-aggressive ambivalence has always left me wondering, 'Why would I feed you?' Actually, Sami was Mary's cat, so when I married Mary the cat was part of the package, like certain furnishings, kitchen utensils, bathroom divisions.

And then I developed an affection for the thing. He kept an eye on me when I was building a fire, knowing there'd be a warm lap to sit on soon. And when he took his position, there was no moving him—the engine purred until I needed to get up. He'd sit on the stool next to me watching me write these letters. When I got up he'd swat my hand with an open paw, claws bared, eliciting from me a 'What the f___ is wrong with you?!"

A couple months ago I noticed that Sami was becoming lethargic, barely moving in the house, eating little. When he'd go outside he just took a few steps and sit, staring in the distance. I told Mary I thought he was dying of old age, but she reminded me that he was only 12. A few days later we became alarmed enough that we took him to the East Hampton Veterinary Group where, after a series of tests, Sami was diagnosed with a blood parasite. We were given a prescription for medication that should eliminate the parasite within 3 weeks.

Hours after giving Sami the first dose of the medication, he disappeared. He went out of the house and didn't return for a day, then another day, and another. He was gone for a week and I thought 'He's gone off to die…they know when it's the end…he's under a bush somewhere.'

And then he appeared again. I walked into the downstairs bathroom 8 mornings later and he was lying on the floor, eyes lifeless, breathing slowly. We kept him inside the house administering the meds and force feeding him some special cat food. But he wouldn't swallow the food and a few days later Sami could barely stand. We took him back to the vet and told the doctor that our assumption was he could not be saved. The doctor massaged the cat's body gently with his hands and after a few moments said he felt a massive tumor in his stomach.

And that was that. Sami seemed relieved when his eyes shut. He seemed to embrace his sleep. I'm just projecting, right? How would I know what he was or was not thinking? We brought him home in a towel and buried him deep in the sand behind the house. Friends told us later, "Oh, it's illegal to bury a pet in your yard." Really? Okay, we didn't do that. Whatever.

There's a cupboard door in the kitchen where we kept Sami's food, and when I open it, the food's still there. We didn't get rid of it yet, just didn't think of it. It's a sad sight so I've gotta do that.

On a brighter note, the ground birds and rabbits have returned to the back yard and don't seem to be looking over their shoulders—or wings—with the usual hesitation.

To common ground,
Lyle Greenfield

———— … ————

December 9, 2013

To The Editor
The East Hampton Star

Dear Mr. Rattray,

I write with glad tidings: This letter is not about me. It's about Aunt Oralee, who lives in my hometown of Rochester, NY. I hadn't spoken with her in a long, long time and thought I should call. It was Thanksgiving, after all.

Aunt Oralee is 92. At 91 she was diagnosed with breast cancer and had surgery to remove it. The operation was successful, but she was told she would need chemotherapy as a followup to make sure that the cancer would not return. Oralee told them, "I'm way too old to start chemotherapy— how long have I got to live?" She was told she would likely have six to twelve months. I said, "Jesus, Oralee…then what?"

"Well, I thought I better sell the house so the kids wouldn't have to be bothered with that when I'm gone." So she sold the home she'd raised her family in and lived in for over 60 years. It went for about a hundred twenty thousand dollars. (Real estate values are pretty depressed in our Rochester suburb.) "And now I'm in an apartment in a senior community—I hate it, really. The only people around me are old…a lot of them can't get around. There are no children in the neighborhood."

And I said, "Good God, what a change that must be. Well you sound pretty good, I have to say!" Now I must mention that Aunt Oralee lost two of her beautiful daughters and one son-in-law to cancer, all at a very young age. She also outlived her husband, my uncle, by 20 years. She has taken all of these losses in stoic stride, relying on her faith and her sense of humor…and a belief that God must have some unknowable sense of humor, too.

"Well, I went back to the hospital for my six-month check-up. They told me the cancer's gone and I can keep on living—can you believe it?!"

"So you were tricked into selling your house! That sucks, Oralee." (She's used to this sort of language from me.)

"Yes, and I didn't even have time to get all of my things out of the house," she cried. "The kids (three living) couldn't take most of it and didn't want me to put furniture in storage for them—I can't even find my Christmas decorations! I found someone's name in the Yellow Pages and he came and emptied the house—he took everything that was left—for $600. Including the piano!"

I was speechless. Well, for me. "Six hundred dollars! What the hell?!"

"Well you can't take it with you, honey. At least I have a nice balcony I can look out from." Oralee still drives, but only in the daylight now. She picks up the ladies for bridge once a week, then drives them home.

"Oralee, you were sent here to do God's work. You are a living saint. By the way, are you excited about the new Pope?" I asked.

"I like him. He seems to be a man of the people and setting an example for the rest of the church— although it really is time for women to be priests."

"You know, the pope drives a Ford Focus."

"Really?"

"Honest to God!" Oralee loves to chat so we talked for another half hour. World affairs, natural disasters, grandchildren getting bigger, crimes against humanity. I think we pretty much solved most of our planet's vexing problems on that call.

"I believe in heaven, but I don't believe there's a hell," she proclaimed during our "crimes" segment.

"You don't? Well what happens to the bad guys then?"

"Everybody goes to heaven, that's what I believe. Jesus died for the sins of all men—so we all go to heaven."

God bless Aunt Oralee. I had hoped there were certain people I wouldn't have to see once I was dead. But I guess I can live with it— as long as there's a beach. I called our local florist in Rochester (the one we call for the funerals) and had a giant red poinsettia sent to Aunt Oralee's apartment. She called me, practically speechless with appreciation—though I couldn't get her off the phone for a half hour.

(Hmmm…was this really about me after all? Apologies to all and to all a good night.)

Lyle Greenfield

———— ··· ————

July 13, 2015

To The Editor
The East Hampton Star

Dear Mr. Rattray:

Please fasten your seatbelt and hold on firmly to the center armrest. I hope you used the restroom before leaving the restaurant. On Saturday evening, in the beautiful sunset hour, Mary and I were driving home from Bridgehampton, back to Amagansett. We'd decided to take the scenic route and avoid highway traffic, heading eastward on Further Lane, windows open, the fragrance of honeysuckle wafting through the car.

Suddenly a black Porsche convertible sped past us, ignoring the double lines, going at least 70 mph. There appeared to be a guy driving and two women in the car. Mary said, "I hope there's a cop up ahead!" And I replied, "Yea…on the other hand if you're young and rich and have a Porsche convertible with two chicks on board, wouldn't you want to pass the old guy in the black Ford Fiesta?" I should point out that I was driving 9 miles per hour over the speed limit. Which is 25. Who's the man?

A moment later we were passing a driveway on the right and there, stopped to open the entrance gate, was the black Porsche. Mary screamed, "Hey, that's Seinfeld!" Sure enough, entering the former residence of Billy Joel, was our famous neighbor.

I responded, "Comedians In Cars Getting Coffee" – he must be jacked up on caffeine."

"What?" was I talking about, Mary wondered. I explained that Mr. Seinfeld had a very successful web series called "Comedians in Cars etc." but that in all the segments I've seen he's driving the speed limit. Probably afraid he'll kill Chris Rock or Mel Brooks. But on Further Lane, fast & furious Jerry.

"What if a baby had jumped out into the road? How does 'Comedians In Cars Running Over Babies On Further Lane' sound?" At that point my wife urged me to stop talking and we continued, safely, on our way.

But that's not why I'm writing, Mr. Rattray, so you can unfasten your seatbelt and exit the car. Let's just talk here for a moment.

The reason Mary and I had been in Bridgehampton was because one of our dearest friends, Dan Kalish, had passed away in his home just hours earlier. We went to be with his wife Carol and beautiful daughter Jocelin, to try to do what you try to do when grief is in the house. You bring food, you hug, tell stories, mention a funny incident, talk about peace at last and a "better place." Nothing does much, but you just want to be there.

Dan fought a 2 year battle with an insidious cancer that simply overwhelmed him over the past few weeks. Yet less than 2 weeks ago he talked, from his home care bed, about helping his twin brother David install a screen door in some lady's house. That's an optimist. That was Dan. People will say "Life is precious—so live each day like it's your last." But I say the hell with that. Live each day as if you'll live forever. Like a bird. Like my friend.

Dan was a builder, carpenter and craftsman who worked on many projects—large and small—for us and for our neighbors and friends over the years. As the son of a third generation potato farmer, he had practical skills in every trade. He worked hard, loved to solve problems, thrived in a time of corporate builders changing our East End landscape. And he told stories—about his daughter's scholastic successes, his camping trips with his wife, his sailboat races out of Breakwater Yacht Club. Every story had a punch line and a laugh.

We built some crazy beautiful things together. We hugged and called each other brother. He was 65.

Sixteen years ago, Mr. Rattray, when your mother was Editor of The Star, I wrote a 2,300-word letter, which she published in two installments. (Don't worry, I won't do that to you...not that you'd publish it anyway.) The letter was my response to a story that had appeared in The New York Times reporting on the shortage of burial plots in the cemeteries of East Hampton. Apparently, this real estate crisis had been caused by the nouveau riche, who were moving into the area, buying blocks of plots for their families and leaving little ground for the locals, who'd been here for generations.

In my illuminating and compassionate letter, I offered a variety of solutions to this vexing dilemma (i.e. a long, narrow cemetery on the grassy median between the highway on Rt. 27 from Manorville to Southampton, with easy on/off access).

I also described in great detail the burial of a dear friend of mine in the Double-Dunes less than a half mile west of Indian Wells Beach in Amagansett. It was a request he had made of his closest confidants and written into his Will, as read upon his death in the Fall of 1996. We accomplished this difficult assignment on a Wednesday night in early November at approximately

3:30 a.m. The beach was empty on this frigid night.

No one commented on this letter, Mr. Rattray. Let me repeat that: No one said anything about the letter or the story! (Which is when I realized that 2,300 words might be a little long for a letter to the editor.)

Then, three months later on a Saturday in early spring, I was in my home in the Dunes when I heard a strong knock on the door. I opened it and faced a tall man in his late 40's. "Are you Mr. Greenfield?"

"Yes," I replied.

"I'm Detective Steve Willis (we'll call him that) from the East Hampton Town Police. May I come in?" He was in plain clothes, no uniform.

I let the detective inside and said, "Is there a problem, Detective Willis?"

"Well…I hope not. Umm, my Captain told me to come here and ask you a few questions. Would that be all right?"

He seemed a little uncomfortable, and I was certainly baffled, but I said, "Sure, what is it?"

"Well, did you write a story in the newspaper about burying someone on the beach, in the dunes?"

With that I literally fell to my knees, laughing. "That was three months ago and no one has said a word about it! Why are you here now?" I asked.

"So you did write the story?" he asked.

"Yes, I did."

"So you buried someone in the dunes."

"No, of course not!" I replied.

"Well why would you write something like that?"

"Because I thought it was a fantastic story and could be told believably. But why are you here all this time after the fact?" Detective Steve explained to me that a resident had contacted the New York State Department of Health, expressing alarm that a body had been buried in their "back yard" (near the current Seinfeld residence, I should add) and the East Hampton Police had been ordered to investigate. In a way I felt bad for the Detective. On the other hand, this seemed way more interesting than a speeding violation.

For the next hour, I gave the officer a sworn statement asserting that I had not, in fact, buried anyone in the dunes. And when we were finished with that, Detective Steve asked me a little bit about what I did for a living (music, commercials, blah blah…). Then he started telling me about himself. He mentioned he was divorced, had a girlfriend in Los Angeles who was a casting agent for TV and film. She'd encouraged him to get his SAG card 'cause he'd be perfect to cast as a fireman, for example. And I said, "Yep, I'm sure she's right!"

Finally, Steve said, "Well I guess I should be going. Thank you for your time. Um, could I ask you one thing?"

"Sure, anything," I said.

"Please don't write about the stuff we were just talking about… that probably wouldn't be good for me."

"I promise I won't write a word about it," I assured him. We wished each other well and he left.

I never told your mother about that encounter, Mr. Rattray. But it's 16 years later—statute of limitations and all. Dan would have laughed his ass off if he'd heard it, so I'm dedicating this letter to him. He'll be buried in the Edgewood Cemetery in Bridgehampton this Friday following a Funeral Mass at Queen of the Most Holy Rosary Church. Wish him a good journey.

Lyle Greenfield

——— ⋯ ———

April 3, 2016

To The Editor
The East Hampton Star

Dear Mr. Rattray,

As you know, I have troubling dreams. Often, in these dreams, I find myself someplace that is vaguely familiar but needing to get back home, or to wherever it is I came from. After taking the street or path that I believe leads to where I need to go I soon arrive at a dead end, or wander further and further into strange territory. I enter a building, am given directions, but again, a corridor I've taken, or a staircase that should lead to the correct exit opens into yet another unfamiliar place. I start to panic.

Then I wake up and say, "What the f***?! Where the hell did this dream come from?" Mary suggests that there must be some unresolved "issues"—something in my life that's incomplete, not finished, and I haven't found a solution and/or don't have control over the outcome. My thought is that would be just about everything, but I don't regard it as a unique condition. So I say, "I don't know…I don't want to think about it too much." So there I am, not "facing" it, whatever it is.

I know what you're thinking, Mr. Rattray. "Why do I keep printing these letters?" You're right, it's your fault. So I'll continue. On the morning of Good Friday, I received an email from a longtime colleague, friend and occasional client. I was one of perhaps 12 recipients on the email, mostly business associates, and our colleague poignantly wrote that his mother had died the night before, that he'd been by her side, and felt both the loss and relief of her passing. This was a very touching note and I was pleased to have been included in the sharing.

It was difficult knowing how to respond—I didn't want to "reply all," so I simply replied with a short, sympathetic email remembering the passing of my own mother, and more recently of my wonderful mother-in-law Jean Hantz. And I said that he, his family and mom would be in my prayers that Good Friday.

Later that afternoon I realized I hadn't, in fact, prayed as I had promised, and I started to feel guilty. So I decided to take a walk around the Lanes and down to the ocean, and I would pray for the family. But I kept getting distracted and found my thoughts drifting to business matters, wondering why my company didn't get more work from my friend and what it would take. Mr. Rattray, I don't know if you're familiar with praying, but I assure you, this line of thinking on my part is the opposite of praying. I'm having these thoughts on Good Friday—Jesus cannot possibly appreciate this. I will be nailed with more bad dreams, of that I'm certain.

So I stopped and faced an open area on Meeting House Lane, stared at the brush and trees and prayed for my friend, his mom, his family, hoping they would find peace and happiness in this and, in her case, the next life. I tried to keep thinking this over and over, yet the feeling that I was also covering for my previous inappropriate thoughts kept creeping into my head. Brutal. And here I am walking around the Lanes on Good Friday. Sweet Jesus,

have mercy!

Mary wanted to attend the Easter Vigil Mass at Most Holy Trinity Church the following Saturday evening, to feel the "spirit" of the Holiday more fully. I was happy to accompany her—I mean, how would it look if I said, "Hey, I'll meet you later." Not good. Plus, I really was happy to attend the Mass.

Each of the congregants was given a candle as we entered the church, and each of the candles was lit by members of the church choir. It was beautiful and the effect was calming and meditative. This, I thought, is what is vital about places of worship. The collective focus of minds and spirits on prayerful thoughts. The room felt sacred to me—a sanctuary.

This was a long Mass, which included a number of sacraments, including a Baptism and, of course, Communion. There were also a number of readings from the Gospel, and a sermon. I can't recall the chapter/verse of the passages, but one concerned God's creation of Earth and all the living things and "on the seventh day He rested…" that one. Another one was about Moses leading the Jews out of Egypt, through the parted Red Sea, and the waters enveloping and drowning all of the Egyptian soldiers who came after them on their chariots. Like some dream that I would have, Mr. Rattray.

And, again, I found myself in

not-praying mode, thinking about these readings and wondering why the Mass couldn't focus more on the example of Christ's life and teachings and less on the mythology of the Gospel literature. And then I tried to stop having those thoughts and simply embrace the peaceful feeling in the room.

At one point early in the service, when a hymn was being sung by the congregation, a baby took that as a cue and started singing "Happy Birthday." Now that I think back, that was the Easter moment for me.

Sweet dreams,
Lyle Greenfield

———— ··· ————

August 9, 2017

To The Editor
The East Hampton Star

Dear Mr. Rattray,

I recently encountered Joan Tulp at the annual AVIS "Summer Splash" fundraiser gala. It was impossible not to encounter her— she was taking and selling tickets at the front door of the South Fork Country Club. As you know, Joan is one of the two most beautiful women in Amagansett. As I handed her a fistful of cash, she said, "Lyle, I haven't seen one of your letters in The Star lately—I miss them!" I told her she was too kind and promised I'd try to write something soon.

In truth, I've missed them too, Mr. Rattray. I always open the Commentary pages of The Star to see if there's anything by me among the Letters—week after week I've been disappointed. Maybe I was upset that you never responded to my email complimenting you and Mr. Biddle Duke on the look

and content of your recent issue of EAST. Not even a "Thanks, Lyle!" I know, you're so busy editing the Letters. Totally get it. So don't blame yourself for yet another thoughtless oversight. (Is that redundant?)

But here is a letter to The Star, and it's dedicated to the beautiful Joan Tulp. Eleven days ago a few of us were enjoying a sublime afternoon on the beach. Mary, who'd been tutoring in Southampton, joined us late in the day, but by 6:30 it was time to walk back to the house for showers and the "getting ready" for dinner thing. Fifteen minutes later, Mary announced, "I can't find my phone!" We looked everywhere in the house it could possibly be, twice. I called her number, but the ringer couldn't be heard. We checked her car. Nothing. "I know I had it when I got back from Southampton—maybe it's on the beach!" I hated that idea, but she and I returned to where we'd been sitting in the sand and looked carefully. Some neighbors joined us, offering wine to fuel the search. Still no phone, so back to the house, dejected. Think of all the "stuff" your phone contains. Thousands of photos, contacts…no back up. Nightmare.

The next morning, at the suggestion of her brilliant daughter, Sophie, Mary turned on her iPad and did that "Find My iPhone" app thing, believing that the two devices were synched. And they indeed were. "It's on the beach!! My phone's on the beach!! Look!" she screamed excitedly. Sure enough, that little red pin on her iPad screen was planted on the beach! Time, approximately 7:40 a.m. So we went back to the beach to search again, but I said, "Wait, let me get the clam rake first." Who's a genius, Mr. Rattray? Say it. Louder! "You are, Lyle!" Damn right, now shut up and I'll continue.

Few people were on the beach at that hour. A couple dog walkers, hopefully carrying little green plastic bags. And Mary and I. We went to the area we'd been the afternoon before, near a large driftwood tree trunk. The high tide had come close to where we'd lounged in the sand. Not good. Clam rake in hand I began raking the beach just west and north of the target area and worked my way east in adjacent parallel lines, like mowing a lawn. I kept the prongs of the rake at a depth of about 3 inches. Back and forth, back and forth. After grooming an area of about 200 sq. ft. up popped an iPhone from the dry sand. Amazing! "Mary, look! Your phone!" She screamed at the sight. Very loud for that hour. I reached for the phone and said, "Hold on a second," and, brushing the sand from the screen, pushed that little "on" button. The screen came to life immediately, announcing "8:09 a.m." We did that awkward white person high-five and agreed that no matter what else happened that day, it was already a great day. Technology + clam rake.

But that's not why I'm writing, Mr. Rattray. I'm writing because, for the ninth year in a row, you have failed to extend good wishes on the occasion of my birthday. July 30th (as you well know). 70! 840 months! I have personally sent The Star over 100,000 words in the form of Letters, each word carefully selected by me so that each letter would "Shine for all." Still, nothing. Nor did you write a "Congratulations, Mary!" on the arrival of her first grandchild 2 months ago. When that beautiful baby is my age, the year will be 2087—think about that.

Okay, that was inappropriate…I apologize. Instead of ranting about what you've failed to do, I've decided to make this easier for you and draft a birthday letter, from you to me. Simple. All you have to do is have someone at The Star print it out and mail it to PO Box

440, Amagansett, etc. Here you go: "Dear Lyle, Let me be the first to offer my heartiest congratulations and good wishes on your 70th birthday. What a milestone! It's been an honor to know you over your letter-writing years and I'm grateful for the content you've generously contributed to The Star, even recognizing that most of it has had no particular relevance or value to the community and much of it has been personally offensive to me. Still, many of your 49 readers (Is that the correct number?) seem to be amused and since it is the policy of this newspaper to print every letter, I've bitten the bullet and swallowed my pride for the greater good. But, like you, I digress. Good wishes always. And try to keep it to 500 words for god's sake! Love always, David"

You're welcome! And thanks in advance for sending it—what a lovely sentiment. Also, my T-shirt size is medium. And as your reward for sending the letter, I'll share a little story I know you'll enjoy because it involves my own public humiliation. Please be seated. Okay: A week before my birthday celebration I went to the Town

Clerk's office to fill out the forms for a Mass Gathering Permit (in case over 50 people showed up and a fight broke out…whatever). While at the Clerk's counter a woman approached me and asked, "Is that your red Jeep in the parking lot?" And I admitted that it was indeed red, and mine. "It just rolled into a police vehicle!" Oh shit, I thought, excused myself from the application process and rushed outside to the parking lot. Sure enough, the Jeep had rolled 15 feet and into the back end of a new Town of East Hampton Chevy Volt. Damage to Volt, minimal. Minor scrape. Damage to the mighty Jeep: $3,145.00 for a new left fender. Two Town Police officers were already there to write up the "accident report," which happened within 100 ft. of the police station. I explained that I'd failed to engage the emergency brake before going inside to apply for a Mass Gathering Permit for the 70th birthday party. "Happy Birthday!" the officer said as he handed me my copy of the report.

Yours, truly
Lyle Greenfield

——— … ———

November 24, 2017

To The Editor
The East Hampton Star

Dear Mr. Rattray,

I hope you had a Happy Thanksgiving. And I should have written that the way I felt it, with an exclamation point. A Happy Thanksgiving! Make that two: !!

You have much to be thankful for, sir, including the fact that this year, for the first time, you were able to eat an organic Butterball turkey while showing your support for the growing factory-to-table movement. Bravo! We, on the other hand, feasted on a locally raised, free-range, privately schooled turkey that had not been injected with butter, nor with opiates. We are blessed.

I love this time of year. Especially this particular year. Think of the recent hurricanes, floods, earthquakes, fires, mass shootings, sexual abuses, protests and political warfare we've had to endure, some of us directly, all of us emotionally. Overwhelming. When the death of Charles Manson seems like the "feel good" story of the day, you know it's time to talk turkey.

I have so much to be grateful for, Mr. Rattray. And not just Sade or Chance the Rapper. Only last week my partner Brian, who is very tall and from Wyoming, told me about the Greater Green River Intergalactic Spaceport in Green River, WY. My first reaction was, "The what?" So he repeated it slowly. So I repeated, "The what?" slowly. Touché.

Now here's the story: In 1994 a report was sent to NASA about the possibility that fragments from the Shoemaker-Levy 9 Comet were potentially on a trajectory to crash into the rings of Jupiter. This information was brought to the attention of the city council of Green River by one of the councilpersons, who suggested that the town rename its sole landing strip, which for decades since WWII had simply been known as Green River 48U. His idea was to name the 5,000 ft. long dirt runway "Greater Green River Intergalactic Spaceport" as a way of providing fleeing beings from Jupiter (or elsewhere in the known and unknown universe) with a hospitable port of entry to our great planet, Earth.

The resolution passed by unanimous vote of the council. Amazing. And what's more amazing: The Federal Aviation Administration (FAA) approved the re-naming. In truth, the town of Green River had hoped that this action might encourage more private air traffic to the newly named spaceport and also stimulate a bump in tourism to the region. Sadly, even 23 years after the official designation, this has not happened. The dirt landing strip still has a single windsock (which does not conform to FAA regulations) and is marked only by the official green sign (which keeps getting stolen). There is no terminal at the Intergalactic Spaceport. No baggage claim. No restrooms.

So why, this Thanksgiving, am I thankful to have learned, belatedly, of the Greater Green River Intergalactic Spaceport? Duh.

Because if Green River, WY can get the FAA to approve that name for its airstrip, the Town of East Hampton can certainly be granted control of the ground rules (and above-ground rules) that apply to our own airstrip. Could it mean that we will be required, as a condition of said control, to welcome visitors from other parts of the galaxy? That is possible, of course. But they would be informed that visiting hours are from 8:00 a.m. to 7:00 p.m., EDT, no exceptions. You're welcome!

I was even more thankful this season for the early arrival on the airwaves of holiday music. (For our purposes here, Mr. Rattray, let's just call it Christmas music. I mean, it's beginning to look a lot like what? And we're rockin' around the what? Case closed. But if it makes you feel any better, "White Christmas" was written by Irving Berlin, a Jew—and according to the Guinness Book of Records, it's the best selling song of all time. Mazel tov, Irving!)

Mary and I were driving back from Vermont two weeks ago, trying to get some radio reception in the mountains. Three choices: classic rock, bad country or "Casey Kasem's Countdown of the 40 Best Selling Christmas Songs of All Time." Now, Mary respects my historic wish to NOT start listening to Christmas music BEFORE Thanksgiving.

However for reasons previously noted I was very happy to get into the "spirit of the season" this year. So we went for the countdown. It was also an opportunity for us to rekindle the annual arguments: Is Paul McCartney's "Wonderful Christmas Time" a true "Christmas classic?" (I say Yes, she says No.) What about George Michael's "Last Christmas?" (I say Yes, she says No.) You get the idea. And there we were, heading out of Manchester, singing those songs. It's just not that heartwarming singing AC/DC's "Highway To Hell." Don't know why. I mean, I love "Highway To Hell!" Probably a seasonal thing.

Anyway, as we got to Number 3 on the countdown (let's hear it for "Little Drummer Boy!") I said to Mary, "I'm pretty sure Casey Kasem is dead." (not to be a downer on our listening experience).

And Mary said, "Are you sure? I mean, that's him talking, right?" So she did the Google thing and sure enough, Casey passed in 2014. But they've digitally re-mastered all of his yearly "Countdowns," which are presently in syndication everywhere. So I'm thankful that Mr. Kasem, like Mr. Crosby, will be with us forever and ever. Rock on, Casey!

Thanks,
Lyle

--- ... ---

February 19, 2018

To The Editor
The East Hampton Star

Dear Mr. Rattray,

Several people have taken me to task for not writing letters (or "articles" as one so kindly put it) to The Star frequently enough. Honestly, I've tried to pull back on the impulse to write something, um, clever, but at your expense. Which isn't nice of me in spite of the pleasure I take from it. But you're welcome.

Which brings me to the subject of this letter, Mr. Rattray. Mr. Rattray? Wake up—it's a letter! Thank you. Okay, as previously reported by me in these pages, I'm often plagued with troubling dreams. When I say often, I mean every night. Two nights ago my troubling dream involved my participation in the Winter Olympics in Pyeong Chang, South Korea. Sounds wonderful, doesn't it? A "dream" come true for a sub-intermediate skier, forward-motion only skater and out-of-control toboggan rider? Nightmare. In my dream, I participated in four (4) Olympic sports: Figure Skating, Snowboarding (Halfpipe and Big Air), the Alpine Super G and the Skeleton (which is like a backward bobsled, head first).

It did not go well for me. I did not "medal," as they say. First was my Long-Program figure skating event, early in the games. (My partner in the dream has asked not to be named in this letter, as she is, in fact, a very good skater. I will honor her wishes. Mary.) To begin, figure skating commentators Johnny Weir and Tara Lipinski made unflattering remarks about my outfit and the choice of music. (We came out as Mighty Mouse and Mini Mouse respectively, and skated to Beyonce's "Single Ladies (Put A Ring On It)." Johnny said, "Slap me, Tara! Are they really wearing that?! Are they really skating to that??!" To which Tara replied, "Only if you slap me, Johnny—so inappropriate. So wrong!"

And that was just the start, Mr. Rattray. As we were beginning to execute our first quad jump, in which I hurl Mini into the air, she spins four times and I catch her, I fell backward onto the ice hard and cracked my head open. My partner kept spinning, with no one to catch her, and also landed unceremoniously on the ice. Luckily she was not injured, but we did not complete our long program (though "Single Ladies" continued playing in the arena). I promise you, there were no little stuffed Pooh Bears thrown onto the ice as we staggered off the rink. Humiliating.

Fortunately, the Alpine Super G is a solo event, so no "partner" could be at risk in a bad performance. I knew my time needed to be at least 2:30 to be "in the running" for a medal. Unfortunately, I did not anticipate that there were turns in the course and I'm not that great at holding an edge. For the first 70 feet, I was golden and gaining some confidence as I shot straight ahead. And then…there was a curve! I plowed off the course, hurtling into spectators, iPhones flying in my wake. (Luckily most people lining the hillside dove out of the way and no Americans tourists were injured.) I was disqualified from the event and commentator Bode Miller simply said, "Well that was disappointing." (He's so boring.)

In the dream, I was initially excited to demonstrate my chops in the Half-pipe. I thought since I'd practiced the frontside 540 hundreds of times I should easily stick it. Stick it indeed. I shot out of the gate on my board picking up plenty of speed before my first trick, but got up to the lip of the pipe and flew over the other side. Where there are no cameras. So basically, I was gone from the picture—just an empty halfpipe left on screen

for millions to see and marvel at. Did anyone even care? Sure. My sponsor, Blue Quail Chardonnay cared. Canceled. Was I hurt? Yes, thank you for asking. I'd broken my shoulder in 3 places, forcing me to withdraw from the Big Air event.

But the team physicians said I could still enter the Skeleton if I was up for it. You run hard, land on your little sled and fly down the ice chute, head first. What could be so bad? And I was representing our flag. There was no question I would go for it. If I could hit an average speed of 84 mph, I could make it to the podium, Mr. Rattray. Bring home some metal. At the gun, I ran like the wind with my sled, threw it down and jumped on top in one seamless motion. But soon I felt some vibrating, was hopping back and forth in the tube alarmingly. I heard a siren-like sound—those European horns, but Korean. Then I woke up and went to the bathroom.

To the beautiful dreamers…I say go for it!

Lyle Greenfield

———— … ————

March 4, 2018

The Editor
The East Hampton Star

Dear Mr. Rattray,

The other day Mary and I were walking somewhere without purpose. She was singing that song

"Sundown" by Gordon Lightfoot. "Sundown, you better take care If I find you been creeping 'round my back stairs" blah blah… Unrelated to her singing I spontaneously burst out laughing. "What's so funny?" she asked.

"Nothing really," I said. Then

started laughing again, harder.

"Seriously, what's so funny? What are you laughing about?"

"Well it's probably stupid, but I just thought of a funny first sentence for a letter to The Star."

"Okay, what is it?"

"All right, here it is: 'Dear Mr. Rattray, First of all, I have to ask you to stop calling me 'Frosty.' That's it, the first sentence." And with that I began laughing again.

"So you think that's funny."

"I do."

"Has David Rattray ever called you 'Frosty'?"

"No."

"Has anyone ever called you Frosty?"

"No." Now I'm laughing-coughing uncontrollably.

"Do you want to be called Frosty?"

"Not really."

"Honestly, I don't think it's that funny."

At this point I was buckled over, holding my sides.

Sincerely,
Lyle Greenfield

———— ··· ————

ACKNOWLEDGMENTS

I'm thankful for the lives, love and shared experiences of the people referenced (if not named) in these stories and letters, including my daughter Jessica, grandson Joseph, sister Joan and brother Doug, our mother and dad, Jeanne and Sid, my mother-in-law Jean Hantz and most of all my exuberant, inspiring and tolerant wife, Mary Jane Hantz Greenfield.

I'm deeply grateful for the friendship, encouragement and inappropriate sense of humor of my partner, Brian Jones. And for the gentle, occasionally not gentle prodding of friends near and far, including Bunny Dell and Jeff Rosner (as mentioned in the Foreword), and Ed Kleban, Tom Dakin, Rusty Leaver and David Mead, who all heard and championed *What Vienna Saw* years ago.

I must acknowledge, again, the historic policy of *The East Hampton Star* newspaper of publishing every letter submitted which, outside of the internet, is about as free as freedom of speech gets. And thank you, *Star* Food Editor, Laura Donnelly, for alerting me to this policy 20 years ago— they have *you* to blame.

And finally, a toast to my dearly beloved, dearly departed art director, John Dignam, who actually lettered the sign in "Signs," and whom I may have buried in the Dunes in Amagansett. The Atlantic has not yet breached the dune, John!

ABOUT THE AUTHOR

Lyle Greenfield was born in Rochester, New York where he was raised Catholic and attended St. Margaret Mary grade school. He went to Confession every two weeks and each time confessed the same sins.

Lyle received a Bachelor of Arts degree in English from Bowling Green University. He wrote a weekly humor column for the student newspaper and syndicated it to fifteen other college papers. (His heroes were the columnists Art Buchwald and Russell Baker.) He began his career in New York City as a copywriter for the ad agency J. Walter Thompson, later moving to Saatchi as creative director on the Jeep account.

In 1980 Lyle purchased a low-lying plot of farmland in Bridgehampton, Long Island and planted a vineyard. He then built The Bridgehampton Winery, the first winery in the Hamptons, but after a 15-year battle between climate and site, the vineyard failed; not, however, before its winemaker, Richard Olsen-Harbich, had won over 100 awards for the wines in National and International competitions. (The winery closed in 1995 and is now home of the South Fork Natural History Museum.)

In 1989, Lyle started Bang Music in New York, a company that today provides original music and audio services across all broadcast media. He is a founding member and former president of the Association of Music Producers (AMP) and co-creator of the AMP Awards for Music and Sound.

Lyle is a frequent contributor to the ad and entertainment industry magazine SHOOT, writing about music and popular culture. He is also a somewhat notorious writer of letters to *The East Hampton Star*, a selection of which appears in this volume. He resides with his wife, Mary Jane Hantz Greenfield, in Amagansett and New York City.